WEST ISLAND

WEST ISLAND

Five twentieth-century
New Zealanders in Australia

STEPHANIE JOHNSON

For my Australian family

Published by Otago University Press
Level 1, 398 Cumberland Street
Dunedin, New Zealand
university.press@otago.ac.nz
www.otago.ac.nz/press

First published 2019
Copyright © Stephanie Johnson
The moral rights of the author have been asserted

ISBN 978-1-98-853157-1

Published with the assistance of Creative New Zealand

Editor: Jane Parkin
Index: Diane Lowther
Cover art: Anna Crichton
Author photograph: Annabel Lomas

Printed in China through Asia Pacific Offset

Contents

A Gathering of New Zealanders and Australians in 1940s Sydney

D ress warmly now, you visitors from the future, because tonight we're going out into a Sydney winter of around 70 years ago, pre-climate change, when the world was several degrees colder. The streets are dark because it's towards the end of World War II and the city is in blackout. A couple of years ago three Japanese midget submarines entered the harbour and bombarded the port as well as a few houses, taking 21 lives. Afterwards, they scuttled their ships and, in Japanese martial tradition, committed suicide. As if plotting further attacks, the mother subs remained off the coast for weeks, which in Sydney caused real alarm and fear. Children were sent away to safer refuge further west, fathers armed themselves with guns, families moved away. The bodies of the Japanese submariners, when they were recovered from the deep water, were given funerals with full naval honours. People talk disapprovingly about that, not understanding Prime Minister Curtin's motives: if he treated the Japanese with respect, it might improve conditions for the many Australian POWs, of whom my husband's grandfather is one.

Curtin's respect for the drowned Japanese submariners hasn't worked. The prisoners go on starving to death, the Pacific war goes on with fresh atrocities every day, and even though Sydney has not been attacked again no one is taking any chances.

Watch your step here – the paths are icy and a little uneven.

Down Macquarie Street we go, past the tumbledown Hyde Park Barracks, designed by convict architect Francis Greenway. It will be another 40 years before the handsome building is recognised for its unique beauty and an attempt is made to restore it to its original 1817 state. Next door is the Mint Building which, like the barracks, is in poor condition, giving no hint of its history as the New South Wales branch of the Royal Mint, striking millions of pounds worth of coins from the state's gold mines. In the 1980s, when Sydney starts to value its nineteenth-century history, this building too will be restored. And here is Sydney Hospital, the oldest hospital in Australasia, with its elegant verdigris-covered cupolae and arched stone porticoes – handsome Victoriana to our twenty-first-century eye but despised mid-twentieth century, and striking fear into the hearts of the ailing for its too-recent past of unrelieved pain. The hospital's neighbour Parliament House with its long wrought-iron verandas has also rung with yells and screams, all masculine, but in rage or victory.

Next is the new Mitchell Library wing of the State Library, opened just weeks after the submarine attacks. All is in darkness, but we can climb the grand stone steps and pass between the giant Ionic columns to peer through. There are the three bronze-framed double doors that lead to the glass-ceilinged reading room, and before that the wide marble foyer with its commemorations of explorers and Aboriginal people. This is an era when the building of a new library can comfort and consolidate a city, a state and possibly an entire nation. The Mitchell holds much of the history of Australia, and not a little of New Zealand's.

Back we go, down to the street and cross into Hunter Street. Note the absence of skyscrapers and the relative quiet of the night. The monstrous late-80s Chifley Tower in Chifley Square – that tower so often miscalled Chiefly by New Zealanders, who not only are more familiar with the concept than are Australians and so misread the word, but also have no reason to remember popular Prime Minister Ben Chifley who will come into office at war's end – may not yet even be imagined.

Here – turn right at Bligh Street and about halfway along we come to number 19, Strathkyle House Chambers. According to the city records it is an iron-roofed brick building of seven floors and 76 rooms, landlord one S.M. Dempster. In the 1940s it is a substantial building, one of the tallest in this part of town. Most famously, it is the premises of Macquarie

Galleries, a private emporium established in 1925 and one which will survive, in various guises, into the twenty-first century.

Inside we go. Already the gallery is crowded with viewers. Keep an eye out for the artist, Roland Wakelin. He's not a big man and won't stand out from the crowd, but he was the first artist ever to exhibit with Macquarie and has returned frequently ever since to exhibit again. Not all the painters who show here can attract so many punters, but Wakelin is well loved and much respected, not only for his early revolutionary paintings but also for the man he is: solid, dependable, decent, a loving husband and father, a true and loyal friend. Not the usual characteristics for an artist – in fact, we could say that some artists born with those traits do their best to dispense with them in order to be taken seriously. By the end of the century the artists' narcissistic temperament will be desired by many, and not all of them artists. Wakelin is not bothered with any of that nonsense. He is, as it happens, by birth and nature, a New Zealander ...

What's that? How can he be 'by nature a New Zealander'? He's not Māori, is he? And even then, how may we attribute certain characteristics to a racial group without risking racism?

Let's not quibble about that now – we have plenty of time to discuss national characteristics later. They do exist, though acknowledgement of them has fallen from favour.

Observe how newcomers respond to the crowded room. Some have come for the party and so ignore the art, looking around immediately for people they know, or have heard of, or would like to meet. Others go straight to the pictures, as we do.

The closest painting is 'The Artist's Wife and Daughter Reading', 1938, oil on board. It tells us much about Wakelin, how he values domestic peace. He portrays the mother and daughter in warm colours, orange and red, with an earthy wall behind them. The open book and magazine or news-paper are deep cream. There is no visible clock but it's almost as though we can hear it, slowly ticking away the hours of an afternoon spent with his family. And a little further on, another tribute to life's simple pleasures, valued by many during wartime. This is 'Sunday Walk' from around 1939, also oil on board, with a car and the street disappearing into the infinite distance. There are stairs up to a block of flats, and terrace houses on the other side of the street. It is a late-afternoon urban landscape, with a man and a woman arm in arm crossing the street. Imbued in the scene is a sense of anticipation for the coming evening. The couple are on their way home, or on their way to visit friends or family. Despite its dark, wintry hues, the painting is comforting, almost cosy.

Ah – I can sense you are impatient to begin mingling and talking, and meeting some of the guests. It's not every day we can walk through a door into an art gallery of the past. Just one last painting before we get a drink – one of my favourites. 'Estelle Wakelin Reading', 1940, oil on canvas. Estelle is Roland's much-loved wife, and this is one of the works he made as they grew old together. It is a successful marriage, by all accounts. Do you know how they met? It was soon after he'd arrived in Sydney as a young man, and he was living in a boarding house in Kirribilli. One day, as he walked along the footpath under her balcony where she was untangling her hair, she dropped her comb. He picked it up, returned it to its owner and fell in love. Like something from a fairy tale, don't you agree?

See how he doesn't flinch from portraying her as she is now – grey hair, glasses, the softening of her jaw line. On a reflective round mahogany table glow flame-like flowers. There is colour too in Estelle's pink dress and the orange curtains that frame a view of the bright Sydney sky and neighbouring roofs. The painting radiates peace, wellbeing and the artist's affection for his wife.

Old man's paintings, you might think. Wives and daughters, afternoon walks. May as well paint his cat.

Well. It's true that Wakelin is no longer the pioneer and trailblazer he once was, but then not many artists are still trailblazing when they're in their late fifties. In fact, some people say that Wakelin's later art is not nearly as interesting as the stuff he began to paint soon after he arrived with all the curiosity and energy of the immigrant. That was in 1912, when he was 26 years old. By the 1920s he was a famous innovator in the Australian art scene, and could count among his friends and colleagues every prominent Australian painter of the era – Roy De Maistre, Grace Cossington Smith, William Dobell, Arthur Streeton, New Zealand-born Godfrey Miller, his close friend Lloyd Rees – I beg your pardon?

Oh yes. Over there, that's Roland. The tall, thin woman with him? I do believe that's the communist novelist Jean Devanny. And seated over there, holding court with those young poets, that's the famous Douglas Stewart. Who would you like to meet first? Jean?

No great beauty, Devanny, but interesting. Very tall and opinionated, abrasive. *Cocksure*, I've heard her described as, which has a number of meanings, if you think about it. Keen on sex. Recently expelled from the Communist Party but I hear they're thinking of having her back. We haven't seen much of her lately – she's been living in Queensland, apparently writing another book. The police up there like to harass her for her political beliefs – they keep her under surveillance. Her husband Hal is still in Sydney and has another woman, which Devanny can't get too upset about since she was involved for years of their marriage with J.B. Miles, general secretary of the Communist Party. A kind of open secret among those on the left ... yes, sorry, gossip. But this circle thrives on gossip! Apart from being a New Zealander, Devanny has one more thing in common with Wakelin – she did her most controversial work when she was young. But then, don't we all? Her 1926 novel *The Butcher Shop*, banned in New Zealand, and a couple of her later ones, *Cindie* and *Sugar Heaven*, ruffled no end of feathers.

If you're wanting to get on in Sydney, to succeed, and let's assume you are – you're another New Zealand writer, aren't you? – then Stewart is the one you need to know. Enormously influential. He's the editor of the 'Red Page' in the *Bulletin* – you can get the *Bulletin* over there in New Zealand. Stewart grew up in the Taranaki, reading the Bushman's Bible, as they call the magazine here. The 'Red Page' is the literary side of it. And he's a writer himself, of course. His radio play *The Golden Lover* won the Australian Broadcasting Corporation competition in 1942, and his book of short stories, *A Girl With Red Hair*, was published not long ago in New Zealand. The ABC recently performed *An Earthquake Shakes the Land*. A lot of his inspiration comes from the country of his birth. For instance, *The Golden Lover* is based on the legend of Hinemoa and Tūtānekai. In our time we'd call him out for cultural misappropriation – but we mustn't judge these New Zealanders by the standards of the future. Stewart wrote the play with all good intentions and was unaware of any negative Māori response to his work. In fact, a Māori theatre company will perform that play in the 60s. Later, when we spend some time with him, we'll hear what Witi Ihimaera thought when he read one of Stewart's 'Māori' stories in primary school.

A kerfuffle at the door – and it's two more New Zealanders. One is Queen of Bohemia Dulcie Deamer, writer and bonne vivante, arriving in her skin-tight leopard-skin suit, which is starting to look a little worse for wear. Later on, after enough liquid refreshment, she may well do the splits. She's famous for it. Right now she's hanging decorously on the arm of journalist Eric Baume, who is wearing one of his 20 ludicrous, fantasy, self-designed uniforms clanking with medals, although he's seen no active service. As one of his biographers will point out, other men were jailed for wearing medals they hadn't won. But Baume seems to get away with anything – adultery, appalling novels dictated at tens of thousands of words a day, and false news reports filed during his years as war correspondent. Recently, Douglas Stewart's 'Red Page' published the shortest book review ever, in response to the second volume of Baume's memoirs, *I Have Lived Another Year*. The review read, simply:

'Why?'

Yes, very amusing. By all means, go and chat to them. And as you circulate, you will meet other New Zealanders mingling with the Australians. Following along behind Dulcie is her friend Rosaleen Norton, the Witch of Kings Cross. See how the crowd part to let her through, some of them with real consternation. You couldn't miss her with her heavy red lipstick and dyed black hair, her colourful clothes – and see, when she smiles, her teeth are filed down to points to match her pointy, witchy ears. And the poets William Hart-Smith and David McKee Wright, the latter unfortunately three sheets to the wind in conversation with Will Lawson – no relation to the more famous Henry. Will is a New Zealand poet famous for his Australian ballads. The renowned black and white artist Unk White, real name Cecil John White, appreciatively cruises the paintings, accompanied by his lifetime companion Sid Keys. The composer Alfred Hill, a classical musician, is here, and over there in full cowboy rig is Nelson-born singer Tex Morton. By the 1940s he's a pioneering country and western artist, incorporating Australian motifs and imagery into his songs. There are also other New Zealanders who might not be recognised for their work, since they publish under pseudonyms. Bellerive, whose real name is Joseph Tishler, famous Poet Laureate of the *Bulletin*'s 'Answers to Correspondents', and Nora Kelly, who publishes as John Egan. She tried to get her stories published under her own name – but found she had more success as a man. Sound familiar?

That's quite enough people to meet in one hit. There are a great many New Zealand writers and artists in Sydney in the 1940s – I could go on and on: novelist Ruth Park who will achieve real fame; poets Anne Elder and Elizabeth Riddell who will have small but loyal followings. There are iconographic photographer Harold Cazneaux, and prominent painters Nancy Borlase, Godfrey Miller and Elioth Gruner. Perhaps we can't include the latter, since he was only one year old when he crossed the Tasman. I could introduce you to a thousand – but you'd never remember them all. The people we are concerning ourselves with, all first-generation Pākehā (not that that word is common currency at this time), and none of them forgetting where they came from, are Roland Wakelin, Dulcie Deamer, Eric Baume, Jean Devanny and Douglas Stewart.

Why?

n July 2016 I wrote to Tim Curnow, the renowned Australian literary agent and son of New Zealand poet Allen Curnow, for permission to read some of his father's papers held in the National Library, Wellington. He was curious enough to ask what I was up to. I explained that I was writing a book that spun around five early- to mid-twentieth-century New Zealanders who made their homes in Australia, all of whom to a greater or lesser extent became household names in their new home and all of whom, pretty much, are forgotten. 'An odd collection of people,' he responded. He did not ask the question the *Bulletin*'s review asked of Baume, but others have.

'Why?'

The answer is complex and also, in some ways, extremely personal.

Like many New Zealanders I have a strong affection for Australia, both for its land and its people. My husband Tim Woodhouse is Australian and my son, the singer-songwriter Skyscraper Stan, is a contemporary equivalent to any of the young musicians who might have curiously come along to the Macquarie Galleries in the 1940s. Had he been born some 90 years earlier, Stan may well have been there, along with his cousin, singer and guitarist Oskar Herbig, and who knows how many hundreds of others. My generation wore a jet trail across the Tasman to Sydney. Stan and Oskar's contemporaries go to Melbourne. Much like Auckland, Sydney has been 'Manhattan-ised' – that is, rents and the general cost of living are far too high for young New Zealanders arriving with small savings and a currency perennially worth less than the Australian. Despite the rapidly rising cost of living in Melbourne, that city somehow retains its Boho artistic character. The music scene thrives in the face of multiple closures of longstanding venues in gentrifying areas. Alternative theatre struggles on, despite savage cuts to the federal and state arts budgets. To New Zealand eyes, there are jobs in every field advertised in dazzling numbers. Our young travellers try their luck: Melbourne is their Mecca.

How many of them, packing their bags and taking the flight, contemplate how they are the present manifestation of a long procession of New Zealanders who did the same thing? In the first decades of the nineteenth century, we made our way by barque and clipper, trading seal fur, kauri spars and flax. It was around this time that Māori began visiting Australia, sometimes taking up residence, in ever-increasing numbers. By the early twentieth century Māori were so much a part of the Australian scene they were included in the celebrations for Federation. Marjorie Quinn, a Sydney-sider, wrote in her memoir:

> When Federation was proclaimed on 1 January 1901, there was an elaborate procession through the streets of Sydney, starting at 11 am from the Domain. Led by shearers, there were many floats illustrating aspects of Australian life. Maoris sat statue-like on great horses; there were Indians on their spirited horses, superb figures. There were bursts of thunderous applause from crowds of onlookers … [The procession] passed along Macquarie Street under decorated arches of coal, wool and wheat, and moved toward St Mary's Cathedral.[1]

Quinn's almost subconscious inclusion of Māori in this description is perhaps proof of public awareness of the deliberations concerning the inclusion of New Zealand in the Federation. It was decided that it would not be, and this led to lengthy trade negotiations between the two nations. More curious in Quinn's description is the absence of Aboriginal people. That they were omitted from Federation celebrations demonstrates, yet again, how ignored and marginalised the first Australians were.

Many of the New Zealanders past and present who thrived and prospered across the Tasman allowed history to forget that they were born much further south. They either felt no strong affiliation with the country of their birth or wanted strongly to be accepted as genuinely Australian. The five New Zealanders who are the subjects of this book did not forget their origins. Even so, they are, for the most part, forgotten at home. This is a common phenomenon. Make it big across the ditch, and back in the archipelago it's as if you were never born at all.

While New Zealand writers and artists who came to prominence in Australia are likely to be ignored at home, almost out of spite, in the literary world this established pattern was recently disrupted. In 2016 our one and only book prize, the Ockham, was awarded to Stephen Daisley, a New Zealander by birth who has lived all his life in Australia. The year before, the Michael King Award, a $100,000 grant made to enable a writer to work on a non-fiction project for two years, was awarded to Martin Edmond, a New Zealander who has lived in Sydney for more than three decades. Both are excellent writers, so whether they were deserving recipients is not debatable here. What is curious is that these awards were made to expatriates who have access to far greater and more numerous funds in their richer, adopted country and, further, that there was very little kvetching from their much poorer and equally deserving resident peers.

I have chosen my five subjects from the many contenders not only because they retained their national identity but also because they were all, curiously, through mother, father or both, first-generation New Zealanders of European descent. Their families had not been in New Zealand for long enough for a strong sense of national identity to have developed, yet they believed they had one. They were New Zealanders. Whatever their difference or particular fields of creative endeavour, they shared the common attribute of wanting to define themselves as fundamentally different from the Australians among whom they lived and worked. They may even have shared the same opinion, deep down, that New Zealand was superior to its giant neighbour culturally, politically and geographically: a kind of small island arrogance that would never be tolerated in Australia. Or could it have been part of the early conviction, now weakened, that no matter how recently your family had established itself in New Zealand, individuals have every right to lay claim to the soil as deeply and spiritually as do tangata whenua?

When Dulcie Deamer left New Zealand in 1908 the country's population was nudging one million, an increase of 120,451 from the census of 1901 seven years earlier. This contrasts wildly with immigration in our time, the biggest onslaught since the nineteenth century: over five hundred thousand new chums in the nine years of the Key administration, and these only the immigrants who have been granted permanent residency. The true number is much higher. In the face of this influx, many non-Māori experience a sense of dislocation and alarm that approaches the lower slopes of Māori upheaval during and since colonisation. Overwhelming development to house the new arrivals occurs all over the country in places that are held commonly as a kind of public tūrangawaewae – around once pristine lakes and rivers already suffering from a bovine population explosion, and around our wild coast. Wealthy Americans, twenty-first-century Riddifords and Butlers richer than the locals, buy up the South Island. In Auckland the nineteenth-century fear of 'blow-ins' from New South Wales, venal and probably of convict descent, is mirrored by widespread disconcertion at the arrival of Chinese, Taiwanese, Thais, Malays, Koreans and all others we clumsily think of as 'Asian', a word that begins to take on the British meaning that includes Indians.

Over the years my Pākehā subjects emigrated west, New Zealand was Māori and European, with a small Han Chinese population. Dulcie, Doug, Eric, Jean and Roland understood what they were part of, and what they were leaving behind: an imported hodge-podge of mostly Irish, England, Scottish and Welsh who had achieved a degree of homogeneity alongside a mostly geographically distant Māori presence. None of the subjects I have chosen for this book is Māori because I am interested in how a national identity rises among recent immigrants, who then migrate somewhere else within the memory of two generations. Māori have an enviable right to belong in Aotearoa.

*

In a *Listener* interview of 1999 I talked about Pākehā guilt and remarked how I had always envied Māori their sense of belonging, just as many non-Māori do. When actor Rawiri Paratene told me that Pākehā guilt had always been advantageous for Māori in their need to retain land and conserve their culture, I felt that I had at last been of some use. Many of my novels have Māori characters and I have not stepped on any toes, as far as I am aware.

For much of my adult life I felt seared by guilt for the actions of my forefathers. Great-great-granduncle Thomas Henry Smith was a judge in the Native Land Court, a fluent speaker of te reo, whose second, much-loved wife was Māori, but nevertheless he acted on the part of the colonial government in freeing up land for British settlement. Among his papers in the Auckland War Memorial Museum are letters to his brother full of discomfort and anguish after the passing of the 1865 Native Land Act, which enabled individual Māori to sell land without consultation with iwi or hapū. Smith was aware of the devastation the new legislation would incur but went ahead regardless.

On my maternal side, a great-grandfather was a timber miller, responsible for the loss of hundreds, possibly thousands, of acres of virgin bush in the Kaimai Ranges and the Mount Pirongia district in the late nineteenth and early twentieth centuries. In his time the bush was there to be conquered, torn down, replaced by cattle and sheep, corn, passive pastureland, orchards and pine. There was a widely held misconception that the forest would rejuvenate, that it was in endless supply.

To have ancestors responsible for such 'crimes' is not unusual in post-colonial societies. If your family is of several generations' standing then it is likely that at least one pale-skinned antecedent is responsible for helping to destroy the natural environment or of acquiring land by nefarious means. Those of us of successive Pākehā generations can only lobby governments for recompense for Māori loss and support ongoing Treaty reparations.

Soon after my son returned at age 21 to live in the land of his birth but not his upbringing, he remarked during a phone call that he had felt his guilt slough away. Stan started school in Auckland in 1993, a time when it was possible for Pākehā children to believe that they had no 'culture', or at least none worth preserving, and that they were in some way personally responsible for the ongoing disparities between Pākehā and Māori in health, education and employment. He felt this keenly, as did many of his non-Māori friends from this time.

Guilt on a national scale does neither side any favours. It lessens us, makes us into boobies, and clouds the issue with emotion that is not constructive. It could be argued that it was a toxic by-product of this guilt that got Don Brash up on the stage for his infamous 2004 Orewa speech to the local Rotary Club. In some twisted way, he could have been trying to scorch a deep, unacknowledged sense of guilt by assuming a higher moral ground. Otherwise, why would a supposedly intelligent, informed man make accusations about Māori having 'special treatment'? On the lighter side, it is perhaps insidious guilt that creates the character that is the butt of so many jokes in Australia: the quiet, indirect, apologetic New Zealander. Vincent O'Sullivan, a senior and much-loved New Zealand writer who frequently spends periods of time across the Tasman, tells a story of how an Australian once remarked to him that if you step on a New Zealander's foot he's the one who says sorry.

So much for guilt. What about envy, which is the other side of the same coin? It's simple really. Māori belong in New Zealand. There was a lengthy period in our history when the plight of the Moriori was used to equalise Māori and Pākehā. We were the second colonisers, doing to Māori only what they had done to Moriori, but more humanely. School children were taught from the early twentieth century on a version first enshrined in a 1916 *School Journal* that Moriori were an inferior race, darker and with flatter noses, and that they had all died out. That myth has itself died out now – we know that Māori settled New Zealand in successive waves from Hawaiki, and that Moriori were the earliest wave some centuries before.

'We're all immigrants,' say New Zealanders opposed to further Treaty settlements. Arguments wax and wane about the exact number of years Māori were here before 'us'. Historian Michael King pegged it at about six hundred; some Maori scholars believe it more like a thousand. The length of time is surely irrelevant. The point is, Māori are Pacific people and those of us whose ancestors came later in the nineteenth century are not. I would love to be able to stand on New Zealand soil and feel that I absolutely belong. The fact that I feel little or no connection to Britain doesn't bring a corresponding genetic claim to the islands of Aotearoa. It means, despite my relative acknowledgement as a New Zealand writer, and the whakapapa of seven family generations born here, that I truly belong nowhere.

In 2008 I made a trip to London for the final stages of research for my novel *The Open World*, a fictionalised account of the life of my great-great-great-grandmother Elizabeth Horlock Smith, mother of Thomas Henry. One evening I went out to dinner with academic and New Zealandophile

Dr Ian Conrich. Through much of the 1990s and early 2000s, Dr Conrich championed New Zealand culture in Europe and the UK, establishing the now-defunct Centre for New Zealand Studies at Birkbeck College, University of London, and organising conferences that highlighted the work and achievements of New Zealand writers, film-makers, academics and artists. The evening after I had given a lecture at the centre, he and I went to a restaurant in Islington called Gallipoli. My ancestor, before she boarded the *Tomatin* in 1841 as part of Bishop Selwyn's party, had lived in rooms in Cross Street, a stone's throw away. I told Ian about that as we ate our falafels.

'You're a real Londoner!' he exclaimed. 'My family came here from Poland after the war. You're more of a Londoner than I am.'

A sudden, powerful sense of belonging infused my veins, a delicious, golden feeling of belonging that I had never known before. These are the streets my ancestors trod. I need feel no guilt. This is my place.

The epiphany fled as quickly as it had arrived. That granny was a long way back and, when you do the sums, each of us has sixteen great-great-great-grandmothers. Who were they, really? The others could have come from anywhere.

When I interviewed the Chinese writer Xu Xinran at the 2015 Auckland Writers' Festival, she told me she was sure I had Chinese ancestry. When I spent time in London with the Aboriginal activist Bruce Pascoe he asked me several times if I was Māori. Māori friends have asked me the same question. I have never had the controversial racial heritage swab test to prove I'm anything other than another member of the drifting, white-skinned, blue-eyed diaspora. Family lore, patchy as it is, doesn't take in an ancestor from anywhere other than the British Isles.

My husband's family have been in Australia for far less time than mine in New Zealand, but still, when my son went to live there he felt immediately at home in the same way, I imagine, as did Wakelin, Deamer, Baume, Devanny and Stewart.

Points of Origin

Roland Wakelin

BORN GREYTOWN 1887, DIED SYDNEY 1971

Contemporaries Roland Wakelin and Dulcie Deamer grew up in small neighbouring towns in the fertile Wairarapa Valley, northeast of Wellington over the Rimutaka Ranges. Locals in the district refer still to the Rimutakas as 'the hill' – a vivid example of New Zealand understatement, once a celebrated cultural trait. The Rimutakas are craggy and forbidding and in the depths of winter may be made impassable by snow. The road, which has a summit of 555 metres, winds around precipitous corners and climbs steep slopes; accidents are common. Keen trampers can almost double their ascent by climbing to the top of 940-metre Mt Matthews.

It was in 1856, 30 years before Roland's birth, that the first road, little more than a bridle track, was opened to take wool and prodigious Wairarapa produce into Wellington. It was 1917 before the road was widened and the mid-30s before it was sealed.

For little Roland and Dulcie, then, Greytown and Featherston were isolated towns, servicing the farms and orchards of the district. The railway was the main means of land transport and Wellington the nearest metropolis. Today, Greytown is one of a chain of small towns on the northern side of the Rimutaka Ranges that have been gentrified, to greater or lesser extents, by an influx of money from viticulture and retirees from Wellington and further afield.

The main street of Greytown has been almost universally renovated to reflect the town's Victorian and Edwardian past. Cafés, gift shops and boutiques appeal to tourists' sense of nostalgia as well as to their pockets. At a midpoint stands Wakelin House, a small villa with kauri floors and double-hung windows, which serves as both a restaurant and a delicatessen selling local produce. On the day I visited, in the winter of 2016, nobody on the premises could tell me why the house carried the name, or whom it was named after. It was a demonstration of the lack of curiosity and memory that has often characterised New Zealand, as if what Pākehā history we have is not worth hanging on to or is embarrassing to recall. The history of our early settlers in particular brings conflict: should we be proud of the courage and hard work of the pioneers, or condemn them for 'invasion', which better describes 'colonisation', and for the catastrophic disease and poverty suffered subsequently by Māori? It is this powerful moral dilemma that forms the main engine of the current amnesia.

In fact, Wakelin House by circuitous route takes its name from Richard Wakelin, Roland's paternal grandfather, who was a town founder. In 1850 he and his wife Mary arrived in Wellington on the barque *Eden*, the last of the New Zealand Company ships to bring new immigrants. They had with them four of their eventual five children. Richard left behind an established career in journalism and activism. As an 18-year-old, and then again at the age of 22, he had made tours of America speaking on temperance. He was a Chartist, an early forerunner of the trade union movement. It is curious, given the image many of us have of the hard-drinking, take-no-prisoners men of the later union movement, that these two forces – prohibitionism and workers' rights – were once so closely aligned. Grandfather Wakelin's conviction, like that of many others, was spawned and nurtured by rage against the Stamp Tax, an attempt by the British government to control the proliferation of newspapers. Each publication was subject to an initial tax of £500, a vast sum in those days, and then a penny a copy thereafter.

The paper Wakelin was editing at the time of his departure for New Zealand, *The Temperance Gazette*, would have struggled to make a profit, even though the temperance movement was strong. It was particularly well supported by women, many of whom would not have had the financial independence to contribute to his funds. Life was hard and Wakelin may well have been looking for escape. Fortuitously, he knew about the New

Zealand Company, having long been interested in the activities of the Wakefield brothers. We can imagine that he had heard or read the name, so similar to his own, and it had lodged in his memory. He might also have thought that New Zealand was a country more in tune with progressive politics and aspirations than England. This was a period when the dream of New Zealand was of a paradise in which the rights of Māori would be respected, where the rigid, moribund class system could be disbanded. It is ironic that he was attracted to the Wakefields, given that they, more than anyone, were responsible for a kind of vertical immigration where servants accompanied families of means: the class system unloaded at the port along with their boxes and effects.

For a short period after the family's arrival in Wellington the Wakelins took up residence in Te Aro. Richard Wakelin had dreams of starting a public school and wrote to Governor Grey with his proposal. Grey, impressed by his erudite letter, suggested that he instead write for the *Wellington Independent*. Wakelin, mindful of the needs of his wife and four children, abandoned his earlier ambition, as Grey suggested, becoming the Legislative Council reporter for that paper which, in a sense, still survives: the *Dominion Post* can trace its ancestry to the *Independent*. By 1853 Richard Wakelin had risen to editor, a position he would hold for the next three years.

Donald McLean is a highly controversial historical figure. In the year Roland's grandfather became editor, McLean was appointed Chief Land Purchase Commissioner in the newly established Land Purchase Department. Previously he had acted as Native Secretary, a role which had itself evolved out of the Protector of the Aborigines. The Native Secretary was supposed to protect Māori interests. When the land purchase commissioner position was amalgamated with the secretarial role, any notion of protection was officially dispensed with, which suited McLean. In his own right he became a landowner of spectacular greed, buying up vast tracts of land in the middle of the North Island. For this he was widely disliked by Pākehā as well as Māori. 'That scamp McLean', as my ancestor Elizabeth Smith described him in a letter to her son, who knew him well.[1] In the early 1850s, by fair means but mostly foul, McLean was getting hold of land in the Wairarapa.

In anticipation of McLean's success, the Wairarapa Small Farm Association was formed in Wellington. Richard Wakelin and his brother Thomas became staunch supporters, using money they had brought with them from England that was probably part of their inheritance. Here they could abandon, or at least dilute, their previous politics and become approximations of squires. Each was awarded a 40-acre (16ha) block, which included a 'town acre' – an acre inside the new town limits. Not one but two new towns were planned, Greytown and Masterton, and both were to take the shape of the cross.

Roland's father, Richard Alfred Wakelin, would have been 10 or 11 years old when the family finally made it over the Rimutakas to take up their new life in the Wairarapa. At five years of age, he had made the rigorous and no doubt character-building voyage from England. He would grow to be a man of great energy and innovation. Father to six sons and a daughter, he was a popular and hardworking member of the community. Not only was he a local councillor who served twice as mayor of Greytown but he was also a successful builder and sawmiller. The original Greytown hospital, the town's Bank of New Zealand, St John's Anglican Church in Featherston, and various farmhouses and cottages were designed and constructed by him: the builder architect was the norm at the turn of the last century. Many of these buildings still stand and form part of the historical appeal that draws thousands of tourists, some of them, like I was, curious about Wakelin House on Main Street. Greytown historian Frank Fyfe suggests that the cottage was built by Thomas in anticipation of his brother's arrival in 1856, and that it accommodated the family for many years, being incorporated into a bigger structure in 1872.

Roland Wakelin the artist inherited many traits from his father, adherence to the work ethic being one of them. As a boy, he would have seen his father working on building plans, and perhaps the sight of him bent over great sheets of paper, pen and ink at hand, planted the seeds for his own future as an artist. Or possibly the greatest family influence on Roland, at least in terms of his deciding to become an artist, was his paternal uncle George, farmer, wood carver and watercolourist. In an interview of 1967, Wakelin recalled how his uncle had scandalised the district: 'When my Uncle made his Nude Woman, which he placed alongside a bird bath, there was a hell of a to-do in that little village I remember.'² The nude woman had companions. There was a giant Māori warrior, which would no doubt not meet today's exacting kaupapa. From the top of the nearby gateway a wooden Ajax shook his fist at a bolt of lightning. A life-size wooden woman bending over a washing tub was so realistic that a lost American tourist on horseback stopped to ask directions of her and was even more convinced of our taciturn national character when she refused to answer him. Today, the only surviving carvings are proudly displayed in the Greytown Museum. They are a crouching lion and a praying Florence Nightingale. They have been painted rather garishly, with what looks like house paint.

A further influence not to be underestimated is Roland's second name, Shakespeare. Grandfather Richard believed himself to be descended from the Elizabethan playwright. Great things are expected of Shakespeares and the name was distributed around the family. Perhaps bearing the moniker aided Roland in believing he could become an artist.

Members of the family recognised his talent early on. His brothers Norman and Francis bought him his first oil paints and boards when he was 13. Two years later, Roland won a scholarship to Wellington Technical College. The whole family shifted from Greytown to Wellington so that he could make the best of his opportunity. In Wellington Roland studied for the Civil Service Exam, which he passed in 1903, and went out to work for the Taxation Department. His wages enabled him to take art lessons at the Technical College. He recalled, 'Things were cheap in those days, I took a room, managed to rent a house for next to nothing with a number of other art students. There we had our life classes on most nights and on Saturday and Sunday. We paid model fees as well, and ate well enough.'³

This was to establish a pattern that would sustain him for most of his life. Wakelin, like all of the subjects in this book, worked for a living at the same time as practising his art. Arts council grants didn't exist on either side of the Tasman and, even if they had, Wakelin may not have felt he deserved to take advantage of them. He worked out ways of supporting himself and his family until his late middle age, when at last he was able to stop either teaching or working as a commercial artist and focus solely on his art. He may well have agreed with Baume that the notion of state sponsorship for the arts is an abomination. Many New Zealanders of the period held that position, on both sides of the political camp. You sank or you swam. You valued your work – or tried to – by the value the market put on it.

Five more years were to pass in Wellington before Wakelin made the trip west to Australia. In the interim, he rented a light-filled studio upstairs from a draper's shop, and studied under Henri Bastings and H. Linley Richardson. These, his earliest tutors, are widely believed to have had little or no influence on his work. A closer examination shows this not to be the case.

Bastings was a Dunedin-born, Sydney-trained architect who also worked as a draftsman in Melbourne. When he returned to New Zealand in 1910 he established his own architectural practice in Greymouth before moving to Wellington in 1915, but painting was possibly always his greatest love. He exhibited with the New Zealand Academy of Fine Arts from late in the nineteenth century, and served as the academy's secretary until 1910. A 1916 photograph shows him as an older man in a stylish Homburg hat and a nicely cut coat with the collar turned up.[4] He has a direct stare and a full moustache. Few of his paintings survive, but those that do – for example, his oil of Dunedin's promontory Lawyer's Head, asking for a new owner in 2016 – show him as a conventional landscape painter.

H. Linley Richardson was better known than Bastings and also far more radical. Born in England in 1878, he trained in London and Paris before settling for seven years in London from late 1900. He did well, prospering as an artist and teacher, painting and illustrating books and magazines. So respected was he that in 1905 he was elected a member of the Royal Society of British Artists. But he must have been hankering for change, as only two years later he was appointed art instructor at the Wellington Technical College. Newly married, he voyaged across the world to the country he would call home for the rest of his life. H. Linley Richardson was remembered by those who knew him as a disappointed, sad man. He perhaps spent too much time wondering why he had ever got on the ship that took him away from the bright lights, and yearned for the life he might have led if he'd never left – a common ex-pat British malaise that persists even when fame is unlikely.

Roland Wakelin as a young man. The date of this portrait is unknown, and it could have been taken in either Wellington or Sydney. The photographer, May Moore, was a New Zealander who emigrated to Australia in 1910 and set up a successful studio.

May Moore photographer, Art Gallery of New South Wales

Wakelin's early landscapes have much in common with the almost universal style of landscape painting in the late nineteenth and early twentieth centuries. Richardson, at the time of their association, had not yet begun painting the radical works he later did, including his portrait of Sir James Carroll as a tiny figure set in a large-scale, dramatic rendition of the landscape of Carroll's Wairoa, but the influences for that later work, brought with him from Europe, may well have been in evidence during his classes. Likewise, Richardson's career as stamp designer, most famous for his radical notion of including Māori motifs in the border, was way in the future. Both he and Bastings were conservative artists who provided Wakelin with time-honoured, invaluable tools and techniques.

They would also have influenced Wakelin with their brand of international cosmopolitanism. Richardson, fresh from an escalating career in London and not yet aware that emigration was not just a way of putting the brake on but a way of seizing up the engine altogether, would have talked of the artist's life in Europe. Bastings' paintings of Australian scenes, some of which he had exhibited in New Zealand, might have served to arouse further curiosity about its nearest neighbour.

Late in life Wakelin wrote a short document for the Auckland Art Gallery after the institution bought one of his paintings. The document begins: 'The New Zealand Art World [his caps] of my day was a dreary enough affair. There was a New Zealand Academy of Fine Arts directed by lawyers and doctors as artists were not considered capable of managing their own affairs. An Annual Exhibition was held at the little gallery in Whitmore Street. If these were no better than the one I saw in 1951, they must have been very bad.' He goes on to name the painters he thought stood out above all others at the time, both of them imports – Scotsman James McLachlan Nairn and Dutchman Petrus Van der Velden. Returning to the years of his youth he goes on: 'We knew practically nothing of what went on in other parts of the world. Each year the Royal Academy Pictures came out and there were little octavo books with black and white illustrations on Turner, Constable, Landseer and other English painters. Of the great Italians we knew nothing, and little of French impressionism. Frances Hodgkins made quite a name in England but her native land ignored her work.'[5] Wakelin would be relieved to know, were he alive today, Hodgkins has been restored to her proper place, most recently through the efforts of Dr Joanne Drayton.[6] It seems he was not aware of the earlier definitive biography by E.H. McCormick, *The Expatriate*, published in 1951.

In the summer of 1908–09 Wakelin travelled with his brother Norman to Australia to visit their older brother Frank, who was working for Woods Great Peppermint Cure, based in Sydney. Given prime billing in many a family medicine cupboard, the Peppermint Cure was panacea for all manner of ills – coughs, colds, toothache, colic, windy spasms, stomach pain, asthma and even 'Sense of Undue Fullness After Eating.' Thousands swore of its efficacy from late in the nineteenth century until the end of the 1950s. Today a version of it is manufactured in Malaysia.

Wakelin's first taste of Australia could be seen as yet another property of the medicine – it cured him of Wellington. Certainly the holiday was enough to make him want to head west as soon as he could and stay there. He did, and in 50 years made only one trip home. This is the clue, if one were needed, to why Wakelin has been so thoroughly forgotten in New Zealand. If he had returned and exhibited, if he had painted more New Zealand scenes, then he may have retained a degree of celebration. In Wakelin's day, just as to a lesser extent it is in ours, a trans-Tasman career needed careful nurturing. Many New Zealanders have tried and failed; a few have succeeded. Success in New Zealand was not, it seems, important to Wakelin – although the dilemma may not have risen in his mind. At the end of 1912 the painter departed for good. By this time both his parents had passed away and his brothers were grown and gone – there was nothing to hold him in the land of his birth.

Dulcie Deamer

BORN CHRISTCHURCH 1890, GREW UP IN FEATHERSTON,
DIED SYDNEY 1972

Mary Elizabeth Kathleen Dulcie Deamer came to live in Featherston in 1901, when she was 11 years old. Had her parents decided
to stay in Christchurch, where Dulcie was born, they might have
had an easier time of it. The English, it is often said, have a greater
tolerance of eccentricity, and Dulcie's parents were certainly eccentric.
Christchurch, the most English of all New Zealand cities, with its central
cathedral, its imported class system and heavy smog, may well have turned
a blind eye to free-thinkers like the Deamers. It may also have provided
some like-minded companions, at least for Dulcie's parents. Her grandfather was a pioneer doctor and her father followed suit, educated first
at Christ's College, Christchurch, before training in Scotland, which at
that time led the world in medicine. In the colonies doctors enjoyed (and,
it could be argued, still do enjoy) almost the status of nobility – a class
in which eccentricity was tolerated more than in any other, even if that
eccentricity was cultivated. Especially if cultivated, perhaps, since unconscious eccentricity is dangerously close to madness.

Recalling her earliest years Deamer wrote, 'Our seclusion was absolute.'[7] The family lived at 173 Armagh Street until Dulcie was six, then
moved to 213 Madras Street. It must be the Armagh Street house she
refers to in her autobiography when she describes a 'shabby bungalow'
beside the Avon, since Madras Street is not close to the river.[8] Neither she

nor her sister ever attended school. Instead they were educated at home by their mother Isabel Mabel, daughter of Colonel Reader, late of the British army, who had grown up mostly in Wellington. Mabel was an amateur actress with a love of reading, storytelling, nudity and ghosts. She herself had 'hated school' and resolved that none of her children should have to endure it.[9] 'We were very happy apes,' wrote Deamer in her autobiography. She was raised in 'Rabelaisian candour' and by her own definition had been 'unshockable ever since'.[10]

The late nineteenth and early twentieth centuries saw the dying phase of the Victorian fetishisation of death, and Dulcie, despite her apparent seclusion, was in love with it. A universal childhood game is the devising of elaborate funeral rites for dead pets, or for animals discovered lifeless. Dulcie went one step further by drowning the soon to be mourned rats in the Avon, or perhaps in the circular fountain that stood beside the house. A respectful and inventive funeral would always follow. A year into the family's new life in Featherston, 12-year-old Dulcie penned a poem, 'Death':

> Gently He laid His hand upon her brow –
> She slept. And still she lies, and white, and cold.
> She was as we are but an hour ago
> Whom now His wings forever to enfold.
>
> How did it come? A whisper of the night
> Rustlings among the lilies by the lawn,
> As the faint echo of a half-heard voice
> Falling across the stillness of the dawn?
>
> Death walked among the dewy fields last night,
> The poppies stirred beside the garden gate,
> Then, in the silence of the moonless dark,
> A voice cried 'Come thou!' and she said 'I wait.'[11]

The fascination with death would have been deepened by her reading – by the age of eight she was allowed free access to every book in the extensive family library, reading Sir Walter Scott and Lord Lytton. 'We had more books than furniture,' she recalled.[12] She may also have heard tales of death and dying from her father, who would have attended many deathbeds in the course of his work. He also made jokes about bodies and sex, and blushing visitors would be 'shocked to the bottom of their Victorian souls'.[13] According to Dulcie, his charm would win them over again.

Dr Deamer was well liked by his Christchurch patients, but this was not to be the case when the family moved to Featherston. 'There was also Doctor G.E. Deamer who practised part time during the 1905–1910 period,' writes Wairarapa historian David Yerex, 'but apparently was not in great favour with the locals. During this period Featherston residents may have preferred to seek medical aid from Dr Bey in Greytown.'[14]

'Ted' to his friends, charming, good-looking and hopeless with money, Dr Deamer was less interested in his patients than he was in Egyptology, what he could examine with his microscope, and the last years of an extraordinary time in literature: the era of the Victorian novel. As a reading man he would have devoured the greats – Dickens, Thackeray, the Brontës, Jane Austen. Dulcie remembered her mother crying over unpaid bills.

The move to Featherston, made apparently on Mabel's initiative, would at least have made it easier to manage. Fresh produce offered by the surrounding farmlands, the small town, the temperate climate, the fact that the children could run free and frequently naked, the fresh air, lake, forest and mountains, and all the surrounding beauty of the Wairarapa would have been good for everyone in the family, except Dulcie. She would recall that she was 'bored stupid' and that the town's inhabitants were like 'rather comic shadows'.[15]

From the 1890s until recently, the town doctor enjoyed the very fine two-storey residence on the corner of Bell Street and Johnston Street. Known locally as 'The Doctor's House', it has a small, now disused, hospital attached, though this was built long after the Deamers' departure. The house would more properly be described as a mansion. In 2016 it sold for well over $1 million, having been restored and made into a luxury home, complete with swimming pool and powder room. The vendor's young granddaughter described it as a 'castle'.

It was not always so. Deamer describes the house as being of rotting timbers, and makes no mention of its being specially built for the doctor. Not only was it rotting, it was also haunted. By her account there were at least four ghosts. Two were the uneasy spirits of people who had been murdered there, one in a bedroom and the other drowned in the decommissioned well in the garden. These sleepless spirits were believed to be the generators of the footsteps and shadows witnessed by all the family. In addition there was a poltergeist, which had a fondness for hurling teacups in broad daylight, rattling door handles and flinging doors open. The last shade belonged to Dr Deamer's deceased brother who had come along with them when they made the shift from the South Island. A banshee is not strictly a ghost, but there was one of those hanging about as well. It kept them awake by wailing at the second-floor windows.

Since the beginning of time mothers have soothed their frightened children during the night by telling them, 'It's only the wind, darlings.' Some of these ghostly activities would have been due to gusts of wind, whistling drafts and loose, banging roof tiles: Featherston is scientifically agreed to be the third most windy town on the planet. But Dulcie's mother, who was delighted with the ghosts and apparent paranormal activity, encouraged the children's faith in them. 'Listen to the banshee, dears,' she may have said.

Dulcie was terrified – although her interest in the paranormal stayed with her for life. In Sydney she was to become, as we witnessed at the Macquarie Galleries, a great friend of fellow New Zealander Rosaleen Norton, the infamous Witch of Kings Cross.

For now, though, there were the earthly pleasures of the little town with its one general store and the delight of running naked in the bush and swimming in the icy waters of Lake Wairarapa and local rivers. The enjoyment of swimming would never leave her. How sad she would be if she could see the polluted, cow manure-thick, dead Wairarapa streams and rivers of today, their lifeless decline caused by the intensification of dairy farming. None of the local rivers are now fit for swimming.

Also enduring were her interests in the occult and writing. In those paradisiacal days there was the sensing of a 'presence' in the bush and the pleasure of composing poems. Deamer did not enjoy every stage of the conception of a poem, particularly the one she called 'fermenting'. This made her 'perfectly miserable'.[16] On one occasion, busy fermenting, she dropped and smashed a huge pile of dinner plates en route from the kitchen to the dining room. Her parents, always understanding, excused her from every carrying plates again lest the loss be repeated.

There were lessons at her mother's knee, and not all to do with reading and writing. 'If a man says he loves you and doesn't ask you to marry him, it's an insult,' Mabel told her daughters, a common enough teaching of the time. There were other variants – if a man kisses you and doesn't ask you to marry him it's an insult; if a man asks you to walk out with him likewise. Deamer's later penchant for kissing competitions must have shocked even free-thinking Mabel, who was well aware of her adult daughter's behaviour in Sydney.

The Deamers had enough money to make sure Dulcie and her sister experienced a little of life in the cities as they grew up. There were elocution and ballet lessons in Wellington; the girls were debutantes in Dunedin. The elocution lessons, along with lessons in fencing, dancing and deportment, held. In the de Berg interview of 1965 and in *Stations of the Cross*, a 1962 ABC documentary about Kings Cross, Deamer is very finely spoken, almost with a plum in her mouth. She would claim she liked her own accent – it isn't a New Zealand one – and it wasn't dislodged either by the periods of time she spent in America or her long years in Australia. The only hint of an Australian accent is the long 'a' on 'freelance' and 'chancy'.

Despite the frequent 'fermentings' of poetry, Dulcie's mother had ambitions for her daughter to become an actress. Even after Deamer won a major Australasian short story competition at the age of 16, she pursued that career, touring New Zealand with the Taylor-Carrington Dramatic Company: 'barnstorming', as they called it then. It was hard work, arriving in a town and showing for only one night, packing out afterwards and leaving the next day. Dulcie loved it, and kept it up for four months in 1907, a time of great excitement that surely peaked with her literary win.

The short story competition was run by *Lone Hand*, a literary magazine associated with the *Bulletin*. 'As it was in the beginning', a historical fiction about 'nearly naked people', was published first in the host journal and then in the Australian *Truth*. *New Zealand Truth* wrote that the story 'is an indication of genius which may develop into something abnormal or wither in maturity like numberless samples of juvenile precocity in the dim and distant past'. It quoted from the story a description of the hero: his 'six feet of hairy manhood was belted with a strip of fawn skin suppled with grease. Save for this, he was naked.' The hirsute hero was on the hunt for a woman. When he found her, he 'sprang, lion-like, and struck her down,

DULCIE DEAMER : AUTHORESS.

TACKLES A TOUGH PROPOSITION.

Sweet Sixteen on the Sex Subject.

"As it was in the Beginning."

How will it be in the End?

Dulcie Deamer, of Featherston, is a youthful prodigy who writes beyond her years. For a girl of sixteen to tackle successfully the immeasurable difficulties of the sex problem, as Dulcie has done in her prize story in the "Lone Hand," is an indication of genius which may develop into something abnormal or wither in maturity like numberless samples of juvenile precocity in the dim and distant past. "As It Was In The Beginning" depicts things in the era when there were no clothes to speak of, and when the law of natural selection made the gentle art of wooing a simple process of reducing the lady to abject servility by pure brute force. Costume had no part in the programme. The Strong Man's "six feet of hairy manhood was belted with a strip of fawn skin suppled with grease. Save for this, he was naked, but beside him lay a spear, beaded with chipped jasper and a coil of deer-skin thongs. He was a dark man with fierce grey eyes, and his long black hair fell all about his shoulders. The reason for being where he was was very simple. He wanted a wife.

The woman—she was young, a girl still, and well-grown. Her only garment was a belt of red deer's hide, and she was fresh with the freshness of all young animals that have not known mother-hood, as a sleek heifer or young hind knee-deep in fern." The woman loves strength, but strength without tenderness is as nought, for love is the mainspring of existence. How he got her: "The strong man sprang, lion-like, and struck her down, and stifled her first scream as it was born. When she was dragged into the shelter, of the gorse he squeezed her throat till she lay gasping, and as she blinked up at him, her eyes, green as a cat's, were wild with hate and fear. Very swiftly he bound her with raw thongs, until she was more helpless than a new-born babe. Then the captor's hand closed again upon her throat, and when they loosened the captive was insensible from suffocation." It wasn't entirely successful. "He had mated as the beasts mate, brutally and by force, but things had not turned out as If, in his dim mind had expected. So If had broken several tough wood splinters in the endeavor to set them right." The woman didn't appreciate him. It was when the strong man felled a lion at one blow, then slipped beneath the yellow-white fangs of a cub-despoiled lioness, that the woman awoke to her responsibilities. She speared the lioness and saved her lord, and thereafter love entered into the business with satisfactory results. The strength of the story is its simplicity, but the phraseology is astonishingly apt and graphic. "Among the water-courses the gorse burned like golden fire and licked the edge of the current with vivid lips." What could be more expressive and luminous? It is the daring of the sketch that commands admiration and inspires amazement at its production by a demure miss, who might not write thus, embarrassed by sex knowledge born of the experience of maturer years. The story has given artist Norman Lindsay an opportunity to idealise the brute in man.

Dulcie Deamer, who is the golden-haired daughter of a Featherston medico, had previously attained purely local fame by the unusual histrionic aptitude displayed in recitations on Wairarapa concert platforms, and in private theatricals. In dramatic impersonation she did not go beyond the family circle, and shared with other Featherston young ladies, some of whom took male parts, the enthusiastically expressed approbation of a favored few auditors. Her future will be watched with curiosity.

This article appeared in *New Zealand Truth*, 18 January 1908. Deamer is cited as tackling 'successfully the immeasurable difficulties of the sex problem'.

and stifled her first scream as it was born. When she was dragged into the shelter of the gorse he squeezed her throat till she lay gasping, and as she blinked up at him, her eyes, green as a cat's, were wild with hate and fear.' Shortly, they mate. 'He had mated as the beasts mate, brutally and by force, but things had not turned out as he, in his dim mind had expected.' Afterwards the man is attacked by a lion and the woman saves him. Love blooms. The 'phraseology is astonishingly apt and graphic', said the *Truth* writer, quoting another a passage from the story: 'Among the water-courses the gorse burned like golden fire and licked the edge of the current with vivid lips.' The reviewer asked: 'What could be more expressive and luminous?'[17]

Critics raved about her talent and how extraordinary it was in one so young. She was to write three follow-ups, all of which were illustrated by controversial artist and novelist Norman Lindsay, and sold well partly because of their notoriety. The stories were open about sex, and Lindsay's illustrations showed breast and leg.

It was while Dulcie was touring with the Taylor-Carringtons that she met her future husband, Albert Goldie, the advance manager and publicity writer for Sydney-based J.C. Williamson. The Williamson's company was a dominant force in Australasian theatre in the early twentieth century, providing work for mostly Australian casts and sometimes engendering resentment within the fledgling New Zealand theatrical industry. Dulcie would have been dazzled by Albert's connections as well as by the attentions of a man 15 years her senior. She fell wildly in love with him. He was only a little taller than her, and she was tiny. He was a fast talker, a Melbourne-born charmer who had changed his surname from Goldberg to hide his Jewish ancestry. He was exotic and interesting. He was her ticket out.

Luckily for Dulcie her feelings were reciprocated. Albert came to Featherston one weekend and asked Mabel for her daughter's hand. Time was of the essence because he was about to depart for a new job as business manager of Hugh Ward's London Comedy Company in India. Mabel gave the union her blessing, and the happy couple sailed for Perth, where they were married. Three months short of her eighteenth birthday, Deamer was a married woman and a published author. She was never to return to New Zealand.

Douglas Stewart

BORN ELTHAM 1913, DIED SYDNEY 1985

ouglas Stewart's early life, as described in his autobiography *Spring-time in Taranaki* (1977) and earlier volume *The Seven Rivers* (1966), was idyllic. It was the kind of childhood that has now all but vanished. He fished, built tree houses, went on excursions over hill and dale, swam in the rivers. He knew all the local people by name. He had dogs, cats, rabbits, guinea pigs, pet sparrows and even, for a short period, a leveret.

The second oldest of an Australian-born country lawyer and devoted, light-hearted mother who liked a laugh and a song, Doug was one of five children. They lived in the small town of Eltham in the province of Taranaki, on the western side of the North Island, close to Hawera and New Plymouth.

The volcano Mt Taranaki, which Doug knew by its now abandoned colonialist name Mt Egmont, rises magically above the plains. It is not part of a range but stands proudly alone. On a clear day on the road from New Plymouth to Eltham you can enjoy seeing Mt Ruapehu and his brother Tongariro away to the north: three snowy peaks – one close in, the other two at a distance – rising high above the green plains. In Māori legend the mountains are gods who once all lived together in the centre of Te-Ika-a-Māui (the fish of Māui, or the North Island) but fought over nearby Pihanga, the only mountain goddess among them. At the close of the battle Tongariro sent the loser Taranaki to stand all by himself near the coast, as far to the west as he could go. And stand there he does. In Stewart's words, the majestic, breath-taking mountain 'made the whole world miraculous'.[1]

For Eltham, the mountain is the one constant. So much has changed. In Stewart's day the town was a thriving, close-knit community. There were two banks – the Bank of New Plymouth and the Bank of New South Wales. There was a draper, a butcher, a grocer, a dentist, a doctor, a pharmacist, a fine town hall and substantial courthouse, two practices of lawyers, two hotels, a newspaper office, a Presbyterian church, a Roman Catholic church and, just out of town, on the road back to Stratford, a park that contained exotic animals for entertainment on Sunday afternoons.

Today Eltham is a charming but melancholy example of true rural decline. On Bridge Street, the main shopping street since the town was founded, the majority of shopfronts are boarded up. Most of those that remain open sell second-hand clothes, collectibles and junk. There are no banks, no butcher, no grocer, no dentist, no pharmacy, newspaper office or legal practice. On a lower corner of the street spreads a large lurid-green franchised seed and garden merchant. This is the site that once held Chew Chong's business. Chew Chong was the enterprising businessman who first created the pound of butter as a means to package and export the commodity to England, a move that ensured a good part of the nation's wealth for over a century and for which, it could be argued, he should be celebrated rather than forgotten. Chew Chong was perhaps the father of the man Stewart remembered: 'the humble nameless Chinese vegetable man who sold us crackers and skyrockets in season and, at all times, lettuces for threepence'.[2]

Next door to the old Chew Chong site is the courthouse, with its imposing entrance, Doric columns, ornate pediment and crenellations. It was officially opened by Prime Minister Sir Joseph Ward in 1908. It hints at the dashed hopes and failed ambitions of those fin-de-siècle townspeople. By the early 1950s it was very apparent that the town was not going to grow, and with improved technology and transport the courthouse was no longer needed: lawyers and criminals alike could make the journey to New Plymouth or Hawera or even further afield. The court-

Elrham. F.G.R.4184.

Bridge Street, Eltham. The photograph was taken around 1913, the year Douglas Stewart was born in the Taranaki town. *Frederick George Radcliffe photographer, ref. 1/2-006046-G, Alexander Turnbull Library, Wellington*

house was closed and only a short time later converted into an imposing veterinary clinic. The building retains that function today.

Unlike many small towns in New Zealand fallen prey to the wrecker's ball, Eltham preserves many Victorian and early twentieth-century shop-fronts and old buildings, and they are consciously preserved. With only a little dressing, Bridge Street has been used as a set for films and television drama. Perhaps as more and more young New Zealanders find it increasingly difficult to survive in our major cities, towns like Eltham will be not only revived but loved and treasured as they were in Stewart's day.

So who were the people who lived in Eltham during Stewart's boyhood? Māori, of course, although not to the extent his readers and listeners might have assumed given the prominence of Māori culture in much of his New Zealand-inspired poetry and work for radio and stage. In a possibly unintentionally tragic passage in *Springtime in Taranaki* he recalls: 'Plump Maori ladies, with tattooed chins and bare feet, came and sold us kit-bags made of flax, and purple, carthy kumaras, and treat beyond all treats, beautiful fresh whitebait which they would have netted,

I suppose, at the mouth of the Waingonoro near Hawera, where they lived. Often, lords of the land as they had once been, they would ask for old clothes in exchange for their wares.'³ There were Dalmatians and Austrians too, employed to dig ditches to drain swamp for farmland. It's possible that some of these families called 'Austrian' were Croatian but misidentified because they were members of the Hapsburg Empire. A man with the Croatian surname Radisch (more likely Radich) was the fishmonger.

It was the more usual, bog-standard English, Irish and Scottish immigrant stock that closely surrounded Stewart as he grew up. His own family were of Scots extraction. His grandfather, Rev Alexander Stewart, was a Presbyterian minister. Having tried Dunedin for a short period, he went to live in Geelong and then Melbourne where he married the daughter of a wealthy landowner and raised his family. Rev Alexander was no ordinary minister. Ambitious, hardworking and clever, he rose to be Moderator of the General Assembly of the Presbyterian Church in Australia.

There appears to have been some tension between Stewart's father, another Alexander, and the minister. The cause of the quarrel is not known but it may perhaps have been about the academically gifted young Alexander studying medicine instead of entering the Church. At any rate, it resulted in Stewart's father leaving Melbourne. When he arrived in Auckland, his knowledge of the classics meant he was able to obtain a position teaching Greek and Latin at King's School, Remuera. Another position followed at a country school in the Hauraki Plains town of Waihi, which is where he met and married Mary FitzGerald. After their marriage the couple moved to Rawhiritoa, in Taranaki, where Alexander taught at the small local school and studied law at night. Soon after qualifying he and his young wife moved to nearby Eltham. He became a partner in a practice with two other lawyers, and stayed in the town for the rest of his life.

In Stewart's account, his father was a contented man. He did not inherit his own father's ambition, happy instead to practise law in a small country town. He kept limited hours, refused big criminal cases such as they were, and confined his business to conveyancing and minor offences. Stewart remembered his mother encouraging her husband to go back to work in the afternoon after lunch, when he would rather sit and read in the sun or adjourn to the golf course. The family house was in Meuli Street, which abuts the only hill in the district apart from the distant mountain.

A photograph shows it complete with veranda and an iconic cabbage tree in the front yard.

They were wealthy enough to afford housemaids drawn from one local family, and a gardener. These days perhaps we would credit Alexander Stewart with advanced E.I. (emotional intelligence) and a healthy work-life balance. He had what he wanted – a beloved wife, a healthy family, a pretty house set in half an acre of gardens, a job he liked better than teaching, golf and plenty of books. He also had, at a time when car ownership was rare, a Buick, which conveyed the family to Opunake beach for long summer holidays.

In keeping with their middle-class position in the small society of Eltham, Douglas Stewart attended a private primary school from the time he was five until he was eight. This was presided over by a Miss Hooper, who was strict but firm, and 'given to laughter'. After three years of her benign tutelage, Eltham Public School was a rude shock, particularly since the schoolmistress there was fond of the strap. By his own count, Miss Papps gave him some three hundred cuts in the first year. All of us educated before the 1980s have memories of the drawer in the teacher's desk in which the regulation-issue strap was kept, and how ominous it was when the teacher removed it for use. Astonishing as it now seems, getting the strap was part of the quotidian existence.

Miss Papps can't have been all bad, because she encouraged Stewart in his first attempts at writing. It was a story from the point of view of an old, rusted umbrella lying discarded in the washhouse, and he recalled that, basking in her praise, he thought he might become an author. It was an ambition that was to fade for a number of years.

Young New Zealanders of the twenty-first century are very aware of the historical tensions between Māori and Pākehā. Less do they know of the historical mutual antipathy between Catholic and Protestant factions. Children nationwide would call out to one another, depending on which side they were on:

> Cattle dogs
> Jump like frogs
> Don't eat meat on Fridays!

Or:

Catholic, Catholic ring the bell
While the Protestant goes to hell.[4]

As a boy, then, Stewart would have been aware of the divisions between Catholic and Protestant, between Māori and Pākehā, and also between the two nationalities absorbed into his family. Of all of the five subjects of this book, Stewart would have been the most familiar with not only the idea of Australia but the reality of it.

Most importantly, there was a real live emissary from West Island. Granny would come to stay – a kind, gentle woman who was in possession of a purse bulging with pennies and sixpences, and who welcomed the children who jumped into bed with her in the morning for a cuddle. In Stewart's recall the family seem more demonstrative than many in this era when it was not uncommon for Pākehā children, and especially boys, to receive no physical affection at all.

Letters would have gone back and forth between Eltham and Melbourne, bringing family news of West Island. By far the greater source of Australian information on a national scale was the weekly *Bulletin*. Stewart's father subscribed to it at a time when it was one of the most widely read magazines in Australasia. Published in various formats between 1889 and 2008, the *Bulletin* was an opinion-maker on politics, commerce, arts and literature.

Stewart, being an observant child and very fond of his father, would have learnt from an early age that the *Bulletin* was, for him, very close to a holy book. He would also have known that in Australia the magazine was fondly known as the Bushman's Bible. In imitation of his father he would have studied it closely, from its now highly controversial masthead, *Australia for the White Man*, to its cartoons and funny stories and, most importantly, the 'Red Page', the *Bulletin*'s literary component. Poems, literary gossip and reviews in what looks to a modern eye like crowded typography filled its pages. Much of it would have made little sense to a small boy, even a literate small boy, in a small town in New Zealand, but it would have encouraged his already strong perception of Australia as a place of ideas and stories.

The enviable childhood went on. After the war, FitzGerald uncles and aunts came to settle in Eltham to be close to Stewart's mother, who was the fulcrum of the family. The Meuli Street front parlour was used for the Glee Club – entertainment in the days before radio and television. The locals interested in music would gather around the piano to sing 'surprisingly juvenile items' – rounds like 'Humpty Dumpty', 'Three Blind Mice', 'Ten Green Bottles'.[5] Folk songs and Gaelic songs were also part of the repertoire. Stewart's father would parade up and down singing, pretending to play the bagpipes. Stewart remembered not only the participants but also the quality of their voices: Harold Northover from the box factory, for example, with his 'husky baritone'.

In his introduction to *Springtime in Taranaki*, long-time friend and literary agent Tim Curnow remarks on Stewart's prodigious recall for names. It is perhaps one of the most extraordinary aspects of what is, apart from some standout passages of nature writing – which was Stewart's true gift – a very ordinary account of an ordinary middle-class rural childhood. Aside from family, he recalled some 25 full names of tradespeople and professionals in the town

'How innocent and merry and companionable were the pleasures of life in Eltham!' Stewart remarked.[6] There were the usual less innocent children's pastimes and experiences, which he recalled with great humour and candour. He remembered playing games of 'Rudey' with a friend of his sister's, 'inspecting with great interest such differences as were to be detected between little boys and little girls; and then, since we knew nothing of the more enterprising games we might have attempted, decorating any crevices we could find in each other with ivy leaves. It was rather a charming game, now I come to think of it, and I am sorry we did not play it more often.'[7] On holidays with family friends who were farmers, he and his mate shared quarters with farmhand Phil. This man was 'blessed with the most enormous doodle ever worn by mortal man. Really, he was like a stallion. As he invariably went to bed wearing only his singlet, we saw a good deal of this mighty object, swinging about and casting long shadows in the candlelight or gruesomely dangling in the dawn, and we never failed to be impressed by it.'[8]

*

The year Stewart turned 13 he was sent some 30 kilometres west to board at New Plymouth Boys' High School, where he would remain for the next five years. The school sits high on the hill overlooking the small city of New Plymouth and with a panoramic view of the sea. It is a handsome institution, with buildings of the same vintage and style as those of other prestigious grammar schools in New Zealand such as Mount Albert Grammar in Auckland.

New Plymouth Boys' is still a boarding school, though the original boarding house is long demolished. The senior housemaster occupies a gracious, late-nineteenth-century two-storey house at the memorial gate. The high white gate is itself impressive, a sombre monument to former pupils killed in World War I. Among the many old buildings still in use is a gymnasium with gabled roof and turret. There are new classrooms and facilities for the boarders, mature trees, music rooms and playing fields. One field occupies the top of a hill, and another called The Gully is exactly that, with high eastern and western terraces carved into the banks for spectators. Walking around the deserted grounds one Labour Weekend, I had the sense of a school well cared for and treasured by its community.

Stewart's years at New Plymouth Boys' seem to have been, in the main, happy ones. After being asked to write a poem for the school magazine he found not only that he could write poetry but that he loved it, and 'so changed the universe'.[9] This was a poem of around 30 lines, a dialogue between an angler and the stream he fished: evidence of his two life-long passions – fishing and poetry – taking hold. All students were given *Smith's Book of Verse*, a standard text of the time, which contained carefully chosen extracts from the works of Shakespeare, Herrick, Milton, Wordsworth, Burns, Byron, Shelley, Keats, Browning and Tennyson. Stewart read it so often that he knew much of it off by heart.

Many of us are grateful to the one teacher during our high school years who saved our lives if we were having a difficult time, or who recognised where our strengths lay and so gave us direction. Stewart's saviour was a Scottish master, Jas Leggat, his English teacher. Leggat arranged for him to join the New Plymouth Public Library, where he could read more poetry than the school offered. It was there that he discovered the more recent poets, the men (and they were all men) deemed to be influencing the next generation of bards: Yeats, Walter de la Mare, W.H. Davies, Edmund Blunden, Siegfried Sassoon, Richard Church, Humbert Wolfe and Rupert Brooke.

The reading inspired him and gave him further confidence. He sent a newly penned sonnet to the *Taranaki News* and was mortified when it was published in the Children's Page. At school he made friends with the young Denis Glover, though doesn't relate whether at this stage Glover had ambition to write. He remembered him as 'a shrill, pink-faced boy ... who was always my great rival in French and English'.[10]

So confident was he of his own abilities that at age 15 he started to send poems to the *Bulletin*. Later, under the auspices of Pat Lawlor, the *Bulletin* would have a New Zealand office situated in Wellington; at this time, however, the magazine was generated from Sydney. Stewart sent so many poems across the Tasman that he would later describe it as a bombardment. In the same year he began submitting to the *Bulletin*, the school asked him to write new words for the school song. He regarded this as a great honour. Many years later he would return to New Plymouth Boys' High to rejuvenate these lyrics, removing from them the imperialist sensibility that had infused the first ones. New Zealand in the 1920s, or at least the majority Anglo-Saxon New Zealanders of the 20s, regarded the country as a far-flung archipelago of the British Isles. By the 1970s this was, for young New Zealanders, a distant memory. The values the school attempts to instil in students – fortitude, clear thinking and mateship – feature strongly in the lyrics, with the recurring strain 'Comradeship, valour and wisdom'. The last verse even harks back to the Roman Empire:

> We will fight for the right, honour the brave,
> We will keep till we sleep to the rule that Rome gave,
> Comradeship, valour and wisdom, Comradeship, valour and wisdom.

Life at boarding school was not all study and the writing of poetry. The great mystery of sex was unfolded for him by a school housemaid, whom he took out to a local park called The Meeting of the Waters in his father's Baby Austin, and where 'very expertly and intriguingly she instructed' him in the art of love.[11] He managed for the most part to avoid other physical activities such as sport, for which he had no interest or aptitude.

In early 1931 Stewart left Taranaki for what must have seemed a racing, glittery metropolis – Wellington – to follow in his father's footsteps by studying for a law degree. In hindsight he was able to describe it as 'the bleak, windy city of Wellington', and it is true that the place has an unappealing climate.[12] The outlying areas are less windy, but the city itself is built on precipitous hills above Cook Strait, one of the most turbulent bodies of water in the world. It faces into southerly gales while also weathering howling storms from the north, particularly in the spring. Even in these days of global warming, Wellington winters are icy and sleety, and in Stewart's day heating of the uninsulated wooden buildings would have been rudimentary.

The law bored him to death. So much so that he failed everything, even the few papers for which he had actually attended lectures. He was far more interested in racing his Baby Austin back and forth from Wellington to Eltham for his holidays, and exploring the works of writers introduced to him by a new friend: James Joyce, Edith Sitwell, Wyndham Lewis, D.H. Lawrence and Bertrand Russell, among others. Prime among these was Australian Norman Lindsay, with his 'baffling but wildly stimulating Creative Effort and his much more approachable "Redheap" (which doesn't seem to have been banned in New Zealand as it was in Australia, and which we enormously enjoyed for its comedies of adolescent love in an Australian small town, so very like the comedies of Eltham)'.[13]

Stewart must also have spent a fair amount of time gazing out to sea, just as he must have done during his years at New Plymouth Boys', except that this time he was focused towards the south or east, rather than northwest. Gazing out to sea is a time-honoured New Zealand pastime, eyes resting on the horizon while contemplating either escape or the arrival of visitors. 'We felt with ever increasing urgency that beyond the rocky headlands of Wellington Harbour lay the great world, and we must see it.'[14]

His sentiments were expressed in an early poem, probably published in the *Bulletin*. Evident is the influence of the poets he was reading at the time, particularly in the repetition of 'cold' in the last line. Unmentioned in the list he recalled is, possibly, T.S. Eliot:

> Morning at Wellington
> Thin stone is in this chill wind from the south:
> Thin stone, an essence of those bleak, hard hills
> That bulk between the town and the cold surf.
> Yes, though it gets its coldness from the sea
> That, snowed with moonlight, icicled with foam,
> Antarctically glistened all night long,

This current, in its planes like panes of glass
That vertically shear between sheer walls,
Is hardened and made sour with those huge hills,
As though the sharp spurs jutting through the grass
Exhale their own dank breath into the wind.

Like the lean soul of steel, like spinsters' lips
It has an acid taste, unhumanised.
I think it will be hard for the young birds,
And children's lips will blue because of it.
If you had ears like mine you'd hear it now,

Bitter with a thin sound that stone might make,
And icy with the far-off ocean breaking,
A cataclysm of surf with frost toned bells,
Coldly on crag and stone and coldly on cold shells.[15]

The poet gave his location as 'Maoriland'. This was not only a hangover from the nineteenth century but also a kind of literary affectation on the part of non-Māori writers from New Zealand.

The opportunity to escape the thin stone and chill spinster's lips of Wellington (although by his own account he had a beautiful dark-haired, dark-eyed girlfriend to kiss at this time) was not so far away, hastened by his total failure at law school. The results came while he was on holiday with his family. It is an insight into the character of his father that Stewart was not made to feel like a failure generally, as fathers commonly do when their sons disappoint them. Instead, he was allowed to come home and think about his future. During this time he got his first job as a journalist, as sole reporter on the *Eltham Argus*. This was a tiny daily newspaper of four pages, and cost one penny. Stewart was responsible for a column called 'Tut tut', which exercised the humour of the period. For example, when he wrote up the window display of woollen underwear in the local draper's he gave it the headline 'Winter is drawing on' – a play on the old word 'drawers' for undies.[16] Hilarious. He had fans, locals who wrote to the paper to congratulate him on his wit.

The *Argus* building still stands in Eltham, tattered and abandoned. Someone has started to paint the facade green but either gave up or ran out of paint at the last minute. Beyond the painter's reach the scruffy pediment, mossy and cracked, announces proudly *1897 Eltham Argus*. A sten-cilled graffiti to one side reads DUDES, the name of a popular Auckland band of the late 1970s. Both newspaper and band are consigned to history.

The country journalist suffered a few romantic misadventures, one of which inspired a poem that brought him his longed-for publication in the *Bulletin*. Pat Lawlor had begun to man a *Bulletin* office in Wellington and it's possible he was looking for New Zealand talent. It was a poem about love and the loss of it. But Stewart was restless. There he was, back in Eltham, a failure at law school, and living with Mum and Dad. He wanted freedom and the open road: the life of the roaming bard.

Fortuitously, a man called Charlie Davey arrived in Eltham with his merry-go-round, and needed an assistant. Stewart left the *Argus* without a backward glance and toured the North Island, or at least as far as Auckland, where the merry-go-round became an adjunct to a touring circus. In Ōtāhuhu, then an outlying town, he and Charlie had a falling-out. Not willing to return to Eltham, Stewart, a failure yet again, headed north. In the Kaipara he was taken in by an elderly Māori couple, with whom he lived for a week or so.

In his first collection *A Girl With Red Hair* (1944), published 10 years after this experience, Stewart included a story about his hosts. An excerpt reads:

> I looked at the old couple, nodding by the fire, the light on their dark faces. What did I really know about them? What went on in those secretive Maori minds? They weren't animals. They had their own thoughts, based on a conception of life beyond my understanding. What possible communion could there be between the white man and the native? The memory of that deep, mindless sympathy when we sat quietly by the fire on the wet night was uncannily disturbing, horrible. The friendly little whare was a prison.

He was not to know that it was this story, full of the prejudices of the time, that would incense and inspire Witi Ihimaera, one of the foremost New Zealand writers of the twentieth century and beyond. It is interesting to compare Stewart's recollection of the story's inspiration and then to look at how Ihimaera, as a schoolboy forced to read it, responded. Here is Stewart, writing about that adventure in *Springtime in Taranaki*:

And they fed me, the old couple, next day in their own whare, where the fire smouldered all day on the earth under its smoke hole in the corrugated iron roof, and the big black kettle swung on its iron hook, and, perpetually simmering with what must have been about the most lethal black brew ever known to mortal man, the fat enamel teapot stood by the embers, never emptied of its accumulated tea-leaves but occasionally replenished with a handful of fresh leaves if the liquid seemed insufficiently tarry. We ate oiled watercress, a stringy vegetable; and flat damper bread; and cockles or pipis which were kept, still vaguely alive, in a kerosene tin in a corner and which somebody had gathered a week or two earlier from the Kaipara. They strike me now as a most dangerous form of nourishment, though they never did us any harm. We cooked them, briefly, the shells opened, over the fire. We ate, too, delicious boiled kumaras, with purple skins and soft floury yellow flesh, the king of all sweet potatoes.[17]

He goes on to describe how the fleas tortured him on his mats in the wharepuni, and how at night he would scrape them from his legs by the handful and chuck them in the fire. 'The old chief and his wife seemed more or less immune from them,' he writes, 'and only very occasionally, when some particularly penetrating bite really got through to him, the old man would say he would pour boiling water over them "tomorrow". But that tomorrow never came, and the fleas flourished and bit. They were a torment ... They were in the wharepuni, too, by the million: in the mats of my bed. I could not sleep for them.'[18]

He recollects how the couple talked about finding him a Māori wife, and how he helped harvest the kūmara crop by riding a horse down the hill to where the women dug and laboured. They would lay a sack of kūmara over his horse and he would return up the hill to where the men were laying the kūmara in fern-lined pits to preserve them.

Here is Ihimaera, remembering the time he read the story at school during the early 1950s:

I had the same attitude to the story that the Nigerian novelist Chinua Achebe had when he read Joyce Cary's novel Mister Johnston: 'It began to dawn on me that although fiction was undoubtedly fictitious, it could also be true or false.'

What was Mrs Bradley thinking? Was she trying to rub our noses in our own pathetic lives? I found the story poisonous, the setting demonic and the Maori characters demeaning. As my Māori schoolmates ducked for cover I was incensed enough to ask Mrs Bradley, 'Why have you made us read this story?' Despite her protestations that New Zealand Short Stories represented the best of our writers, I threw the book out the window. Quite rightly, she hauled me before Mr Allen and he gave me six of the best.

My ambition to be a writer was voiced that day. I said I was going to write a book about Māori people, not just because it had to be done but because I needed to unpoison the stories already written about Māori, and it would be taught in every school in New Zealand, whether they wanted it or not.[19]

Ihimaera's rage and determination are obvious. We could, in a way, thank Stewart for setting Ihimaera on the road, even though it was a bitter stirrup cup he offered.

I should add here that when Stewart's daughter Meg read a draft of this chapter she was saddened by Ihimaera's boyhood response to the story and wrote to me: 'If Dad was alive to today I'm sure he would be deeply distressed to learn of the affront that the heightened language and sentiment of a short story written by him decades earlier caused to the young Witi Ihimaera. Obviously Dad never intended (as you acknowledge) his words in that story or any of his works to be so offensive or wounding to Ihimaera or other Māori readers (including the Māori members of our own family) and I apologise to them on his behalf.'[20]

What is clear, from Stewart's letters, diaries, poetry and plays, is that he was not an overt racist. If the charge of racism is to be made against him it is of the same innate type that infected all new New Zealanders of the time. On his return from the Kaipara he wrote this poem, reproduced in *Springtime in Taranaki*:

Talk lewder now, and turn the radio
Louder, and shout the whirling darkness down,
And someone lock the door against the snow.
So in a bleak time once I reached the end
Of troubling and pianoing desire.
And dead as stone in age-old leathery silence
Crouched with two savages beside a fire
And as a dog knows, knew them both for friend.
Corncobs and drying shark were hung on wall
And sooty kettle swung from a black chain.

And rain outside, and shadows in. The woman
Jabbed at the embers. And then was still again.[21]

Had Ihimaera read this his resolve to become a writer would doubtless
have been even stronger. In the 1930s the term 'savage' was passing from
use, and it was certainly archaic by the time Stewart wrote his autobiography. This might well be why he added: '"Savage" was hardly the word for
these two gentle souls.'[22]

Living 'among the Maori' was not for Stewart. He returned to the
Taranaki where he thought he had a girl waiting for him. She was not. He
endured his first real heartache and even contemplated suicide, though
not for so long or so intensely that he couldn't fall in love with someone
else three months later. Meanwhile, he worked as a journalist on the
Hawera Daily News and took up drinking. He continued to send poems
to the *Bulletin* and was regularly published. One such effort is 'Watching
the Milking', the first verse of which is:

> In the ashen evening of a bird's song spouts in silver
> That swirls to the shed where an engine spits and chugs.
> The yard is muddy; sunk to the knees, the cows
> Await the sucking cups, the hand that tugs,
> Content and chewing; and not afraid of man
> Or the weird machine that robs their swollen dugs.[23]

Breasts, ovine and human, are always a source of fascination for masculine young poets. Here is an excerpt from 'Two Studies':

> The four girls frolic in the water
> and their flesh grows warm at the subtle caress of the current
> two of them, meeting in the pool
> stop
> and stand face to face
> each with hands on the other's delicate breasts.[24]

All young poets, perhaps, should destroy their juvenilia.

Stewart enjoyed his time in Hawera. He reported on all issues,
including on one memorable occasion a journey to Patea to interview
the prophet T.W. Ratana. His record of this, as set down in *Springtime*,
is rather sneering and not worth reproducing. This was a time of heavy

drinking and youthful behaviour, and in February 1931 he was given the sack.

Poetry was all. He wrote prodigiously, sending poems off to magazines in New Zealand and Australia. He grew a thick skin – necessary, perhaps, given the wording of some of his rejections. In September 1931, when he queried a rejection by the *New Zealand Magazine*, established in 1921 as *New Zealand Life*, the editor responded in a handwritten note:

Dear Sir,

You ask in your letter: did I find the poem unamusing, dull? To be perfectly frank, I did; and that is why I advised against publication … If you are writing for your own pleasure, well and good; if you are writing for publication (other people's pleasure) then I think your venture hopeless.

Yours sincerely
The Editor NZM[25]

Another letter preserved among his papers, not quite a rejection, stands as an example of the kind of response today's young writers rarely receive. It is dated 10 August 1931 and typed in dashing blue.

University Tutorial School
Masonic Chambers,
Wellington Terrace, Wellington.

Dear Mr Stewart,

I have read the Ms of your burlesque epic with great amusement and a keen appreciation of your felicity in handling an extensive vocabulary. Occasionally you have trouvailles in verbal prestidigitation that a verse writer in Punch might envy … I am inclined to think that your appeal would be more effective if you retained that half of the whole which is best; a heavy demand, as it would involve rewriting a large number of stanzas. After all, not much happens to your hero that could not be put on a sheet of note-paper, and if you rely wholly on your skill with words to interest your readers, that skill must be kept as nearly as possible at its highest level throughout. Your work seems to me good enough to be worth the labour of making it shorter.

Sincerely yours,
GW von Zedlitz[26]

For around 10 years Stewart had been in correspondence with the literary editor of the *Bulletin*, the writer Cecil Mann, not only concerning the publication (or not) of his verse and short stories but also in the hope of a possible job. In 1933 Mann wrote to say that there could well be an opening as staff light verse writer. The letter reads, in part:

> ... as editor of the Mirror I've been accepting your verse for some time: now I'm back with the Bulletin, looking after the short stories, Red Page, 'serious' verse and suchlike literary matters ... I write to see if you'll let me have first choice of your work; I'll return what I don't take so that you may place it elsewhere. Also, are you likely to be over this way? If you are, look me up. You might also tell me what inky experiences you've had, for possible future reference. Have you ever, for instance, written 'light' verse?
>
> All the best intent
> Cecil Mann[27]

Contemporary writers would be envious – imagine being paid to write light verse! Older New Zealanders will remember Whim Wham and others of his ilk. Light verse was a kind of poetic cartoon, a way of making light of the serious issues of the day. Mann believed that the current staff writer of light verse, Andrée Hayward, was about to relinquish his post. Without hesitation Stewart boarded the *Marama* in Wellington and made the five-day voyage across the Tasman. He intended to stay for a while at the People's Palace, a cheap, private hotel run by the Salvation Army, and favoured as safe accommodation for single people as well as families. Built in 1888 on a large site on Pitt Street in the central city, with 600 rooms, it was a New Zealanders' destination for decades. My own mother, making her first brave foray away from home at the age of 20, stayed there with her best friend when they arrived in Sydney in 1959. The building was demolished in the late 80s.

Stewart would likely have thought that staying at the People's Palace was part of the usual Kiwi in Sydney adventure and particularly inspiring to a poet, but it is unlikely he was disappointed when Mann changed his plans and took him across the harbour to Kirribilli to stay in the flat he shared with his wife and two young sons. Stewart's daughter Meg recalls that Mann's flat was 'filled with literary atmosphere as well as a sense of Sydney cultural life'.[28] Bookshelves boasted first editions from Nonesuch

Press, a British publishing company renowned for its handsome editions of John Donne's poetry, as well as the works of writers such as William Wycherley and William Congreve. On the walls were framed drawings and cartoons from the *Bulletin*. Beyond the flat were the strident cries of Australian birds and the hum of cicadas, fiendishly loud to New Zealand ears, and fine houses and gardens that spread to the water's edge. Stewart and Mann went swimming at midnight in the shark-infested harbour, and the following morning drank six bottles of beer. Then it was across the harbour again on the ferry, and on to the *Bulletin* office. 'I walked through the turnstiles at Circular Quay into the world of magic I had dreamed of,' Stewart recalled.[29]

But Andrée Hayward didn't resign. Who could blame him? Jobs writing light verse were rare even then. Stewart, still only 26 years old, went instead to Melbourne where he stayed with relatives and tried for six months to make a go of it as a freelance writer. He went to see fellow New Zealander and editor of the *Sun*, Eric Baume. Stewart recalled his interview: '"Oh, writers," said lordly Baume, lolling back on his chair with his feet on the desk, "I can get writers anywhere. Are you a good sub?" Truthfully, but foolishly perhaps, I said I had had no experience as a sub-editor, and that was that.'[30] He did manage, briefly, to find employment as a reporter – on yacht racing, about which, by his own admission, he knew nothing. After Christmas in Melbourne he returned to Sydney to see if Andrée Hayward would at last relinquish his post, but the situation was the same as it was before.

Back to New Zealand he went, wanting nothing more than to return to Australia as fast as he could. He was excited by the men he had met, the writers and artists, the 'brilliant, hard-drinking men', and especially the poets Kenneth Slessor and Robert D. FitzGerald, who would become close friends.[31]

As we all do when we return from our first journey to Australia, Stewart marvelled at how green and lush the New Zealand countryside is, how different the quality of light. He felt that he had fallen in love with New Zealand all over again.

In a poem 'Haystack', written after his return, he wrote: 'The creamy frost of toi-toi plumes/Above the rushes' blue-green shrilling/Forewarns the farm that winter comes,/But the rich land is not unwilling.'[32] Another poem, 'The Growing Strangeness', contains the evocative line: 'The blunt grey statement of New Zealand hills'.[33]

Love for the beauty of New Zealand, particularly Taranaki, was not so overwhelming that he did not experience an irritation with his homeland. This too is a common phenomenon in young New Zealanders after their first real, adult experience of Australia. It can manifest itself in highly unpleasant ways, annoying family, friends and total strangers, especially if that irritation is published. Stewart tried to publish his. Luckily for him, the piece he submitted at the end of 1933 to the *New Zealand Herald*, 'Nelson in Winter: A drive to Takaka green rivers and black crags', was rejected. It reads, in part:

> 'Where are we now?' I ask. I am being cured of a sentimental predilection for Maori place-names, for in Nelson the English names are all so beautiful that one must believe it was colonised by poets, while the Maori ones are harsh and ugly, sounding as if they were squawked out by quarrelling seagulls. Motueka, Riwaka, Wakapuwaka, and hideous Takaka are the brown man's legacy: but the white pioneers have given us Rainbow Valley, Golden Valley, Dovedale and Pigeon Valley, Bright-water and Ruby Bay. The biggest natural spring in the word ... is still insulted with the ridiculous Maori [erased] name of Pu-Pu ...

He goes on to describe travelling through a valley of inbred idiots and remarks that:

> ... many of the bridges over the big rivers are crazy structures that would not be tolerated in the progressive North ... The Maoris, before they were driven away are said to have had five hundred acres under cultivation around Nelson ... (these days) the country's full of unemployed fossicking on the subsidy. They're making a crust, but these people are different. Three Wellington families, all comfortably off before the depression; went broke, and are making a marvellous fight of it here.[34]

It was during these few years back in Taranaki, before his departure for good, that Stewart made the acquaintance of novelist and poet Eve Langley, an Australian living in New Zealand. He was so dazzled by her writing that he hoped, on their first meeting, they would fall in love. Given her long battle with mental illness, he had a lucky escape. He visited her several times in Auckland and was to say, '[I]t was always the same impression of squalor and down-to-earth peasantry all around her and this vivid flame in the middle of it.'[35] Langley wrote in her journal of him: 'I really do love that boy for his goodness and quiet kindness and his Douglas Stewartness ... his red rimmed eyes, his sad down pulled nervous mouth ...'[36] Their friendship was to endure until Langley's lonely death in her shack near Katoomba, New South Wales, in the winter of 1974. Langley loved Stewart as a brother, often addressing him as such. He helped her out financially, emotionally and practically many times, and was a great admirer of her feverish, image-rich writing. Langley had a brief, unhappy marriage, and bore three children who were put in an orphanage by their father Hilary Clark while Langley was incarcerated in Auckland Psychiatric Hospital. An extract from one of her many, lengthy letters to Stewart, written in the 1930s, gives a strong sense of her voice and state of mind:

My brother you should know by my silence, that I am busy about forbidden things. The angels are always waving Eve out of Eden. In old days I went out alone, but this time I have contrived to drag a companion with me. I have married him, so I suppose that means that he must come, too.

His name is Hilary, he is a tall black bearded art-student of 22 and he lives alone in his garret, like a wolf, and bawls out, 'Who the hell's there?' whenever I go near the door. Therefore, I don't go near it, often.

At odd times he will consent to share the marriage couch, but when the clocks strike the long midnight, he says that he hears a motif in them that he must follow, and paces around the room, complaining, 'god, tonight I feel that I could write a concerto! My Eve, I will away!' and he buckles on his sandals, and with a delicate flutter of white undergarments is gone.

So, Dhas, I am much alone, and working hard, preparing a book of verse for London. Surely to God they'll have the sense to see that it's not worth printing. And a book of fairy tales for the same suffering City, and a book of short stories for the same screaming, outraged place.

Fear and loneliness drive me on, brother, and I will admit them to none but you ... Hilary is a great and glorious drinker; foam lies on his beard, his lips grow rich and wide, and he has a laugh as long as the Wall of China and as loud as a Maori's blazer ... This place at Hernbae (as the Indian greengrocer's calender [sic] has it) is two rooms belonging to a woman who paints, and for seven and tix [sic] a week I have got it from her for three wiks. It is full of the gimcracks that some women love, and which I love, too, for a while. Little cups and plates and things like a mob of cattle of different brands, all yarded in cupboards ... Hilary lives under a big box, for which he pays no rent. It has two rooms, the one below is for him to study and swear and sing and bellow in, and the one above is for the echoes, because his echoes need plenty of space. He really has more belongings than I have, because there is his piano which he rocks like a cradle, and his violin which rocks him, and a bed which is like rocks, and a chair with its jawbone torn out.[37]

Stewart was captivated by the humour, energy and sense of danger in her writing, and always felt very sympathetic towards her, no matter how irked he was by her behaviour. It may have been that Langley first came to his notice in 1934, when he received a letter from Dunedin asking if he would be willing to contribute to a new magazine called *The Golden Fleece*. Its mission was 'to find out literary wealth in New Zealand'. The editor, A.N. Allan, was proud to announce that he had 'five pounds in Dunedin Savings Bank and a guarantee of five pounds that we can call on'. Most importantly, he wrote, 'Eve Langley has given us permission to quote from her "Jason of Argo laughs" on the title page.'[38] For the magazine to go ahead he needed 560 subscribers at £1 each. Stewart may well have contributed financially. His willingness to support other writers and all kinds of literary endeavour was one of his endearing, life-long traits.

Meanwhile he wrote letters to Australian newspapers seeking work. The *Ballarat Courier* replied to say there were no vacancies but that 'Your name has been placed on our list.' A telegram arrived from the *Melbourne Weekly* to say his application had been received; a second telegram announced POSITION FILLED.

Stewart continued sending poems to the *Bulletin*. A 1935 letter from Mann reads, 'Work has been so thick that I've only now got to your verse. Some of it is splendid – Mending the Bridge, Winter Crazed, the Poplar piece and the ... strangeness seemed to me uncommonly full of poetry ... the others enclosed I don't care for so much.'[39]

'Mending the Bridge' is worth reproducing in full for its vigorous energy and imagery. Until the end of his life, Stewart rightly regarded it as one of his best:

> Burnished with copper light, burnished,
> The men are brutal: their bodies jut out square,
> Massive as rock in the lantern's stormy glare
> Against the devastation of the dark.

Now passionate, as if to gouge the stark
Quarry of baleful light still deeper there,
With slow, gigantic chopping rhythm they hack,
Beat back and crumple up and spurn the black
Live night, the marsh black sludgy air.

And clamour the colour of copper light
Swings from their hammering, and speeds, and breaks
Darkness to clots and spattering light, and flakes
Oily, like dazzling snow and storms of oil.
The night that never sleeps, quickens. The soil,
The stones and the grass are alive. The thrush awakes,
Huddles, and finds the leaves gone hard and cool.
The cows in the fields are awake, restless; the bull
Restless. The dogs. A young horse snorts and shakes.

Beneath the square of glaring light
The river still is muttering of flood,
The dark day when thick with ugly mud,
Swirling with logs and swollen beasts (and some
Still alive, drowning) it had come
Snarling, a foul beast chewing living cud,
And grappled with the bridge and tried to rend it,
So now these stronger brutes must sweat to mend it
Labouring in light like orange blood.

Men labour in the city so,
With naked fore-arms singed with copper light
And strangeness on them as with stone they fight,
Each meet for fear, and even the curt drill
Mysterious as trees and a dark hill.
But these are stronger, these oppose their might
To storm and flood and all the land's black power.
Burnished with sweat and lanterns now they tower
Monstrous against the marshes of the night.[40]

On 1 July 1973 an ABC programme called 'The Poems of Douglas Stewart' was broadcast on Sunday Night Radio Two, presented by

Stewart himself. The typescript of the unscripted narration explains the genesis of the poem: '[It] dates away way back to my early youth in New Zealand. Think I was about twenty when I wrote it, and oddly enough, I'd just come back from my first attempt to get a job and live in Australia, and that fell through. And when I went back to New Zealand I seemed to be seeing the place with fresh force, almost for the first time.'

Poets of every generation struggle to get their work published. Stewart went into battle with Whitcombe & Tombs over his first collection, *Green Lions*. Following an initial request that they read the manuscript he received a letter, dated 11 September 1935:

> ... as you probably know, the market for poetry in Australasia is small and as a rule we undertake publication only at author's expense. However, if you care to submit your selection we will consider them and report to you as soon as possible.
>
> Yours faithfully,
> AW Shrimpton,
> Editor[41]

A month later, he received a further communication:

> Dear Sir,
>
> Yours of the 29th of September has been under consideration for some time. We have no wish to incite you to reckless expenditure but as you seem keen to have your verses in print we will see if we can help you ... We will estimate the cost of production in the style say of Jessie Mackay's recent volume, Vigil, which you have no doubt seen.
>
> AW Shrimpton[42]

By 6 November his demands were starting to annoy Shrimpton:

> ... I have to say that your condition re window display is impossible. It would not pay any bookseller to do more than give a little space to a book of poetry, particularly by an unknown author and at the Xmas season. Poetry sells badly at any time and window space is valuable. Few copies are selling of Vigil and Miss Jessie Mackay is well known ... We cannot control window displays by our branches and our Australian houses have no windows. Neither can we dictate to other booksellers, who, of course, fill their windows with stuff for which there is a known demand.

Your other condition re having the book out to catch Xmas sales I regret to say is practically impossible too. You perhaps don't realise that there is no profit for us in this job at the price quoted.[43]

It seems that that Stewart asked his father for help in this regard – and that he had already suggested his father read *The Wasteland* so that he had some conception of what his son was on about. A letter from his mother confirms:

We'll think hard about 'Green Lions' and act in due course.
Pop's got to find out what kind of book T.S. Eliot's Waste Land is before he accepts your kind offer – let you know the result later – suppose it's too indecent![44]

In the end, his loving mother contributed £50 towards his book. Stewart himself would have had additional funds to contribute. When *Green Lions* roared into print in 1936 he was editor of the *Stratford Times*, a job that would have paid not a lot but more than enough to keep a young single man who was living at home. A letter from Mr Shrimpton in January of 1937 informed Stewart that all Whitcombe & Tombs' outlets had been supplied with the book and the rest were in the warehouse awaiting his instructions. Many poets are too self-effacing, lacking in confidence or ignorant of the power of connection to do much more than get their books into print. Possibly because of his years as a journalist, Stewart knew better and didn't waste any time, sending copies not only to the *Observer* and possibly other newspapers but also to poets he admired, most particularly John Powys.

It was the publication of *Green Lions* that gave him the impetus and will to leave – not for Australia, as he'd always planned, but for England. He was flying high: his first book had been published and he was in love with a Taranaki woman called Daphne, whom he intended to marry. Powys also knew about her, which shows that their correspondence was about things personal as well as poetical. Powys may even have met her, since Daphne went to England later in the year.

The main problem that confronts all young New Zealanders going to live in England is how to survive. Stewart, once he started working on it, was well connected. W.J. Green, editor of Wellington newspaper *The Standard*, wrote a letter to Prime Minister Michael Savage in April of 1937:

A studio portrait of Douglas Stewart as a young man, just before he worked his passage to England in 1937. *Brandon Haughton photographer, Hawera*

Mr Douglas Stewart has asked me would I give him a letter of introduction, as he is desirous of covering your movements and your reception in England for THE STANDARD.

Mr Stewart has recently published a book of poems which has been very well received in New Zealand and in Australia, and has been described by 'The Sydney Bulletin' as the best poet in this part of the world today. He is a fully experienced journalist, having worked in both Sydney and Melbourne as well as in New Zealand cities. Prior to leaving for England he was editor of 'The Stratford Evening Post'.

I may mention incidentally that he was a foundation member of the Labour Party branch at Eltham, but his subsequent connection with 'The Stratford Post' forced him to keep his Labour views in the background.[45]

In the same month he obtained two cards from his uncle Maurice FitzGerald, county engineer for the Matamata County Council. FitzGerald's name was printed on the front of the card, with 'Tirau New Zealand' beneath. On the back he had written:

Introducing Douglas Stewart, my much travelled journalistic nephew to

Mr AA Dorliac
15 Rue Bartholde
Boulogne-Sur-Mer
France.[46]

There were identical cards addressing a barrister in Bristol and Sir Seymour Williams of Warmsley Lodge (also a barrister). The cards appear unused, as if Stewart forgot to pack them or make use of them. He also had a letter of introduction dated 27 April from L.M. Moss, a barrister and solicitor in New Plymouth to the High Commissioner for New Zealand, London: 'This letter will introduce Mr DS son of Mr AA Stewart, Barrister and Solicitor of Eltham.' The lawyer goes on to say that he has known the family for many years and that Stewart's newspaper work and *Green Lions* have 'received favourable notice here and in Australia, and although he has had very attractive offers to remain in NZ, I feel sure that he is wise in seeking wider experience in England.'[47]

The day finally came when Stewart boarded the *Doric Star* in Wellington. He was to work his passage to London as Third Pantryman. In Auckland, a journalist went on board to interview him for the *New*

'Like most New Zealand writers of poetry, Douglas Stewart has found it extremely difficult to win any local market for his poems,' wrote Robin Hyde in a newspaper feature as Stewart left the country. New Zealand Observer, *15 July 1937*

Zealand Observer, and headed her article 'To England in the Galley'. The journalist was none other than Robin Hyde. He let her know she would recognise him by what he wore – 'a beer and an aspidistra'. She describes him as looking 'younger than four-and-twenty … small, slight, dark, with very intent eyes, self-possessed manner, decided views, but no suggestion at all of aggressiveness'. She related how Stewart had received a letter from John Cowper Powys and that the English poet thought the New Zealand one a genius, 'but, like most New Zealand writers of poetry, Douglas Stewart has found it extremely difficult to win any local market for his poems, still more so to get paid for them. Brother writers will recognise the symptoms … So another ship goes out, waving a plucky flag.'[48]

Stewart's sojourn in England was to last less than a year. He spent time with Powys, he worked in a bar and made the discovery that most young colonial poets do sooner or later, which is that everything in England seems to have had prior claim laid to it by the centuries of native-born writers who came before us:

> But England, just when I was beginning to feel I could survive in it, increasingly filled me with dismay. I was not writing my customary poem a week. I was not writing anything. Moreover, I could not see where I could ever make a start. In the kind of country writing in which I was interested, everything in both verse and prose seemed to have been said before. 'That's Hardy's moor!' Yes, and that was W.H. Davies' skylark, if it wasn't Shelley's or Wordsworth's or Shakespeare's …[49]

He wrote again to Cecil Mann in Australia, this time suggesting that he take over a page called 'The Long White Cloud', which dealt with New Zealand issues. The *Bulletin* expressed interest, though made no commitment. It was enough to get Stewart on a ship back to Sydney, the city that was to be his home for the rest of his life.

COLLINGWOOD, DUNEDIN AND WELLINGTON

Jean Devanny

BORN FERNTOWN 1894, DIED TOWNSVILLE 1962

For a very long time Jean Devanny was entirely forgotten and her work neglected. This was partly because of her gender, partly because of her trans-Tasman identity – which makes it peculiarly easy to be forgotten at home – and partly because of the didactic nature of her later novels. Add to these ingredients the fact that her first novel was banned for many years and that she was in some regards a scandalous figure, then we have a certain recipe for cultural amnesia. Even Dr Michael O'Leary in his excellent study of New Zealand women writers of the mid-twentieth century, *Wednesday's Women*, omits Devanny because: 'Of her 16 novels, the last 9 were set in Australia, and of those only the last two were published later than 1944. She is relevant, but geography excludes her to a large extent.'[1] This means five of her novels were set in New Zealand – a substantial number but, by his reckoning, not enough to warrant her inclusion.

For me, Devanny loomed large. When I was a young writer I knew some older women writers who had great respect for her. I was party to conversations about that banned, lush, vibrant, melodramatic but groundbreaking novel *The Butcher Shop*, which was championed and edited by academic and writer Heather Roberts. When it was re-published in 1981, I was 20. I did not read the novel then, but I remember playwright and novelist Renée talking about Devanny as an inspirational feminist. In the same year, Drusilla Modjeska published her fascinating *Exiles at Home:*

Australian women writers 1925–1946, which included New Zealand-born Devanny. Another acquaintance, academic and writer Aorewa McLeod, wrote a monograph on her and praised Devanny's novel *Cindie* as a fine work. However, the biggest revival was staged across the Tasman by Carole Ferrier, who not only wrote the definitive biography, *Jean Devanny: Romantic revolutionary* (1999), but also edited Devanny's autobiography, *Point of Departure* (1986), which had languished unpublished in various drafts for over three decades.

There was a lot of talk in the 1970s and 80s about how men were in charge of the 'canon' and excluded works by women writers. The idea of a canon – that there is a set of literary works in which it is necessary for any educated person to be well versed – is quaint, but it is still true that literary fiction read mostly by women is not given the same mana or respect as that mostly enjoyed by men. Male critics may still be disparaging about Devanny. Patrick Evans, in his masculinist 1990 volume *The Penguin History of New Zealand Literature*, makes this rather sneering comment: 'Her main interest is of course in women, who tend in her novels to sound a lot like her (with similar surnames: Divine and Devoy, for example), and in what must be her own struggles to express her sexual and creative identity in a capitalist society which tends especially to crush women.' Elsewhere Evans is more generous, crediting Devanny as a kind of literary pioneer of the 1930s.[2]

*

The one true thing anyone can say of Devanny's life, even in a brief study such as this one, is that she was not crushed. She endured some very difficult times – years of penury and exclusion – and at times certainly felt as if she had been utterly flattened. But she never let the bastards get her down completely. This is in stark contrast to other writers of the period like Robin Hyde (1906–1939), who was so devastated by the difficulties of her life that she committed suicide.

Born in Ferntown, a vanished ghost town in the Nelson district, Jean Devanny was christened Jane Crook, the eighth of 10 children. Her father William was a Londoner, a boilermaker by trade, but could turn his hand to anything, as many tradesmen did in those days. Jane, Jean's mother, was also an immigrant; her father had arrived in New Zealand by way of

India, where he had been a colonel in the British Army. In New Zealand he fought in the so-called 'Maori Wars' of the 1860s. Jane married young, at 17 – a circumstance which poverty would force Jean to replicate.

The family were poor but in Jean's positive account they never went hungry. Food was provided by the surrounding bush:

> [We] gorged ourselves on the edibles available in the forest. Most delectable of these was the gaga or kie kie, the flower of a tough great vine. The size and somewhat the shape of a large water-lily, the flower had several long spikes, projecting from its heart. In summertime the pulpy and juicy petals were eaten, in winter the spikes ... Second in choice to eat were the berries of the lawyer vine; next the heart, the 'rolling pin' of the nikau palm ... Up to eighteen inches long, round and slender, the half of it was hard and juicy, the rest comprised tightly-packed tape-like strings. The drawback to a meal of nikau was that it filled one with wind ...[3]

The bush also provided meat for the table, as it did for many families in the period. Wood pigeons, kākā parrots and even tūī were made use of. Devanny remembered in particular tūī pie, a fairly horrifying prospect today, although not as disturbing as nineteenth-century accounts of early pioneers eating kiwi and finding the skewer they come with very handy for holding the rest of the bird over the fire. Kiwi do not appear to have formed part of the Devanny menu.

Conventional food was also abundant for the Crooks. There was roast beef on Sundays, bread and vegetables, fish and mutton on other days. The week's baking was done on Saturday mornings. Nearby orchards sold off surplus fruit for a shilling a bucketful. It seems Mr Crook's manners were the only distress at the table – Jean loathed the way he drank tea from a saucer and picked his teeth. This is an early indication of a strange snobbishness she had, despite being a champion of the working class. She did not easily forgive or ignore poor manners in people who had had no chance to learn good ones.

The Crook children spent their spare time ranging freely. There was the beach and the forest, the hills and gardens. As in Douglas Stewart's childhood, there was an idyllic element that may make many of us nostalgic for the unspoilt New Zealand of over a century ago.

The Crook children's academic careers were as attenuated as those of most working-class children in the early twentieth century. To help her mother, Jean left school at 13, a fact that would surprise any reader of her fluid, articulate novels. She continued to educate herself, reading widely and passionately. The natural world was always a source of fascination for her, too, as evidenced in many of her novels and particularly the non-fiction *By Tropic Sea and Jungle* (1944) and *Travels in North Queensland* (1951). From childhood on, that consuming curiosity was characteristic. As a young girl she delighted in collecting treasures, bringing home insects, butterflies, pebbles and oddly shaped roots from her wide-ranging rambles. Her mother would ask her, 'Why can't you be like other girls?' Once, to her mother's absolute horror, she arrived home with 'the skull of a Maori child', having trespassed, one supposes, into a burial cave.[4]

The Crooks had a piano and Jean's mother gave her lessons. From a very early age she played at dances in the district, and was paid for her services, but her first real job, though a shortlived one, was as a general maid at a Collingwood boarding house. At only 13 she worked from six in the morning until eight at night. Other temporary jobs followed, the last one as a barmaid in a Collingwood pub when she was 15. The hours here were even worse – five-thirty in the morning until eight at night – and it was the sort of work that demeaned women. Devanny commented that local women did not go behind the bar for fear of how the men in the community would regard them.[5] She seems to have enjoyed the work, though, since another enduring characteristic was her delight in being the centre of attention, a witty barmaid pouring the drinks, cracking the jokes and keeping the men in their place. Not only did she put in those punishing hours, but on a Saturday night she would go on to 'socials' in the local halls and dance until the music stopped. Prodigious energy and a strong constitution were traits she'd inherited, she believed, from her father. Later in life, in her thirties, she was diagnosed with an over-active thyroid and attributed her extraordinary stamina to that complaint.

Just before Jean turned 16, the family moved to Puponga, 20 kilometres from Collingwood. Her father worked in one of two coal mines, which for a time were enormously productive. In 1911, the year after he started work, more than 30,000 tons of coal was shipped, twice the output of 1909.[6] The mine was a problematic one, suffering from periods of serious mismanagement. Hand in hand with the ill-trusted and poor-quality bosses went the mine's emergence as a hotbed for the fledgling labour movement. There had been labour disputes there since 1905. In 1913 the mine suffered a serious mishap when against all expert advice coal pillars were extracted from under the Wiriki Creek and a great volume of water entered the mine. The damage was deemed too expensive to fix if production was to remain profitable. The enterprise limped on under various companies until the 1950s, when the mine was closed for good.

Today Puponga is a holiday destination. There are baches, a Department of Conservation information centre and some old pieces of rusty machinery – the only reminders of the mines and the 250 men who worked them.

When the Crooks moved up the spit to Puponga, some of these 250 men were newly arrived Australians – around 80 of them. They may well have been the first Australians Devanny had met. Two of them were musicians, and possibly better ones than Devanny, since they got the job of playing piano and violin at the Saturday night dances in the miners' hall. They and their compatriots had been brought over with the Ingersoll-Lyner water-boring machine, a new method of mining using water spray, in combination with the pick, to increase production.

The Australians fitted in well with the New Zealanders. Later, when they had gone and their labour was taken up by newly arrived 'Pommies' or Englishmen, the replacements were not liked nearly so much. 'Their speech repelled us,' wrote Devanny, who went on to remark proudly, and with a hint of snobbishness: 'The speech of the New Zealand worker was little removed, in a grammatical sense, from that of the moneyed class, and the general standard of culture was very high.'[7]

By the time the new English labour had arrived, Jean was married, and not to one of the Australians. She chose instead New Zealand miner Hal Devanny, tall, good-looking, political – a man she nevertheless described as 'utterly passive'.[8] A neighbour warned her against marrying him, telling her he was too quiet for her; but, headstrong and determined as ever, she went ahead, becoming Mrs Devanny soon after her seventeenth birthday. Motherhood followed quickly – Karl was born in 1912, just after Jean turned 18.

Coinciding with her son's birth was a political awakening. The miners at Puponga were members of the Federation of Labour, and Hal was one of the most prominent of them. This would have brought him and Jean into contact with many Australians who were at the forefront of workers' movements at this time. For example, when the striking Petone slaughtermen won a 15 per cent wage rise in 1907, the minister of labour told the press he blamed Australian transient workers for the strike.[9] The Attorney-General made reference to 'birds of passage' of an undesirable type, meaning Australians. Further, the mines, particularly those on the West Coast, acted as a kind of political finishing school for several Australians who would later become leading politicians: P.C. Webb, Robert Semple and future New Zealand prime minister Michael Joseph Savage. Webb and Semple were among the many union men who were house guests of the Devannys.

Paddy Webb was a miner involved in a dispute at Blackball, where the first branch of the New Zealand Socialist Party was formed. Blacklisted in Victoria, Webb had emigrated to New Zealand in around 1905. He was the first president of the Federation of Labour and became a member of parliament for the Social Democrat Party in 1913. In 1918 he was imprisoned for refusing military service, but didn't give up on his political career. He stood again, unsuccessfully, in 1932. Finally, in 1945, he became minister for mines and labour in Savage's Labour government.

Robert Semple, a miner of 26 years' experience on the Australian coal and goldfields, emigrated to New Zealand in 1907. He became president of the Federation of Miners the following year, and after its merger with the Federation of Labour became one of its major organisers. He too was imprisoned during World War I for resisting conscription, and later became a cabinet minister in the first Labour government.

The most well known and loved of these three Australians was Micky Savage, who came up the ranks of the Federation of Labour to become New Zealand's first Labour prime minister. But when Jean Devanny was becoming politicised his government was two decades away, following years of social unrest, the Depression and two world wars.

In 1912, the year of Karl Devanny's birth and of the bitter six-month Waihi gold-miners' strike, Liberal leader Bill Massey came into office, a position he was to hold for 16 years. Massey had no sympathy for the working class and even less patience with unions or organised labour. By 1914 he'd crushed the Federation – the so-called Red Feds – by recruiting blue-blooded young men from farming communities to ride as mounted police specials: the so-called Massey's Cossacks. 'Thus over the very years in which Labor emerged as a major governing party in Australia,' writes historian Rollo Arnold, 'the administration of New Zealand was firmly in the hands of a rurally based, strongly anti-Labour party. It is little wonder that for years at government level there was little love lost between New Zealand and Australia.'[10]

How much young Jean was aware of, or even interested in, trans-Tasman relations at this point of her life is debatable. As she looked after her first-born and fretted about the future of her husband's job, she would certainly have known of the Waihi strike. She would have sympathised with the miners, the railway workers, their families and everybody who was suffering. The Devannys, with Hal a union secretary, were in the thick of industrial unrest.

Point of Departure does not go into great detail about this period of Jean's life. However, *Dawn Beloved*, Devanny's fourth novel (actually her first, but published after the first three), provides a great deal of insight into what it was like to be the young wife of a miner. It is the most auto-biographical of her novels, published a year before the Devannys moved to Sydney. Puponga is renamed Paranga and the young husband Valentine Devoy bears many of Hal Devanny's traits – silence, fortitude, self-containment and a refusal to help around the house. He also resembles Hal physically: 5'10", slim, dark hair, 'thinker's brow', 'immense shoulders', 'handsome to a degree rarely seen'. Central character Dawn sees 'the cleanness in him without understanding the quality she saw was cleanness.'[11] By 'cleanness' Devanny means innocence, a quality she found very frustrating in her real-life husband as the years went on. He was never able to see the dark side of people's natures and believed the best of everybody.

While Dawn is pregnant with her first child she declares, '"I can't seem to settle to anything now, but after the baby is born I'll study this socialism."'[12] We can also imagine that Dawn's realisation of how hard married life was for working-class women was also Jean's: 'A working-class woman must ... scrub the floors; get down on her hands and knees and scrub dirty floors. She must stand at the washtub and rub filthy clothes on hard boards. She must stand over a hot stove and bake and cook, often with scraps so inadequate as to worry her to death over the preparation.'[13]

Dawn's character, especially as a child, closely resembles Devanny's own: 'Though savagely alive and physically active, rowdy and quarrelsome with her brothers, she was yet subject to moods of intense melancholy and distress. She was filled to overflowing with virility.'[14] The child Dawn is also embarrassed by her father's drinking tea out of saucer and sucking his moustache, just as Devanny was herself.

Devanny's strange, characteristic snobbishness appears out of place in a novel purporting to present socialist ideals: 'Her childhood was unhappy because she did not know she was above them.' And later: 'If Dawn could only have held to this faith in herself, this understanding of her own superiority.'[15] This is a quality many would remark on through Devanny's life, her arrogance and apparent cast-iron ego. It may have made her difficult to get along with, but it also made her a survivor.

The similarity between Dawn and Devanny is of course one of the points noted by Patrick Evans. It is as if he assumes that male writers do not make the same kinds of connections in their work. Carol Ferrier, when discussing *Dawn Beloved*, comments, 'Jean's early life, as described in her semi-autobiographical novel *Dawn Beloved* and her autobiography, bears many resemblances to the home situation that D.H. Lawrence depicted in *Sons and Lovers* (1913), in a mining community on the other side of the world ...'[16] So there we have it: D.H. Lawrence, a miner's son, wrote it as he saw it, and so did Jean Devanny, a miner's daughter.

By the outbreak of World War I, the Devannys had had two more children, Patricia (born 1913) and Erin (1915). The Puponga mine was temporarily closed and Hal Devanny was forced to seek work elsewhere. Eventually a job came up in Fairfield, a mining town near Dunedin. At first Jean did not accompany him, going instead with the children to Wellington, where she stayed with Bob Semple's wife Margaret and their five children, in Brooklyn. It was a household of women and children: Semple was in prison in Lyttelton. His family were supported by the Miners' Federation.

As many women have discovered throughout history, these hard periods when the menfolk are imprisoned, away at war, or working in other places can also be very liberating. At the end of the day the exhausted wife may have time for her own thoughts and quiet contemplation, rather than dealing with an equally tired and/or demanding husband. She might also make new friends. It was during this period in Wellington that Devanny met Peter Fraser and Harry Holland, two committed socialists who had an enormous influence on her. Fraser was also in jail, convicted on the same charge as Semple. Holland may well have deepened Devanny's interest in Australia, since he was a journalist from New South Wales. Initially he had come to New Zealand to edit the *Maoriland Worker*, the newspaper of the Labour Federation. Holland was a good-looking man and had a withered leg: both attributes likely to quicken Jean's interest and compassion. By 1919 he had become leader of the Labour Party, but would never be prime minister. He died before the party came to office with Savage at the helm.

It is probable, too, that during this period Devanny began to contemplate writing seriously. More certainly, it was during the war years that she first read Marx and Lenin. Her copy of Lenin's *State and Revolution* had been smuggled into the country by radical seamen in 1918.

Tragedy awaited Jean when she joined her husband in Dunedin. In 1919 her youngest daughter, four-year-old Erin, was bitten on the toe by a pig and died of septicaemia. The loss affected Jean deeply. She stopped playing the piano, became reclusive, and the marriage suffered. The years in the southern city were unhappy. To help with her grief, Devanny may well have turned to writing. Before *The Butcher Shop* was published in 1926, she had written at least two other novels, one of which was the published *Lenore Divine*.

At the end of 1921 Jean and Hal returned to Wellington and stayed with the Semples, while Hal began work on the tunnel through the Orongorongo Range. Bob Semple, who had won the contract to build the tunnel, paid his men well, so the Devannys were able to buy a boarding house. But times were still tough, and it might have been this period that John A. Lee refers to in a fairly scurrilous, undated letter to Mrs Olssen, written in 1976 or 1977, while she was working on a project that required short biographies of women writers: 'Jean probably earned a bob or two on her back when times were hard but I would say it was only a case of expecting her friends to pay. Queenie Semple, Bob's daughter boarded with her for a time and told me this. She said Jean would type around the unwashed breakfast dishes. If a man called and interrupted her work she'd get rid of him at once. No nonsense.'[17]

In those few lines Lee reveals more about his own attitudes and those of his generation than he does about Devanny. He links prostitution with leaving the dishes unwashed and dismissing unwanted guests so Devanny could get on with one of the four novels she wrote between 1925 and 1929. And, really, was it prostitution? Devanny had revolutionary ideas about sex and monogamy. If it was 'only a case of expecting her friends to pay', then perhaps there was no 'expecting' at all. It could well have been that the friends she slept with gave her a bit of money to help her, since Hal was away working on the other side of the harbour. Queenie Semple may have witnessed money changing hands and leapt to conclusions. At this time Devanny was in her early thirties, her husband was away for lengthy periods, and she enjoyed sex. She was taking risks, of course, since it was easy for a woman not only to lose all social standing if suspected of immoral behaviour but also to become pregnant with an unwanted child. Devanny liked to say that her recall of this period of her life was murky. It could be that the loss of her daughter Erin propelled her into some kind of sexual excess, and that there were aspects of life in moralistic, judgemental Wellington that she would prefer to forget.

The boarding house was in Knigges Street, Te Aro, an area known for its political foment. In the 1920s it was still as it was when Miles Fairburn described it in essay 'The Farmers Take Over': 'the boarding house area of central Wellington provided the recruiting ground for radical trade unions from 1908–13'.[18] Many of its residents were new immigrants from Australia and further afield.

Both Jean and Hal joined the Labour Party. Jean was disappointed by it: 'At once I recognised that the basis on which the Labour Party was developing was in no way Marxist, in no way revolutionary as I understood the meaning of that word.'[19] She maintained her contact with the party, though, taking part in fundraising events and Labour women's lunches. Wellington's *Evening Post* of 21 September 1925 records Mrs J. Devanny as a winner of the Labour All Nations Fair Guessing competition. She won a baby shawl. She and the other winners were directed to collect their prizes from Trades Hall in Vivian Street.

Money in her pocket, a novel or two taking shape, the boarding house to run, and a growing love of Wellington: Devanny was happier here than she had been in Dunedin. In *Point of Departure* she writes of how one day as she walked in Karori Cemetery she 'came to realise the loveliness of Wellington, a city that seemed to cling and hang, for the most part, to the undulating slopes, even to the crags and escarpments'.[20] In *Dawn Beloved*, the heroine finds that:

Up on Tinakori hills a park had been set out. The native shrubbery embossing the hillsides and making bowers of the tiny valleys had been left flourishing; only paths had been cut out and flowering plants had been used to convert the gravelly banks into charmingly decorated walls. One tiny valley Dawn had claimed for her own; surprisingly few people cared to visit its peace. She could lie in the long fresh grass and look out over the Bay – entirely alone. Young gums, their leaves deliciously red, would make music in the light wind; koromiko, purple mauve and white, would attract hosts of dainty wee butterflies of a golden brown colour. Everywhere would be broom – yellow broom, acres and acres of it ...

'Oh, you little old Country!" she cried, beneath her breath, 'You are indeed a jewel set in Southern seas!'[21]

As many novelists do, Devanny wrote short stories alongside her novels. They explore similar themes – female sexuality, the limitations and realities of married women's lives, and hardships endured by the working class. In 'The Perfect Mother', written in the 1920s, two neighbours in a poor mining village discuss politics, motherhood and sex. One woman's husband is a company clerk, the other's is a miner. The miner's wife confesses one day to her friend: 'I'm not a passionate woman; I could get along for ever without seeing a man ... But more than once I've had another man. It just came my way and I took it.'[22] The clerk's wife is shocked and storms out of the house. The reader assumes that if one of these two women were to leave her drudge-filled life and run away it would be the sensual, plump and untidy miner's wife. Devanny plays with our expectations by having the clerk's wife – tidy, stitched-up and organised – disappear with her lover to pursue a career in politics in America. The miner's wife takes on the deserted children even though she already has four of her own. The story ends with her musing, as she serves up smelly meat out of which she has earlier flicked maggots: 'she subsided back into her old soft, lollopy sweetness and murmured: "Oh, well, two kids won't make much difference."'

Life as a boarding-house landlady, peaceful cemetery visitor and winner of baby shawls was about to come to an abrupt end. The prestigious British publishing house Duckworth wrote to say that it would publish *The*

Butcher Shop. When it appeared in 1926, Devanny was instantly famous. Much has been written about this, her most well-known and controversial novel. It sold 15,000 copies internationally, which is not bad even by today's standards, despite the fact it was banned in its home market, as well as in Boston, Australia and Nazi Germany.

The Butcher Shop is the story of Margaret, who at age 17 goes to work as a maid on a farm near Taihape. Almost immediately she catches the eye of Barry Messenger, the farmer. They fall in love and marry, but it seems he's neither as strong nor as clever as she is. He is, as men like him often are in Devanny's novels, *too nice* and therefore boring. Soon enough Margaret finds herself irresistibly drawn to Glengarry, Messenger's foreman. He is handsome, macho, sexy and a little cruel. What woman could resist him? As confidante Margaret has Jimmy Tutaki, who is Messenger's best friend. Her affair with Glengarry rages while the business of the farm goes on around them – the docking, the shearing and the sending of beasts to the works. Margaret is smart enough to know that she must remain affectionate towards her husband:

> 'You know, Glen, you really must get used to my – my friendliness and affectionate manner with Barry. If I altered he would wonder, and ask questions.'
>
> He smiled back at her sympathetically. 'Yes, of course. Never mind. Don't worry.'
>
> 'You know, Glen, one must like Barry. He is so good … He is pure gold, right through. I should be a bad woman, unfit for any man's love, unfit for motherhood, if I did not appreciate and love him.'
>
> 'Don't!' cried the man sharply.[23]

Glengarry, we are to understand, may not be capable of true love but he is capable of furious jealousy. Love and jealousy and sex – Devanny was not alone of her generation in writing about these fascinating subjects. Then, as now, they are ingredients that will help a novel sell. In the 1920s there was much talk of the 'sex instinct', 'sex-consciousness' or 'sex-nature', and particularly fascinating was that possessed by women. The Victorian era, when women were not supposed to experience any such thing, was not far in the past.

When house guest Miette, a woman blessed with very active sex instinct, decides to go after Tutaki, Devanny writes:

Now Miette had met men of his sex-nature many times – men to whom the sex-act carried no spiritual significance. They had been men of her own race who had left her no room for doubt regarding their attitude towards her. Unequivocally and articulately they had put her in her place, and she had supinely awaited their pleasure.

But here was a man not of her race, a man whose sex traditions differed essentially from the pakeha's. Civilisation demanded from the white man of Jimmy's type at least a semblance of respect and consideration for the Miettes; but two generations had not taught Jimmy the finer points, the niceties of civilisation.[24]

This is where *The Butcher Shop* is shocking to a contemporary reader – not for its descriptions of sex, since we are now mostly oblivious to any shock value in that. We could argue that so trammelled are our 'sex instincts' that any representation of sex between willing parties brings no frisson at all. However, when we read attempts by Pākehā writers to represent Māori thoughts and feelings, most of us see the assumptions of the nineteenth century still making themselves plain.

Prior to the scene quoted from above, Tutaki goes to Wellington to fetch Miette and her husband Ian from the ship. He sits on the wharf and thinks about the state of his people:

Racial emotions stirred within him. He knew the history of the white migration and settlement; in his breast, as in every true Maori's, there burned the never-dying resentment for unavenged wrongs done to his race in those early days. The stolen lands, upon which greedy whites, descendants of the thieves, now lived in splendid opulence, ordering chieftains and chieftain's sons to do their bidding.

It was the march of Progress, Jimmy knew. Progress, which was carried in the hands of the 'pakeha'. Progress made sport of racial extinction. The fittest to survive!

Jimmy, true son of his race ... knew that the law of club and fang was the law of Progress, and yet that Progress was good.

And his heart turned to water, and his eyes spilled over their tears with anguish for the death of his race, for the death of his race which was slowly sinking, sinking, with thinned blood and loosened muscle and sagging belly back into the earth which was the dust from which it had sprung.[25]

In the early twentieth century, white New Zealanders, and a few sad and mourning Māori, did believe that Māori were dying out. John Logan

Campbell's 1906 inspiration for the monument on Auckland's One Tree Hill was to 'smooth the pillow of the dying race' – a much-borrowed phrase, first coined by doctor and politician Isaac Featherston in 1856. In Devanny's defence, she was one of very few writers of her generation, or earlier, who dared even to approach race issues.

Some 26 pages later, when Margaret confronts Tutaki about his dalliance with Miette, Devanny digs herself in deeper:

> Jimmy shuffled about in misery. 'Oh, Lady, what do you know of men and of women such as she? Why, she is only a common - - -'
> Instantly she was a transformed woman ... It was her racial pride, the woman's woman in her. Jimmy did not know. How could he? He thought that it was his use of the vile word before her and was bewildered. It was not like Margaret to –
> 'You – you nigger!' she cried.
> He crumpled up. His face puckered and gave up its life as though he were dying; his head fell forward, his legs bent beneath him and sagged until he was lying in a crumpled heap before her.
> ... Her wrath fled as quickly as it had come ... 'Jimmy! Jimmy! What is it Jimmy? What have I done to you?'
> He began to weep like a little child as he quavered out: 'You have broken my heart.'[26]

Overseas reviewers were particularly enchanted by Tutaki. 'Most lovable is the figure of Jimmy the Maori,' wrote the American *Bookman* reviewer. The *Glasgow Herald* reviewer wrote: 'The character of Tutaki, the cultured Maori, and the pen-picture of him "sitting on the wharf under the shadow of the pakeha's brain and hand", his eyes spilling with anguish for the death of his race, is very fine indeed.'[27]

Needless to say, it wasn't her clumsy handling of race issues or even the purple, sensual turns of phrase when writing excitedly about the 'sex instinct' that got the book banned. There were two scenes that particularly upset the New Zealand censor. One was a depiction of men castrating sheep by biting off the testes. This was deemed to be injurious to our future agricultural trade. The other was a scene inspired by a true story of a drunkard who had invited his equally drunk mate to cut his head off to relieve him of his hangover and the mate obliged. John A. Lee put it best:

Jean Devanny may have been an Australian but her *Butchers Shop*, foolishly banned by the Massey Govt was written in New Zealand, as were her next three books. Alas I haven't kept any and Jean was an apostle of the sex revolution in days when that caused most to freeze at mention of her name. The book published by Duckworth was banned because she fictionally used an incident. A couple of King Country workers went on a drunk. When in a state of semi imbecility one went out, put his head on the chopping block and invited his pal to chop his head off. The other obliged. The Govt reckoned the book did not paint a fair picture of NZ but the case was widely publicised as the executioner was tried. The ban was shameful. I wasn't in parliament 1919–22, and Labour made no protest. Jean was a commo opponent. Pity half a dozen of her books haven't been saved.[28]

In May 1926 the *New Zealand Free Lance* sent a journalist to interview Jean. The article appeared under the headline 'Banned by the censors: *The Butcher Shop* too brutal: Novel by Wellington woman refused admission into New Zealand'. Jean was described as a 'young woman still in her thirties, with sleek black hair, a pale, thoughtful face and large, luminous grey eyes, with curling lashes, she looked as far removed in type from any suggestion of coarseness or brutality as one could well imagine. She was the busy housewife in her cotton working frock, but a quick intelligence, a keen knowledge of life on its rougher side welled to the surface ... [Mrs Devanny] says she chose the title ... because the woman is butchered in life.'[29]

Writers can get overexcited during interviews. The long hours alone, the intimacy with fictional people who may seem more real to the writer than the flesh and blood she comes daily into contact with, and the sudden, intense attention of an articulate, sympathetic journalist can encourage wild statements. The interviewing journalist, Nelle Scanlan, would herself go on to become a novelist – in fact, New Zealand's most popular novelist of the 1930s and 40s with her *Pencarrow* series, a family saga spanning generations. She would have been very interested in who this newly famous writer really was. Emboldened, Devanny announced her plan to write another book 'on the emotional life of the Maoris. It has not yet been done ... "The Sexlife of the Maoris" – a little book ... for the man and woman in the street.'[30] She had already written a book, or said she had, with the compelling title 'The Sex Life of Peoples Ancient and

Modern', in which she followed the evolution of monogamy, beginning with the society of the Ancient Greeks. Her idea was that 'the whole stream of our sexual life today is tending to become debased, tainted, rotten at its source, because our rigid marriage code will not bend to the new demands made on it'.[31]

No wonder people recoiled from her. But it seems her fascination with sex was boiling over. Ferrier quotes a passage from an unpublished manuscript:

> The motor car is not at all a small factor in inducing sensuality in women. The swift rush through the pure air fills the body with vital forces, the moment excites. A country tour ... will in many cases develop a passionate response in the liking or loving wife ... To lie on the grass with trees around, the blue sky above and the sun-shine playing its warmth upon her, will sway her to the passions of any man she likes.[32]

The young woman who wrote this, it seems to me, is in the grip of unrelieved horniness.

The decision to leave New Zealand and try Australia was made in the teeth of the Depression. The reasons Jean gave for the move were both political and personal. The political motivations were to do with frustration with the Labour Party, which was not Marxist enough for her liking. The personal one was to do with her son Karl who had been diagnosed in 1925 with valvular heart trouble, a rheumatic condition and, like his mother, overactivity of the thyroid gland. Jean described him at age 16 as a 'big fellow, six foot two and weighing thirteen stone'. Karl was often bedridden and the Devannys believed the climate in Sydney would be better for him. They also had the misguided idea that the Depression was not as severe in Australia as it was in New Zealand.

Before leaving, Jean travelled with her children to visit her sisters, and then spent six weeks in Auckland, where she spoke at meetings and also cultivated a friendship with Miriam Soljak that would last all her life. Miriam had married Dalmatian Peter Soljak in 1908 and borne him seven children. During World War I he was classified as an alien, which meant she was too. She was fluent in te reo Māori. Apart from a brief period in the 1930s when she became a communist, she was an active member of the Labour Party. The two women had many things in common.

Soljak championed Jean both as an activist and a writer. Six years after Jean's departure for Sydney, she wrote an article for the *New Zealand Observer* titled 'Outspoken New Zealand Novelist'. It begins with some biographical information, goes on to discuss the banning of *The Butcher Shop* and finishes by remarking that Jean Devanny was one of the most interesting people in Sydney.[33]

The day before the Devannys sailed for Sydney, the Auckland women's branch of the Labour Party held a farewell tea for Jean at the Farmer's Trading Company tearooms. She was not the only guest of honour. The other was a Unitarian woman minister, Rev Wilma Constable, who was being welcomed to the city. The final sentence of the article below is indicative of the close association the socialist movement had in the twenties with eugenics: 'Among the [other] guests was Mrs Peter Fraser, of Wellington, a member of the Eugenics Board.' Janet Fraser was wife of the future prime minister, and one of the founding members of the Wellington women's branch. She and Devanny would have been close

LABOUR PARTY TEA

WOMEN'S BRANCH WELCOMES
REV. WILMA CONSTABLE

FAREWELL TO MRS. DEVANNY

The members of the Auckland women's branch of the New Zealand Labour Party and their friends met yesterday afternoon at the Farmers' Trading Company's tea-rooms for the purpose of welcoming the Rev. Wilma Constable, a co-minister of the Unitarian Church, and to bid farewell to Mrs. Jean Devanny, the well-known New Zealand authoress, prior to her departure for Australia and England. Mrs. L. Harrison, president of the branch, in well chosen words, extended to the Rev. Mrs. Constable a hearty welcome, and wished Mrs. Devanny every success in her new field of activities.

Mrs. Emily Gibson also spoke, referring to the need for new workers in the Labour movement, and the loss in the Dominion caused by Mrs. Devanny's departure.

Mr. Gavin Stove, as an old friend of Mr. and Mrs. Devanny and a fellow worker in the movement, also spoke.

The guests of honour responded in feeling terms.

Among the guests was Mrs. Peter Fraser, of Wellington, a member of the Eugenics Board.

associates. Since World War II, the idea of eugenics has struck fear into most hearts. But in the 1920s many left-leaning thinkers in New Zealand and elsewhere were attracted to it because it offered hope to women through its concentration on birth control. Jean was a strong supporter.

Biographer Carole Ferrier asserts that rather than seeing Australia as her destination, Devanny was on her way to Europe, where she thought she would have a greater chance of selling her fiction for sensible money. She had by this stage published five novels, all with New Zealand settings: *The Butcher Shop, Lenore Devine, Old Savage, Dawn Beloved* and *Riven*. She may not have realised it, but she was playing out a failed ambition common to many New Zealanders since the late nineteenth century: using Australia as a stepping-stone to places further afield. She may also have not been aware of an attitude towards New Zealand literature held by Vince and Nettie Palmer, a well-regarded novelist and critic respectively. Eileen Duggan, Jessie Mackay and Katherine Mansfield were greatly admired by Nettie, and Vance Palmer is on record as saying: 'To an outsider the most remarkable thing about Maoriland writing is the originality and strength of the women and the relative feebleness of the men.'[34] Needless to say, this was not an opinion held by male New Zealand writers.

For well over a decade, Devanny had counted Australians like Bob Semple and Peter Fraser among her friends and associates. At 35 years of age it is doubtful she could have been so naïve as to imagine that the West Island was full of men just like them, but it is just possible that the realities of Australian society, much more masculine than Pat Lawlor's oft-quoted description of 'cheery, beery, male bohemia', the conservative penpushers who dominated the New Zealand writing scene, had escaped her. While men did not write the majority of New Zealand books – between the 1920s and 1970s women did – men still believed they were at the fore-front of the literary scene. In Australia men really did dominate in both fields of endeavour that Jean Devanny would participate in: literary and political. She would find that her adopted country offered her plenty of battles on many fronts.

Eric Baume

BORN AUCKLAND 1900, DIED SYDNEY 1967

Frederick Ehrenfried Baume, known throughout his life as Eric, and sometimes as Eric the Bastard, or 'The Beast', was one of four sons born into a politically conservative, unorthodox Jewish family in the gracious inner-city Auckland suburb of Grafton in 1900. As a boy he exhibited the characteristics that would eventually make him one of the first controversial media figures across the Tasman. He was curious, arrogant, ambitious and determined to be noticed. These character traits are common now, aspirational even, but in Baume's day they were not necessarily celebrated. Like Jean Devanny, Baume's personality was polarising. People either adored him or would have liked to shoot him. His legacy to us all are shock jocks and television announcers of the likes of Paul Henry in New Zealand and Alan Jones in Australia.

His parents were colourful, intelligent and active people and it would seem his mother had the greater influence. This is mostly because Eric's father, Frederick Ehrenfried Baume, described by Baume's biographer Arthur Manning as a 'man of rigid convictions and hair-trigger temper', died when his son was only 10 years old.[1] It is unlikely that Baume would have had anything like the freedom he did had his father lived into old age. He may, in fact, have lived an entirely different life. As it was, the son remembered the father as a remote figure, keen on whipping the boys with the buckle-end of the belt.

Until Frederick's early death, the family enjoyed a high standard of living in a two-storey house in Princes Street, grand by colonial standards. At the Baume's residence were a cook, a housemaid and a governess, Miss Taylor. Eric remembered also an elderly gardener who had fought in the New Zealand wars and would regale him with bloodthirsty tales of British soldiers losing their heads to greenstone mere. With staff to run the house and care for her sons, his mother, Rosetta Lulah Baume, had the time to pursue her many civic interests.

Born in San Francisco, Rosetta Leavy graduated from the University of California with a Bachelor of Philosophy in 1891. She met New Zealander Frederick in the city of her birth in 1898 and married him a year later, before voyaging to the South Pacific to make her home in Grafton. Auckland society welcomed her with open arms. The Baumes entertained frequently, and Rosetta was sophisticated, witty, and enjoyed well-informed, lengthy conversation. The affection was probably not reciprocated. Baume was of the opinion that his mother was never truly at home in New Zealand. Certainly, during those years of her first marriage in Auckland she felt that she was an oddity as a university-educated woman. She wasn't totally. Among our famous women graduates are Kate Edger, who graduated from the University of New Zealand with a BA in mathematics and Latin in 1877, 13 years before Rosetta graduated. The year before Rosetta's marriage, New Zealand's first woman doctor, Margaret Cruickshank, went into general practice. It's true women graduates were very rare, but it is possibly a symptom of her sense of displacement that she expressed it as a feeling of being unique. Baume himself wrote:

> She settled down there to the semi-official life of the colony until my father's death in 1910. I don't think she was ever really happy in New Zealand. I think she suddenly found herself, as many other women have, placed among most well-meaning, stiff relatives with whom she had no common interest; who were, perhaps, unknowingly jealous of her for her extraordinary mental ability ... She found herself marooned in some far-off island in Oceania in which even thoughts were modelled upon the old traditions of England; in which every one referred to England as 'home', although she herself had only one home, in the United States ...[2]

Her marriage was a love-match. Frederick was also a brilliant university scholar who went on to be a journalist, lawyer and eventually a politician, and had a life-long taste for amateur dramatics. Known in Auckland for his inspirational public lectures on literature, he was an erudite proponent of Rudyard Kipling's work and therefore also a passionate imperialist and militarist. Two years after Eric's birth, Frederick was elected to parliament as a Liberal for the City of Auckland. From 1905 he represented the Auckland East seat, and served as a member of Joseph Ward's government; he was further honoured in 1907 with an appointment to King's Counsel.

Even as a child Eric would have been aware that his father was a powerful and opinionated man. 'I could have been forgiven in those days of Eton collars and Eton suits,' he wrote, 'for becoming a nasty little class-conscious snob, as most of the men of my generation and opportunity did become up to the outbreak of the war in 1914.'³ His parents would have had high ambitions for their sons.

In 1909, when Eric was only nine years old, his father suffered a serious heart attack and departed with his wife to a spa at Bad Nauheim in Germany to recover. It was not to be. He died there in May of the following year. Rosetta returned briefly to Auckland but was too grief-stricken to stay there. Instead, she took the children home to her native California, where the brothers had more freedom than they had ever had in Grafton. They had perhaps run free in the Domain, the expanse of green at Auckland's heart where some of Te Wherowhero's people still lived. In big, loud, complex San Francisco Baume had encounters with prostitutes, meetings with people who lived on the edge, an underworld. It was this short, intoxicating interlude that opened his eyes to the wider world.

He recalled, 'And from then on the tree ferns and the blue sky faded, the smell of the fresh, damp air rising sluggishly off the harbour of Auckland was soon to be changed to the murky fog of the Golden Gate, from which I never regained the touch of Arcady, my New Zealand heritage.'⁴ He certainly retained an affection for New Zealand, describing the place of his birth as 'on the edge of Paradise'.⁵

The Leavy family in San Francisco were an interesting bunch, fascinating to a boy who had been taught by his mother's example to think of himself as a cut above the rest. One uncle had the smell of greasepaint, and was an impresario, the director of the San Francisco Opera. Another uncle worked on the business side of the Orpheum Theatre. The grandfather had been a captain in the Union Army and had fought at Shiloh

– young Eric listened breathlessly to his stories of bloodshed and glory, which must have resonated a little with the gardener's tales of war in New Zealand. There was a cousin involved in five-and-ten-cents melodrama shows, cheap entertainment in the late nineteenth and early twentieth centuries: five and ten cents refers to the seat prices. The coming of the movies would later destroy the melodrama shows, but perhaps the cousin went on with his other line of trade, which was to do with boxing, cycling and dancing contests. Manning notes: 'This relative taught Baume many things which would have horrified his mother but which were essential subjects in the educational development of a boy who was physically and mentally well in advance of his years.'[6] It is debatable just how 'essential' these subjects were.

Another source of life education was the Lurline Baths, on the corner of Bush and Larkin Streets. Described in 1910 by the *San Francisco Call* as 'one of the most elaborate indoor bathing places in the world', the Lurline had one large pool, grandly named the natatorium, filled with fresh salt water piped in from the sea.[7] There were two slides for boys to plummet down into the water, and if bathers got chilly they could warm up in one of several hot baths. Spectators could fill the galleries and watch the bathers for free. Bathing suits came for hire along with the entrance fee, and on two days a week women were admitted for segregated bathing. In 1910 the pseudo-Greek exterior and fleshy, exuberant interior would have been very new and wild. The more modest Auckland equivalent, the Tepid Baths, would not be built for another three years. Young Eric had seen nothing like it.

Baume describes himself at age 11 as looking 14, by which he implies he had already entered puberty. Perhaps it was at the Lurline that he met a woman almost twice his age: 'I shall never forget the blandishments of one girl, who must have been twenty-six or twenty-seven. She used to take me home to her apartment, feed me on coffee and sweet cakes, say she liked listening to my accent, give me a dollar – one of those great silver cartwheels – and send me home. That is the most polite way of saying I learnt about women from her – knowledge which was to help me hugely in the years which lay ahead.'[8]

Little wonder that after his return to New Zealand in 1912 the world and all its richness – freedom, women and swimming pools – beckoned.

The story of the older woman may or may not be true – Baume was a self-mythologiser, a teller of tall tales who despite (or perhaps because of) his training as a journalist never let the truth get in the way of a good story.

Back in Auckland Rosetta set about persuading her 12-year-old son to devote himself to his studies at school. It was her intention that he follow in his father's footsteps and become a lawyer, though he must have confided in her his desire to become a writer. Discretion and patience were never part of Baume's character.

When his first, adolescent poems were published in the *New Zealand Observer* he felt, as he told his biographer many years later, like a mixture of God and Byron. These early poems are nationalistic and militaristic: inherited, enduring twin obsessions. Grandmother Baume took the headstrong boy in hand and sent him to board at Waitaki Boys' High in Oamaru. Baume loved it, especially the boxing – perhaps he'd learned some killer techniques from the American cousin – and rugby and music. He won an Empire Medal for an essay.

His final year at school was 1916. He returned to Auckland with the intention of going away to the war but was prevented by the doctor, a family friend, who examined him for military service, ripped up Baume's papers in front of him and told him to 'run away and play'.[9] Again, just as we may wonder how Baume's life would have been if his father had lived to quash some of his wild ideas, how different may it have been if the doctor had passed him for enlistment. All his life, Baume was fascinated by war. Perhaps a dose of the trenches, supposing he survived it, would have made him a pacifist and less admiring of the officer class.

A brief period of submitting to his mother's wishes followed. In the days before the existence of law schools, young men were articled to law firms; Baume was signed up to Endean & Holloway, who had bought his late father's firm. But the law was 'hell', as he knew it would be, and it was impossible for him to continue.

Baume talked himself into a job at the *New Zealand Herald*, pushing not a pen but a broom, and earning 15s a week. How paltry this sum must have seemed to him: still at Auckland Grammar, he could earn the same sum in one day playing the E flat bombardon in the band at the races. Promoted quickly during the two years he spent at the *Herald*, he learned many useful things about running a newspaper. He also, sadly for him, learned how to play poker.

Gambling was to become a lifetime obsession, but between times Baume covered court news and reported on fires, which were a regular occurrence in a city mostly built of wood. He was frustrated, feeling that he was not yet valued or acknowledged as a journalist – or not enough. When in 1918 he had his first short story published in the *Sydney Bulletin*, a magazine that would later become one of his arch-enemies, he believed he was well on the way to becoming a respected writer. The story, set in San Francisco, was called 'A Night in Chinatown', and earned him three guineas, which was, as Baume describes it, 'an Olympian sum in those days'.[10] The *Herald*'s editor was not so impressed. He wasn't looking for a fiction writer. He wanted a budding reporter – and proof that the reporter was doing the budding. When Baume put his fiction skills to work and reported on an organ concert that had in fact been cancelled, proprietor Sir Henry Horton told him he would never make a journalist.

Baume was impatient to progress. Eventually fortune smiled and offered him a job as a junior on the Te Awamutu daily, the *Waipa Post*. The job was short-lived, a period of months. Baume experienced not only what it was to write for a provincial newspaper at grassroots level, but also what it was to lose substantial sums of money. Within one week he'd lost £120 playing poker, money he didn't have and had to earn to pay it back.

It was a formative period – he fell in love not just with gambling but, on a visit to Auckland, with a young woman called Mary Stone. She was four years his senior and, as Manning notes, 'knew him to be a playboy'.[11] She was also engaged to another man. After a swift and intensely romantic courtship, Baume persuaded her to marry him. He was not yet 20 – and it is easy to imagine him as an earnest, amusing young man, given to wild gestures. He was tall, dark and handsome, travelled and educated. But she loved him on sight, and Baume's passions would have been intensified by the existence of a competitor, and then by a period of absence – Mary went away to Europe for two years, leaving Baume to pursue his other love of gambling. The marriage, surprisingly perhaps, given what came later, was to endure.

The wedding took place on 17 December 1921 in the Methodist church at Whāngārei. It wasn't until Mary saw the marriage certificate that she learned how young her groom was: he had kept his age a secret. She may not have been particularly concerned. The war had cut a swathe through men of marriageable age; many women of her generation did not marry at all. Perhaps she regarded his relative youth as yet another alluring characteristic of her handsome, unpredictable husband.

The newly-weds moved south to Christchurch, where the *Sun* had offered Baume a job as senior reporter and music critic. Doubtless his new employer hadn't heard of the fake review of the cancelled organ concert. But the job wasn't enough. This clever, ambitious young man, with his eyes on the stars, wanted to be boss. As it happened, the *Timaru Herald* was looking for an editor after the resignation of Oliver Duff. A colleague of Baume's in Christchurch helped him write the letter of application. It must have been a very good letter, because at only 22 he found himself in the chair, apparently the youngest newspaper editor ever in New Zealand. He was also, by far, the youngest on the staff, and was soon locked into an unhappy battle with the paper's dominating general manager, a Mr Doyle. Oliver Duff, who many years later would edit the *Listener*, had not got on with Mr Doyle either – he may even once have kicked him down the stairs – and it was because of Doyle that he had resigned. Baume and Doyle fought every day. Further, Baume's rapid ascendency was resented by his fellow provincial newspapermen, some of whom made life difficult for him. There may have been a degree of anti-Semitism in their behaviour.

Life at home was miserable. Mary was lonely and pregnant, and one day fell in the street. The baby was born prematurely and almost died. Baume, longing for escape, studied the Australian newspapers and wrote away asking for work. He must have felt bitterly trapped: 22 years old, with a sickly baby and miserable wife, a job he hated and clamouring regrets. He called in his resources.

Uncle Sir Arthur Myers, mayor of Auckland (replacing Baume's father, who was his immediate predecessor), was a wealthy man. Baume's connection with him was through his maternal grandmother Catherine Ehrenfried. Sir Arthur was also a connection with Australia: he was born in Ballarat, but moved to Wellington as a child after the death of his father. Throughout his life Baume was very proud of his Ehrenfried relatives, a pride that mutated into a fawning over all things German that would get him into trouble after World War II.

The nephew borrowed £200 from the uncle, and sent his wife and newborn son north to live with Mary's father, who was also a mayor, but of Whāngārei. For himself, Baume recalled: 'Just when the position seemed hopeless I received a wire from Sir Joynton Smith asking me to join the editorial staff of the *Daily Guardian*, a new morning newspaper which was to be produced in Sydney on July 2, 1923.'[12]

It was already June, so with great relief he resigned from the *Timaru Herald*. The offer must have seemed a gift from heaven. Eric Baume, only just 23 and already with a proud newspaper pedigree, sailed west on the ship *Ulimaroa*.

Out into the World

s Australia 'the world'? For many born New Zealanders, Australia is the first taste of it.

On publication of my second book, a collection of short stories, *The Glass Whittler*, I was interviewed in Sydney for a New Zealand newspaper. The sub-editor picked out in bold one quote: 'It's another country.'

Well, yes, of course it is. Shades of the embarrassment Devanny may have felt after publication of her interview with Nelle Scanlan, not that the article revealed anything about my intimate psyche other than a sense of wonder that I was actually in another country, and that it was different. I was reminded of that state of mind in 2014 as I listened to American novelist Lionel Shriver speak at the Auckland Writers' Festival about how, when she was a child, she couldn't believe the rest of the world bore any resemblance to the world she already knew. That other countries had grass, trees, skies and buildings was disappointing to her. She wanted it to be so different it wasn't even fully imaginable.

If we are honest, it is only in the last half century or less that Australia has become a travel destination. Mostly, before that, it was a stepping-stone. Young New Zealanders stopped off there to take advantage of the higher pay scale, lower cost of living and larger job market, and to be initiated into a big-city, cosmopolitan lifestyle, before heading further afield, usually to England, more rarely to Europe or the United States. Douglas Stewart knew of Australia from his father and from swotting the *Bulletin*. Jean Devanny would have picked up information from her prodigious reading and from the Australian leaders in the New Zealand labour movement. Eric Baume, who considered himself a man of the world after his pubescent experience with a San Francisco prostitute, maintained until the end of his life that there was no difference between the two countries. He did recall thinking soon after he arrived that 'Australia breathes freedom at a man' – a sentiment migrants from all over the world have shared.[1]

With the proliferation of images from the mid-twentieth century and into the screen-obsessed twenty-first, we are familiar with representations of Australian flora and fauna, with Aboriginal art, with *Bondi Beach Rescue, Crocodile Dundee, Mad Max, The Voice Australia* and television identities like crooked, hard-drinking Sydney lawyer Rake. But when Dulcie Deamer went to Australia in 1908, the earliest of my five subjects to do so, what would she have known of the country? She had won the short story competition and she had seen Norman Lindsay's risqué illustrations, so perhaps she thought it was a land brimming with freethinkers like her parents. At the very least she would have expected it to be bigger, brighter, more exciting.

When I think back to my impressions of Australia in 1985, when I first crossed the ditch, they are to do with animals and men. Both were very different from what I was used to. Louder, brighter, more exciting. What were left of New Zealand native birds, until the middle class resettled the inner-city suburbs and planted native trees, had relocated to what was left of the bush. Australian birds hung about the city, screaming and scuffling and making themselves known. You didn't have to go far out of town to see wallaby, kangaroo or emu. Australian men were just as loud and exotic. They flirted, made off-colour jokes and let you know if they thought you were gorgeous.

Back home, middle-class educated Pākehā men seemed to be frightened to flirt in case it was seen as sexual assault. Already culturally reticent, they had been further stitched up by a mania about child sex abuse. The lid had been blown off the hidden statistics: child abuse was, and still is, so widespread that one in four girls experience it, and one in six boys. This ugly truth became a kind of national obsession, reflected also in our art and literature. It changed the way men were treated. Fewer went into professions where they would come into contact with children, such as primary school teaching. Many fathers were reluctant to express physical affection towards their children. It was an extremely damaging phenomenon, part of a fervent feminism that was a more vocal part of public discourse than its Australian counterpart. We are seeing a similar movement currently with #MeToo, although its genesis is not grassroots New Zealand, but Hollywood.

A telling demonstration of this trans-Tasman comparison is two cases of middle-class assault. In New Zealand the Mervyn Thompson affair, so called, pre-dated by eight years the 1992 subject of Australian Helen Garner's book *Cast the First Stone*. Thompson was an Auckland University lecturer and theatre director who was abducted and beaten by a group of vigilante feminists because they believed he had raped one of his students. The supposed victim was never publicly named; nor were the women who punished Thompson, apparently on the victim's behalf. The subject of Garner's controversially apologist book, which was hated by many Australian feminists, was a man she called Dr Colin Shepherd, real name Alan Gregory, master of Melbourne University's Ormond College. He had put his hand on a student's breast and subsequently lost his job and social standing. In the process of writing *Cast the First Stone* Garner never spoke to the student or other girls who had been similarly touched by Shepherd, only to Shepherd himself. She is on record for later expressing remorse for her view that his punishment far outweighed the crime. By the time her book was published, New Zealanders had weathered almost a decade of arguing over the ramifications of the Thompson case, which really came to an end only with Thompson's death, relatively young, of cancer, in the same year. We were miles ahead of them, although it is difficult to work out if that is anything to be proud of.

The year I left for Australia the term 'politically correct' was in its heyday in Aotearoa. Jean Devanny was apparently the first person to use this term in the late 1930s. She would enrage friends by telling them, 'But you see dear, you don't understand. That's not correct thinking.' It's doubtful any trans-Tasman argument will ever arise over who used it first, since it's not as alluring as pavlova. In mid-80s Australia the phrase seemed barely coined, or at least not bandied about with the righteous alacrity it was at home, where to accuse someone of political incorrectness was tantamount to calling them a member of the Ku Klux Klan. I remember being tearfully ashamed of myself after being called out for using the playground phrase, 'What's the story Hori?'. I hadn't realised it was racist, or even that the last word was Māori, since I had imagined it spelt Horey or even Whorie. Similarly, it wasn't until I had been living in West Island for some that I learned 'taihoa' was Māori, having had some idea it was an English horsey term from fox-hunting, akin to Tally-ho!, but meaning to rein the horse in, and so a metaphor for pausing, which is in fact what it means. These mistakes would not be made by young New Zealanders today. 'What's the story Hori' is consigned to the dustbin of the truly politically incorrect, and the rudimentary Māori learned at primary school could be enough to help those growing up without te reo to at least recognise a word as Māori.

There have been other curious examples of this kind of confusion. For instance, in the early 2000s there was a small media discussion around the phrase 'big hooer', as in 'I went fishing and caught a big hooer', or 'Move it along, you big fat hooer.' It is a word that Pākehā might be reluctant to use, since it's commonly believed to be Māori and poor use of it could lead similarly to accusations of racism. Sometimes it is spelt hua, which according to the *Reed Dictionary of Modern Māori* has multiple meanings – fruit, egg, profit, outcome, lever, jemmy, outline, asset and answer. Hooer is in fact not at all related to the similarly pronounced hua, but to 'whore', pronounced with a Scottish accent, and a hangover from colonial days when a large percentage of New Zealand's settlers were Scots.

*

When Wakelin, Baume, Devanny and Stewart crossed the Tasman, they were motivated by hopes for better prospects and higher incomes. Dulcie Deamer got on the ship for love, and was married when it docked at Perth. My reasons for going were more like hers than the others', but didn't result in marriage – and just as well.

In 1985 I flew to Sydney at the invitation of a Kiwi erstwhile boyfriend who had returned a month or so before with short-lived declarations of undying love. It was the first time I had ever left my homeland. Until my departure, Australia had held little fascination for me – apart from as the subject of a childhood poem written for a primary school social studies project:

On we go, through and through
Past koala and kangaroo
The long-legged emu cries out 'I see you
and you look just as strange as I!'
Soon so soon we run out of peas
We'll have to go and ask the Aborigines ...

The rest of the poem, perhaps luckily, I can't remember.

My father's brother, a successful businessman, made many trips to Australia through the 60s and 70s and would bring back presents for my siblings and me – koalas of varying sizes made from kangaroo fur, a kangaroo-skin purse that I treasured for years, as well as American and English toys not available in New Zealand. It's likely though not certain that the purse was made from the scrotal sack of a buck kangaroo. I didn't know this at the time and I don't suppose Uncle Doug did either.

For a short while during my childhood we had a living Australian among us in the shape of a small green budgerigar. My great-uncle Eric, a stalwart of the Social Credit Party and breeder of goats in Greenhithe, had for a time an Australian girlfriend. In 1971, when I emerged from Middlemore Hospital after yet another protracted recovery from orthopaedic surgery, the girlfriend gave me Bobby, who spoke with an Australian accent. 'Geedoiy Steefnoie', he said. In our house Bobby learned to speak with a New Zealand accent, and he also learned to say 'Shut your head!', to yell for my brother to get out of bed for his breakfast and for someone to answer the phone. When I practised my cello he would scream at the top of his voice. On sunny days his cage was hung on a hook on the veranda so that he could 'talk to the other birds'. One winter evening I forgot to bring him inside and he died of cold. It was the first and only time I have been responsible for the death of a pet, and among the many creatures I have loved and nurtured through my life there has never another caged bird. The overwhelming feeling I have when observing the plumage or clever chat of a feathered prisoner is one of sadness.

This avuncular and avian evidence of another country so near and so different didn't pique my interest enough to want to go there. I was more curious about the lands of my long-ago forebears, the countries that featured in the playground game of elastics: England, Ireland, Scotland,

Wales, inside, outside, puppy dog tails! Like most New Zealanders of my generation fortunate enough to belong to a library, I grew up on Brothers Grimm fairy tales, on Beatrix Potter and Enid Blyton, Elizabeth Goudge and John Townsend, Roald Dahl, the Brontës, Oscar Wilde, Charles Dickens and D.H. Lawrence – all of whom reflected back a country that was very like home but wasn't. It was enviably different, somehow superior. The new radio station Hauraki played bands from Great Britain; the music I played on the piano and cello came from Europe, which was near England, wasn't it?

As a little girl I desperately wanted to be English or Irish or Scottish, to be more 'real'. A conversation I remember very clearly from when I was about eight years old happened while I was travelling over the Auckland harbour bridge with my grandparents towards our modest three-generation family bach at Torbay, then still rural. I asked my grandmother what we were. 'We're British,' she said firmly, though she was herself second-generation white Fijian. I was relieved. Perhaps I really could have the adventures of the Secret Seven or the Famous Five. Perhaps I really could wake up one morning and see a unicorn in our garden or witness a little swallow plucking the jewelled eyes from a statue.

But I wasn't to go to England until my late thirties. Australia was the country I went to and stayed in for several years – the only country apart from New Zealand in which I have lived for more than a few months. Europe, even after I had had novels published in England, was not to be visited for another 14 years as a side-trip from France when I was the Katherine Mansfield Fellow, by which time I had an Australian husband and three children.

Youthful love affairs are to some degree imaginary – we fall in love with what we know of a man or woman and imagine the rest, which in many cases is glorious, super-human. That way disappointment surely lies. My returning boyfriend had first left New Zealand to seek his fortune as a cameraman. There were no film schools here then, and through our tumultuous years together he had worked on films and television as a clapper-loader or grip. The first time I ever heard those terms I loved them immediately. They were hilarious. Later, as we tore one another apart and I weathered his bits-on-the-side, I came to think of the job descriptions as more descriptive of the man himself. But all that lay ahead.

He'd been gone for over a year and we had finally, I thought, split some months before that. He was my first true love; I loved the bones of him, heart and soul. He was from a small regional North Island city, was slight and graceful, shone with health and curiosity, read widely, talked incessantly and could play the guitar. At the time we met, one blustery afternoon in the Canterbury university library, he was finishing his degree in clinical psychology. We were 19 and 21, and I think it was love at first sight. We shared a textbook for an arts paper and I remember his hands on the page – beautiful, long hands that were larger than my freakishly giant ones.

I had been a very lucky girl, sent by my hard-working father to one of Auckland's most expensive girls' secondary schools which, though it may not mean to, fosters in many of us a life-long delight in the exclusive company of women. In the time since the clapper-loader and I split, I had slid very happily back into a world that at first glance was similar. It was exciting intellectually, politically and sexually – my first love at 11 was a girl, and there had been a couple of adult attachments since then. It wasn't long before I fell in love with a softly spoken, clever gentlewoman from America.

Much of my early work was influenced by the heady feminism of the times. Men, it seemed, were responsible for the parlous state of the environment, endemic violence and child abuse, and it was best to stay away from them. There was a worldwide movement against pornography, which had resulted in an uncomfortable alliance between right wingers, Christians and feminists, and I had written a play, *Accidental Phantasies*, about the issue. Women played men in the play (a fairly novel idea at the time), and it was very funny. Or at least the first act was. At the opening night in Wellington the audience was in stitches, watching Chips in his diner on the Desert Road welcome a group of disparate travellers, all of whom seemed to know something about a car crash up the road. It was rude and sexy. The second act was the car crash itself and this is where the play fell apart. Didactic, preachy, boring – Hugh Hefner and the Marquis de Sade come face to face with Eve, a character based on Jennifer Beard, who was the victim of a high-profile disappearance in 1969.

In the time the clapper-loader had been in the sunburnt country, I had lived in a couple of houses full of musicians, actors, drifters and sensible women who had sensible jobs. I was already establishing what was to be a pattern of feast or famine, working as an actress (we said 'actress' proudly in those days, being mindful of how many centuries it had taken us to get on the stage in the first place) and writing plays and film scripts, sometimes for money. There were employment schemes – PEP schemes – that seem quaint now for their concern for giving young people an occupation, and the result was a grassroots training for actors, writers and musicians, many of whom have gone on to have successful careers. No doubt the schemes could be another reason for the current beleaguered generations to resent the baby-boomers (we were at the tail end of the demographic spike) – this evidence of a caring society, presided over by one Robert Muldoon. From this distance, Muldoon's politics seem bizarrely conflicted – he was at once dictatorial and oddly socialist. He will forever earn the ire of those of us on the left for his immediate dismantling of the New Zealand superannuation scheme in 1975, which by conservative estimates would be worth over $300 billion today. His Think Big plans for mining and industry were controversial; he brought Australia to the fore in the thinking of many with his 1982 free trade agreement with that country, the CER, or Closer Economic Relations. But at least his generation of politicians seemed to understand the concept that they were the people's servants, not bumboys for international corporations. He was old-style National Party – protectionist, fiercely patriotic and still concerned enough for the little man (and woman) to try to make it easier for us now and again.

Life was, on the surface, pretty full and blissful. There was lots of laughter, wild parties and righteous anger – the soon to be victorious anti-nuke movement was in full flower. We angsted about acid rain, overpopulation and sexism, lookism and ageism. I was to write about this time with satirical affection in my 2001 novel *The Shag Incident*. My third play was in rehearsal, I had published some short stories and poetry, I was a regular at the Globe readings where I hobnobbed with all manner of poets and poetesses (yes). I was a founding member of the Women's Political Party. I remember sitting upstairs at Espresso Love, a popular long-gone café in Three Lamps, and looking out towards the blue Waitākeres and thinking I was at the centre of the world.

One afternoon in 1985 I was single again and visiting my parents when my flatmate rang to tell me that my old boyfriend was in town and that he was looking for me. The news was not only puzzling but alarming – what could he possibly want?

Children of the 60s, as in children actually born in the decade and not the older baby-boomers who hold the banner, were enormously influenced by that older generation. To be 'different' was aspirational; to have 'experiences' was a method for living. The first sat uneasily with me – I was a buck-toothed lippy half-crippled skinny girl, who wished desperately to be normal. When my primary school began afternoon ballet classes in the hall, I insisted that my mother take me along. Of course I could do none of the things that were required, not even the skipping, having one leg shorter than the other, and sore, malformed feet barely responding to seven or eight lengthy operations so far. Both my disappointing appearance in the long mirror and the reflected sympathetic glances of other mothers made me furious and sad. I hated being pitied. In the same vein, after the Paradise Rink opened in Avondale when I was about 14, I decided I would take up ice-skating. Only a trip to Mr King the orthopaedic surgeon would dissuade me. It was as if I thought sheer willpower would make me 'normal'. When I read in our ancient copy of Arthur Mee's *The Children's Encyclopaedia* that wild birds will peck to death birds of brighter plumage released from a cage (the reason I would not set Bobby free, though my hand rested often enough on the wire door as he hung on his outside hook), it made perfect sense to me. Of course they would. Nature's way and no use wishing. But why would you want to be different if you weren't? It was a puzzle.

In some of us the legacy of disability and its good friend the playground bully is an almost pathological desire to please, to enter an apologetic state for being so wrong, to try to revert to normalcy. Or is it reversion? It may as easily be that we go forward to it, climb the slope and struggle to triumph on the peak of general acceptance.

I left my parents' house after that phone call in a familiar emotional state: a sense of cleaving, a bifurcation of my self. It was how I could pass in the able-bodied world as one of them – I was an actress, wasn't I, of sorts? – and how I could pass just as easily between lesbian and heterosexual groups of friends, though less and less, since the transition filled me with guilt of almost religious acuity. *People are the same everywhere* ran a piece of common wisdom handed out in the 60s, intended to comfort. Far from *celebrating difference*, as we try to today, the ideal was a smooth, homogeneous society. By the 1980s it was very clear that we weren't the same. There were very real divisions between people, to do with ability, religion, race, class, sexuality and culture, becoming more and more apparent. I seemed to be either ignorant of them or painfully aware.

How would my erstwhile boyfriend see me, as I was now?

I went home, he came around, but only flashes of our reunion remain in my memory. I can see him arriving, walking smiling down the sunny autumn path of my flat. I remember how he took me in his arms and how there was a hunger for me in him that didn't seem to have any connection to who I actually was. It set off dimly ringing (dinner?) bells – *this isn't real* – but suddenly I wanted it to be. I wanted to be beside him again. He had been halfway around the world, he told me, and had never met anyone like me. I would love Sydney; he wanted me to go back with him. He sniffed the nape of my neck. 'You still smell the same.' He loved me. I was confused.

Another memory – sitting on a low windowsill, a hot window behind me, the sound of the sea and the sun glancing off a cork-tiled floor (we must have gone away somewhere together, he and I, although I can't remember where), and hearing myself tell him I was a lesbian now and couldn't live with him, but that I would come to Australia. I remember how disappointed he seemed but how quickly he covered it with his usual tough humour. And also, I had to wait until *Accidental Phantasies* opened at the Depot in Wellington, and that was a month or so off.

Restored to me body and soul, my beloved went back to Sydney. I was familiar again with the urgent longing for him, the gap he left in my life. I went to Wellington, attended the opening night in a tuxedo and bow tie, and was so pissed and overwhelmed that when the audience called 'Author! Author!', no doubt in relief at having survived the second act, I had to be supported between two kind friends who also straightened my bow tie.

Home to Auckland for two days and a going-away party. It was a scandal. I had a lesbian going-away party and I was 'going back to men'. I protested feebly – no, only one man. A woman I barely knew suggested that since I was going to be doing it with him I may as well do it with lots of others and get paid for it. Most friends, particularly older friends, were kind and understanding. There was a generational divide between older and younger: those who called themselves children of the 60s eschewed labels; the true children of the 60s embraced them with fervour. Murky sexual identities were shameful.

My bricklayer Pop had died recently and left me a little hard-earned money that was enough to get me started across the Tasman. My cello and I departed, and took all my confusion with us.

*

At the airport I was met by the clapper-loader in a big white camera van, and on the way into the city he told me in colourful language of how he'd slept with a girl the night before and no matter how much strident effort he put into the exercise he was deprived of an orgasm. I was stunned. I thought we were reunited with dry cheeks, like the Emmylou Harris song. But 'possessiveness' is wrong, isn't it? (Our generation would ask one another earnestly, 'Are you possessive?' just as we would ask, 'Are you ambitious?' Both were negative qualities.)

Then he asked me why I had on so much makeup. I hadn't worn street makeup for years and had forgotten how to do it, if I ever knew. 'You're not a dollybird. You look stupid.'

As I wept copiously at his betrayal my pancake melted, mascara ran, lurid green eyeshadow slipped, and my eyes stung and swelled as if they were poisoned. We drove in silence to a terraced house in Yurong Street, Darlinghurst, which was full of dust-rimed artefacts collected by his land-lord/flatmate from native peoples of New Guinea and Indonesia. Our bedroom was an entirely windowless upstairs room empty of masks and figurines, with thick fetid-smelling shagpile carpet, nanna-ish gold and white wallpaper, his guitar, a ghetto blaster and a mattress on the floor.

As the weeks went by I would wake in the morning and think overly dramatic thoughts like, *I am in enemy territory*, especially after nights spent with Australians who were so vastly different from the New Zealanders I'd left behind. Sexist, derogatory remarks were manifold, as were racist ones (e.g. 'You're so lucky to have the Maoris,' usually said by Australians unhappy with the 'Aboriginal situation'), and I wasn't sure it was cool to have so many native artefacts. Our room was pitch black with the door closed. In the mornings we would reach for one another and for a little while everything would be roses again.

Then during the day, while he clapped and loaded, I wandered around as far as my feet would carry me, searching, with long, painful rests, for peace in the beauty of Hyde Park or Mrs Macquarie's Chair or St Mary's Cathedral. Sydney was beautiful, though frightening. I fell in love with the new quality of light, with swimming at Nielsen Park in the deep, rocky harbour with water the colour of kerosene (on the map the beach is marked 'Shark Bay'), a harbour so different from the muddy, tidal Wait-ematā. I loved the old sandstone buildings and the hints of the convict past. There were lizard-headed ibis, raucous cockatoos, rosellas and kook-aburras, and I thought how lucky Sydneysiders were that their native birds had adjusted better to city life than ours had. The flying foxes that rose at dusk from the Morton Bay fig trees in the botanic gardens were a fairy tale. On a trip away to a farm in the New England tablelands I swam in a creek and a magical platypus went past in a stream of bubbles.

But I was scared. I didn't know who I was anymore. I suspected I had made a big mistake but knew also that when we were good together you couldn't have better. We would have giggling attacks like kids. We would lie close and listen to one another's thoughts ear to ear, or to his collection of cassettes – Keith Jarrett, Phoebe Snow, Joni Mitchell, Eric Clapton, J.J. Cale – touchstone music, which went some way to stilling the clamour in my head.

It wasn't long before I discovered that the best cure for the clamour, as writers have known from the time humans first put chisel to stone, is to write. In New Zealand I had written poetry and plays and had often been in the company of thespians. In Sydney I knew no one except the camera man, and my disability meant I could not do the usual waitressing/bar jobs young New Zealanders take up – jobs that provide not only money but also new friends. I had one attempt as a dishwasher and couldn't walk for days afterwards. I started to write prose, short stories and my first novel, absorbing myself in fictional worlds so that I didn't have to fret about the real one. It was wonderfully liberating – no longer did I have to think about cast sizes, or how to tell a story limited to bodies and voices in a room, helped only by lighting and costuming. I remember a sense of exhilarating freedom – anything was possible. A character could walk upside down on a ceiling; a crowd scene wouldn't blow the budget. I had to work against the instinctive self-doubt that I believe plagues many New

Me at the time of
my departure for
West Island.

Zealanders, particularly of the postwar generations. We are quick to put
ourselves down, slow to believe in ourselves, tempted to dwell on the negative. All I knew was that writing gave me enormous pleasure and comfort,
just as reading always had, and that it was pretty much all I wanted to do
and surprisingly similar. I had always been a story-teller to my younger
siblings and cousins – the dramas would unfurl, the scenes play out in my
mind's eye. Although I had not started to write it at this stage, my first
novel *Crimes of Neglect*, set around Darlinghurst and the Cross, began to
take shape in my mind.

The clapper-loader (now promoted to focus-puller) and I moved to
another house in Surry Hills. My small stash of money was running out
rapidly, even though I eschewed normal human activities like eating. I
would ring up about jobs I saw advertised in the *Sydney Morning Herald*
or the *Trading Post*. One was for a receptionist for a private eye. This
sounded like the dream job.

'You're a New Zealander, aren't ya?' he asked, early on in the convo. 'Look, love – your countrywomen have done you a great disservice. I've had two or three New Zealand housekeepers and they just cleaned me out. Left me with nothing. I belong to Rotary and a few organisations like that – businessmen, you know – and none of us will employ New Zealanders.'

I wondered if they'd signed a pact

'Māori girls. The housekeepers.'

'I'm not Māori.' The words were out of my mouth before I thought further. I was consumed with guilt. I was appealing to his racist instincts.

'Doesn't matter,' he said. 'You're all the same.' He hung up.

It was my first real experience of brazen, racial discrimination and I was entirely unprepared for it. Of course there were all the jokes: What's the definition of a New Zealand virgin? Someone who can run faster than her brother. An Australian, an American and a New Zealander are on a sinking life-raft. Grab anything we don't need and chuck it over, says the American. So the Australian throws the New Zealander into the sea. An Australian in New Zealand comes across a Kiwi fucking a sheep. Back home we shear those, he tells him. Well, you're not sharing any of mine, says the Kiwi. (This is a language joke.) How do you pick the New Zealander in the shoe shop? He's the one trying on the boxes.

Younger New Zealand relatives and friends living in Melbourne – their current go-to city – tell me they never hear any jokes like these. I wonder whether that's generational or the enduring difference between Melbourne and Sydney.

Most of the jokes, and they were legion, were internationally inter-changeable and, just as likely to be bigotry about the Irish/Blacks/mothers-in-law/blondes. The best jokes I knew in response to a laconic wise-cracker were pretty pathetic. Why do seagulls fly upside down over Manly? Because Australians aren't worth shitting on. How many Australians does it take to tile a bathroom floor? Three if you slice them thinly. How many Australians does it take to change the kitchen light bulb? None – let the bitch cook in the dark.

In 1985 I made a brief return trip to New Zealand to collect the Bruce Mason Memorial Playwrights Award, arriving in arctic Wellington in an orange singlet and with inch-long hair. I was graceless at the award cere-mony, never having attended anything like it and not realising a thank-you speech was required. I bumbled around Wellington, bewildered. A strong gust of wind blew my 44-kilo self crashing through an orange safety barrier and into a hole on Lambton Quay. Bruised and bronchial, I returned to Sydney where I felt more at home, or warmer at least, and was very glad of the generosity of the award. I felt guilty, though. Was I obliged to go home, since I had won the prize?

During those first months in Sydney I heard tell of the Kiwi ghetto, which was supposed to centre on Bondi. There, since the 1950s, New Zealanders had occupied brick and tile flats, grotty rooms above shops and rooming houses. They'd partied, surfed, misbehaved and earned an unfortunate reputation for living off the Aussie dole (for which we continued to be eligible until prime ministers John Howard and Helen Clark came to an agreement in 2001). Although I never lived in Bondi and never went surfing, for a short time I fulfilled the other criteria for becoming the classic Kiwi bludger.

Eventually I landed a job as assistant in the news-clipping library of the ABC at Artarmon, and life came into some sort of balance. Self-esteem is difficult to hold on to at any stage of life and more so when you're young – mine was zero. But I was setting off each day on the train to the North Shore and earning some money, and was able to see the road ahead a little more clearly. The focus-puller and I found the strength to finally end our disastrous relationship and I moved out, firstly to the Cross to stay with a New Zealand friend, and then into a succession of flats.

During the following year, I was taken on by Cameron's Agents and was cast in *Dogs in Space*, Richard Lowenstein's semi-autobiographical film shot in Melbourne. I play Erica, who wears a pink boilersuit and tries unsuccessfully to take off with Michael Hutchence's girlfriend. In preparation for the role I studied hard to gain an Australian accent. I wanted one anyway, to stem the wearisome tide of sheep and bludger jokes. The accent took root. Even now, after nearly three decades back home, it will leap out at inopportune moments and overwhelm my native vowels, particularly if I am nervous. It's embarrassing, especially if it happens during an interview or public speech.

With my freshly minted Australian accent I returned to Sydney, where Cameron's literary arm represented me on my first book of short stories, *The Glass Whittler*. And on the dust jacket of the Australian edition I was claimed as one of their own.

Life in West Island

1913

For all our West Islanders 1913 is important. For Douglas Stewart it is possibly most important, since it is the year he is born.

Jean Devanny, mother of two, is living in the tiny mining settlement of Puponga in the northwest of the South Island. This year she will give birth to her third child, daughter Erin, and experience, albeit at a distance, the violent Waihi Strike, which will polarise her politics even further. She learns hard lessons about the drudgery of motherhood and marriage and survival, which will steel her for the difficult years ahead.

Thirteen-year-old Eric Baume is newly returned to Auckland from the United States of America, where he has run wild in the flesh pots of San Francisco and lost his virginity (if he is to be believed) at the age of eleven-and-a-half. Re-inserted into his Eton jacket, striped trousers and bowler hat, he is sent back to Auckland Grammar to resume his education.

Dulcie Deamer is 23, and five years into what will be 14 years of travelling the world with her husband Albert Goldie. Her fairly appalling novel *The Suttee of Safa* is published in New York, and she has now become a mother to two of six children, none of whom she can really be bothered with. Marjorie Quinn recounts a story of being in New York during this auspicious year and Dulcie and Goldie joining them for an evening in their apartment 'minus a couple of babies whom they left peacefully reposing at the hotel ... I'm not saying that the infants had been left alone by their parents. Probably, we'll so surmise, someone was watching over them.'[1] Always the drama queen, Dulcie tells Marjorie that she doesn't like New York, and that she would like to go behind a skyscraper and cut her throat.

But it is Roland Wakelin's 1913 that deserves the most attention. This is the year, consciously or unconsciously, that he becomes an Australian.

The Painter

This is 26-year-old Roland Wakelin's first year on the other side of the wide Tasman Sea; he arrived only in the last month of 1912. He reacquaints himself with the city he loved on first sight in 1908, the city he had vowed to return to as soon as he could. It is the realisation of a four-year dream. Since his first visit both of his parents have died and the rest of his immediate family have scattered. He is a first-generation New Zealander and has no roots to hold him in that southern archipelago.

The Sydney of his arrival has a population of 694,000 in the metropolitan area, and only 116,406 centrally.[2] A map of the period shows the young city clinging to the harbour edge, extending only as far as Marrickville and Ashfield in the west and as far as Willoughby on the North Shore. The train line runs to Parramatta; the harbour bridge is non-existent; and the Spit is a ferry terminal. Out in the wider world, George V is the king of the British Empire; nationally, Australian prime ministers will change twice – Labor's Joseph Cook coming in in January, only to be replaced by Liberal Andrew Fisher in the May elections. Women wear hats, blouses and long skirts; men have beards and waistcoats; the horse and cart is still the most common means of land transport. Among their funnels and smoke stacks, steamships at rest in the harbour carry soon to be redundant masts. Sydney Stadium is a small, round structure dumped in the middle of a paddock in 1908. Weekend crowds flood popular White City Amusement Park for the rides and freak shows. Parlours and drawing rooms bristle with Victorian-style aspidistras and parlour palms, uncomfortable furniture and floral carpets; gas lamps light the streets. Broadcast radio will not arrive for another decade.

Within weeks of arrival, Wakelin joins the Royal Art Society and finds a job with the Land Tax Department in order to pay the bills. Full of the enthusiasm of the young immigrant, he has no idea how virulent the criticism and response to his future art will be. He spends time with his brother, and starts art classes in bohemian Rowe Street with the 'little Italian', Antonio Dattilo Rubbo, who will become an important mentor.

Well versed in European traditions and innovations, Rubbo is a fiery and loyal friend to his students. At the time he and Wakelin meet, he is in his early forties. He emigrated from Naples to Australia in 1878, establishing his art school the following year. At his Rowe Street studio, Rubbo teaches 'ladies during the day and regular art students in the evening'.[3] The 'regular art students', we can only assume, are men.

Wakelin will say of Rubbo years later, 'He fought many battles on behalf of his students and was, with his virile personality and boundless enthusiasm, an inspiration for us all.'[4] He will also recall Rubbo's ever-present green eyeshade and brandished feather duster: '... if he didn't like a painting he would say "no good, that! Make laugh – a da fowls!" and would obliterate the drawing with a duster'.[5] In New Zealand Wakelin had painted in the open air and begun experimenting with colour. Rubbo encourages more of this, guiding and encouraging him to follow the French impressionists, already deceased artists whose practice has not yet reached Australia.

There is some crossover between the two genders, however, because it is at this time that Wakelin makes the acquaintance of Rubbo's student Grace Cossington Smith, who will become a loyal and lifetime friend, referring to him most usually as 'Dear Mr Wakelin' and treasuring a large collection of his paintings. In the same period he forms relationships with other student artists who will mutually sustain one another throughout their lives, most importantly Geoff Townshend, Lloyd Rees and Roy De Maistre. Home is a boarding house in Waruda Street, Kirribilli, which Townshend also occupies. Estelle Robinson, she of the dropped comb, is a neighbour. The comb falls at Wakelin's feet, he returns it, falls in love, and marries his Rapunzel in October.

In this auspicious year of 1913, Wakelin also meets 18-year-old artist Norah Simpson, who possibly has the greatest, most long-lasting effect on his life's work. Norah has returned from a trip to Europe, where she had gazed upon the works of Cézanne, Van Gogh, Gaugin, Matisse and Picasso, as well as French pointillists such as Seurat. She brings home a suitcase packed with art books and reproductions to show her artist friends.

As the twenty-first century wears on it will become increasingly difficult for us to imagine not only how slowly fashions in art and textiles travelled across the world in the early twentieth century, but also how image-poor life was, and how astonishing it must have been for Norah's artist friends to witness the opening of the suitcase – the spilling out of images, of colour, of techniques and styles. Wakelin, Cossington Smith and De Maistre are enormously influenced by seeing copies of these works for the first time. They have heard of them, of course, seen black and white images of some of them – but such a feast is mind-blowing, a welcome relief from the 'burnt sienna and rotten eggs', which is how the group describe Australian painting of their period.[6]

Around the same time, possibly a little earlier, Wakelin sees a photograph of Marcel Duchamp's 'Nude Descending a Staircase' published in the *Sunday Sun*. The painting is a chromatic, cubist rendition of a descending abstract figure, in browns and black, an attempt to demonstrate the subject's movement second by second. Duchamp is a controversial figure, one of the first modernists. At the Parisian Salon des Indépendants of 1912, 'Nude Descending a Staircase' was rejected by the cubists themselves as too futurist. The uproar is a news story around the world. It is this grainy but startling newspaper image that Wakelin will later say was his true introduction to modern art, which is not to say that he wasn't also influenced by Norah Simpson's enthusiasm, though her own practice, in European terms, was already behind the times.

Wakelin continues to experiment with colour and the method of application of paint. The next greatest influence after Norah's suitcase and Duchamp's appearance in the newspaper is E. Phillips Fox, an artist and tutor at Melbourne's National Art School, who trained in Paris and lived and worked in Europe for long periods. On Fox's return from France in 1913, an exhibition of around 70 works is held in Sydney. Wakelin says of this show: 'We'd never seen colour like that before ... painting had been on the brown side – more tone than colour – this was expression through colour; we'd never seen it before.'[7]

It is innovation in colour more than in form that motivates Wakelin, who is remembered as one of Australia's foremost colour theorists. In his early career he is struggling not only to establish himself as an artist but also to introduce what is, in this part of the world, a revolutionary art form. The works he submits to the Royal Art Society in 1913 are rejected. Perhaps, given his gruff, sensible New Zealand character that many are to appreciate and love throughout his life, Wakelin rolls with the punches and feels kindred to Duchamp. He paints on, with the same enthusiasm and excitement that has motivated him since he was a boy. He believes, as he will state in 1924, that great painting comes not from accuracy or method but from the heart.

In 1915 after a long battle waged by Rubbo, Wakelin's painting, 'The Fruit Seller of Farm Cove' (oil on canvas), is accepted by the society, as is Grace Cossington Smith's 'The Sock Knitter'. The *Sun* critic Howard Ashton, Wakelin's lifetime opponent, responds to 'The Fruit Seller' as 'a positive nightmare' and 'deliberate frightfulness'.[8] This almost equates to the *Bulletin*'s response to Baume's early work: 'Why?' Baume's bombastic, self-aggrandising book may well deserve the epithet, but Wakelin's works will stand the test of time. Ashton will keep up his criticism of Wakelin even into their old age. It seems as though he made a decision to go after him early in their respective careers and never wavered from his aim.

Art reviewers now rarely resort to such responses, even when they possibly should. Wakelin would regard current mainstream criticism, such as it is, with astonishment, since most of it is reduced to blandishments and the endeavour to 'understand', with all the simplification of the artistic process that this implies. Many young artists must long for that intensity of attention from a critic, even if it only amounts to 'Why?' – far better than the deafening silence or murmurs of sporting encouragement.

By contrast, the young Grace Cossington Smith will come to regard critical neglect as normal. While Wakelin receives attention, she receives none. This is because she is a woman painter and her subjects are domestic. Even the prices asked for her works show gender-based discrepancy. After the Royal Art Society exhibition, 'The Fruit Seller' remains unsold at 75 guineas and 'The Sock Knitter' at 15.

For the contemporary viewer, Wakelin's 'The Fruit Seller of Farm Cove' is an exercise in nostalgia for a long-gone Sydney that none of us ever knew. The setting is a tiny inlet between Mrs Macquarie's Chair and Bennelong Point on Sydney's foreshore. Even today Farm Cove remains an oasis of green, though skyscrapers and tower buildings fill the skyline. On sunny days there are bicycles, throngs of tourists, joggers and giant push-chairs conveying screen-intent toddlers. The deep rocky harbour glints kerosene blue, striped white with water traffic. Lizard-headed tip-turkeys rifle the rubbish; gangs of magpies and gulls settle and lift away. If you visit at dusk you will see fruit bats rising in great clouds from the Moreton Bay fig trees high on Mrs Macquarie's Chair. In the dying light they wheel and dart, winding themselves up for a night on the town. There is the roar of the bridge, the Cahill Expressway and the clogged canyons of the city. Rosellas and cockatoos scream from the gums and palms with, as New Zealander Ruth Park noted memorably, the voices of boys. The air fizzes.

Wakelin's scene is quiet. It is a fairly large painting, 91 x 116.5cm, and so was probably painted in a studio. Wakelin described his process: 'At the end of 1914 I took the sketch I had made at Pearl Bay the year before and painted a new version, using only alizarin crimson, French blue, and cadmium yellow with white, and applying the colours in small dabs in imitation of the impressionist method of stimulating the vibration of light. Encouraged by the success of this experiment, I set to work on a four-foot by three-foot canvas of "The Fruit Seller at Farm Cove".'[9]

It seems that Wakelin wants to reproduce winter morning light, low in the sky from the east. Everyone has their backs to us, except for a man in profile who relaxes on the sea wall, fashionable in his plus-fours and cheesecutter. A little redheaded girl in a white dress and hat waits with the other customers. A man in a panama hat examines the produce. Beside him stands a man in a sailor suit. There's a dowdy ageless woman – the provider – with a string bag, showing us her perusing back. The slope behind the stall seems foreshortened, buildings brought closer. It is this composite way of painting, where Wakelin moves buildings or objects, altering the perspective, that rocks Ashton's boat as much as the artist's use of colour. The conservatorium cupola and arches are faithfully repro-duced. It is a piece of Sydney and a group of its people, lovingly rendered in warm, glowing colours.

Two years later another painting, 'Down the Hills to Berry's Bay', a large, bright landscape and harbour scene, is accepted into the 1916 Royal Art Society exhibition, but only after Wakelin's champion Rubbo has successfully challenged one member of the society to a duel with pistols, swords or fists. Details of this duel, if it took place at all, are sketchy, but the story demonstrates how passionately artists and their critics are willing to protest their case, since Rubbo or his opponent may well have been killed. Art, it is believed, is supposed to reflect nature, not rely on any expression of the artist's process. Wakelin and his contemporaries are at the very beginning of a journey that tests viewers' aesthetic boundaries – a journey that ends, perhaps, with the current predominance of conceptual art in contemporary galleries.

'Colour became the liberating force for Wakelin,' writes Walton. Never was this truer than during these first years in Sydney, when Wakelin becomes friendly with Roy De Maistre, who in the late 1910s is experimenting with colour music. The early twentieth century abounds with theories on everything, and Wakelin is fascinated by De Maistre's idea that colours of the spectrum correspond with the eight notes of the musical scale. Fellow painter Douglas Dundas describes Wakelin's small paintings of this period as unique and quite beautiful.

One of these paintings, 'Landscape with Red Shed' (1918), will sell in 2008 for $24,000. It is tiny, only 17 x 11cm, a vibrant impressionistic rendering of a landscape in blues and greens. In the foreground there are two tree trunks, one yellow, the other purple. In the mid-ground a shed glares fire-engine red. An example from Wakelin's 'much sought after period,' announces the dealer. How Wakelin would laugh if he knew. His arch-enemy Howard Ashton, having perused an exhibition of these works in August 1919, declares the work to be 'elaborate bosh'.[10]

Another example of work from this colour-theory period is 'Synchromy in Orange Major' (1919), a coastal scene with a small bay, the hills around it in vivid greens and blues and pinks. The structures are yellow and orange, simple forms. In 1983 this tiny, jewel-like painting is bequeathed to the New South Wales Art Gallery. When I visit in early March 2017, it hangs as one of 10 of Wakelin's paintings on display in the twentieth-century Australian collection. Almost a century after its execution, it is still arresting. More vibrant still is another of his 1919 works, 'Causeway, Tuggerah', the colours and geometric shapes accentuating the man-made structure. Nearby hangs a painting from 1917, another recent acquisition. This is 'Narellan', an oil on canvas on hardboard. Bruised purple clouds show a neon-pink underbelly, while the sunsets glow green and pink and yellow. The land below is in shadowy dark greens and blues, the spectrum pushed out of a naturalistic rendering but still true to the colours suggested by the natural world.

At an exhibition in August 1919 Wakelin shows other paintings inspired by De Maistre's theory. Among them are 'Still Life Study in Blue Violet', 'Minor Key' and 'The Bridge'. Howard Ashton responds with fury, suggesting the artist has 'the Gladesville touch', a reference to a lunatic asylum in that suburb.[11]

Douglas Dundas, writing in *Art and Australia* in March 1967, recalls Wakelin's next period as being swayed by Max Meldrum, a Melbourne-based teacher and artist who eschewed colour. His influence on Australian artists in the 1920s cannot be underestimated. 'Beneficial as Meldrum's dogma has been in the case of some painters', Dundas writes, 'there is always the danger of its becoming an obsession. How fortunate it was for Wakelin that his sense of structure both in form and colour had been so well established before he came under an influence which in many instances had led to disregard of colour and of formal values!'

In fact, the influence is short-lived, though Wakelin believes he can see a correlation between his adored Cézanne and the Melbournian Meldrum. (As he had never seen a colour reproduction of a Cézanne until Norah Simpson opened her suitcase, he may well have later abandoned that notion.) More significantly, Wakelin is at this time two years into a job working as a commercial artist, as he will do for many years, this time with a firm called Smith & Julius. It is an occupation he does not particularly enjoy, but it puts food on the table for Estelle and their son Roland, born in 1914. Perhaps it is this enforced consideration of colour and form that prevents him from becoming a member of Meldrum's school.

TO EUROPE AND BACK AGAIN

In 1922 Wakelin left Australia for London on the one-class liner *Largs Bay*. He took with him Estelle, eight-year-old Roland Jnr and £70, £60 of which was the profit from the most recent exhibition. Husband and father must have wondered how soon it would be before penury forced a return to the South Pacific. In the end they stayed for three years, much of the time in fairly straitened circumstances. In London, as in Sydney, he scraped together a living as a commercial artist. It must have been soul destroying, because he believed he was never very good at it, lacking 'the slick touch'. He recalled that 'most of the stuff I had to do was pretty dead and uninspired', though he thought that European commercial art was way ahead of the Australian.[12]

There were high points, however. One of the companies he worked for, Cinads, was pioneering the first advertising films. Wakelin's brief was to work as an illustrator and scenario writer, which allowed him to travel through England and Ireland. He also went to Paris, and took himself off on weekend jaunts to sketch and paint. With his own eyes he saw paintings he'd only seen in reproductions, and most of these monochrome. In 1923 he saw an exhibition of Gaugin's work, and another of Van Gogh. He wrote of the Van Gogh exhibition: 'It burst upon me like an explosion … It was a revelation; none of the few prints we had seen in Sydney could reproduce the vitality in the paint itself.'[13]

For the rest of his life, these seminal viewings influenced his own practice. Although his commentators like to identify periods in Roland's work – that influenced by Roy De Maistre, by Meldrum, by Cézanne – it seems to have been more fluid than that. Even a cursory glance through the work sees him return to Meldrum's ideas as late as the 1950s ('South Melbourne Pier', 'The Starch Factory') and paintings influenced by colour theory in the same decade. It seems more natural for an artist, particularly after a long and fruitful career, to experiment again and again with different ideas and not necessarily in the same time frame.

Biographer Leslie Walton has it that Wakelin struggled in England to adapt to the soft European light. But could it also be that the quality of light reminded him, if only subconsciously, of the softer, rainier light of winter in his homeland? Antipodean painters past and present are often quoted on the subject of adapting to the light. When I suggested to New Zealand painter Richard McWhannell that Wakelin may have not found it so difficult to adapt, he related his own experience of painting Don McKinnon's portrait in London in 2006. 'It is true,' he told me, 'It's very different.' He described the light as 'smoky' and lacking clarity.

Back in Sydney in 1925, Wakelin found the art world not much moved on from where it was when he left. The March issue of *Art in Australia* of that year has him criticising the painters and critics of his adopted country for their ignorance: 'Monet's "Water-lily" pictures are not very good representations of water lilies from the botanical standpoint. But they are beautiful poems of light and colour, for Monet is here portraying the beauty he felt rather than the things he saw.'[14]

Macquarie Galleries showed the English pictures soon after his return. The exhibition was opened by Ethel Anderson, an Australian poet who had recently returned from Europe. She too gave some idea of artists' struggles to bring the Australian public up to speed on innovations and changes in the wider art world when she wrote, 'Roland Wakelin is a modern: he offers this exhibition to the public after an absence of three years from this city. He asks you to judge and accept these works for their aesthetic qualities rather than the pictorial.'[15]

The Wakelins made their home first in Dee Why, now a Northern Beaches suburb. In the 1920s it was mostly bush. Estelle found it too lonely, so around the time of the birth of their second child, Judith, the family moved south to Chatswood and later to Waverton. Berry's Bay was close at hand and became a regular haunt for Wakelin on his Sunday painting excursions. Beautiful Sydney Harbour inspired more of his work than any other location.

The same year Judith was born, 1926, saw the establishment of The Contemporary Group, which would, despite the scepticism of contemporary critics, become the most influential force in the country. George Lambert and Thea Proctor were at the helm, though their own work was more conservative than that of other group members, and were encouraging of the younger artists who gathered around them – a set that included Roy De Maistre, Margaret Preston, Elioth Gruner and Wakelin. The group swelled in the early 30s to include other post-impressionists such as Grace Crowley, Arnold Shore and George Bell.

Had Wakelin stayed in New Zealand and been surrounded instead by the likes of Rita Angus, Doris Lusk and Leo Bensemann, would his painting have developed in a different direction? To a New Zealand eye, 'Portrait of Roland Wakelin Jr' (c. 1933) shows an influence that could be that of Rita Angus. It could also have a hint of Picasso to it. Post-impressionism took shape and gathered practitioners all over the world, and in the era before instant communication and image proliferation each coterie of artists was able to believe that it was at the vanguard. Even Wakelin's colour theory of the late 1910s had precursors in the early years of that decade: two Americans in Paris, Morgan Russell and Stanton MacDonald Wright, had come up with a similar idea, which they dubbed synchronism.

Not every critic was antipathetic towards The Contemporary Group, or to individuals within it. Wakelin had his champions, including Ethel Anderson who wrote in the *Sydney Morning Herald* that 'Mr Wakelin's art is individual, personal in its expression ...'[16] So taken was she by Mr Wakelin that in September 1930 she opened her home in Turramurra for an exhibition of his works. The viewers crowded in, far more than she had expected – nearly a thousand of them. People picnicked in the garden and police were called to control the traffic.

By now the Depression had taken hold. Many commercial artists were out of work. Wakelin's employers cut his working hours to one week in three, and the family subsisted on half his previous salary. There was one glimmer of a silver lining – he had plenty of time to paint. But the canvasses and boards piled up: few people had the money to buy art. The Sydney Harbour Bridge was at this time under construction and a popular subject for many artists, Wakelin among them. Today those works, if they come up for auction, sell for thousands of dollars, money the Wakelins could never have dreamed of. In 1994 his 'The Bridge Under Construction' (1928) sold at Sotheby's for A$178,500.

Around 1930 Roland Jr left school and went out to work. But still Estelle, like many artist's wives, was required to manage the household on very little – and did so admirably. Daughter Judith elaborated on this, remarking that her mother always decorated the rented places they lived in, painting walls and furniture in strong colours. Each home had a studio for Wakelin, meaning that Judith rarely had her own room. Sometimes she had to sleep on the veranda, which was likely closed in to provide further accommodation, a common practice during those years. Colin McCahon's daughters, two decades later, slept in bunks under the house so that their father could have a studio, with the difference that this space was not closed in. By the time Judith was 15, she had lived at 12 different addresses.

By 1934 the Depression was lifting, and Ethel Anderson helped to organise another exhibition of Wakelin's work at the Macquarie Galleries.

This consisted of 29 oils and six watercolours. It was, at long last, an exhibition that garnered critical approval, even though it did not make much money.

Financial matters did not improve greatly after the beginning of the war. Commercial artists were still struggling. In late 1940 Wakelin lost his job and the family moved again, this time to a smaller flat. Judith, who had been briefly at East Sydney Tech studying art, was compelled to train as a secretary. She became the main wage earner for the family and only returned to Tech to attend art classes held by her father, a long time afterwards. As the war went on, Roland Jr went to fight in New Guinea and perhaps some of his wages went towards the family economy. This is a common enough situation for artists' families, many of whom have to struggle with not only their father's insolvency but also his drinking and/or drug abuse. Roland Wakelin was never that kind of artist. He was temperate, gentle, generous and reliable. Many of his students adored him, and he made friends for life. It wasn't until after the war that he was able to give up work as a commercial artist, augmenting his income with intermittent bouts of teaching in Sydney or Melbourne.

At war's end Wakelin was 58 years old. He had suddenly become part of the establishment. Critics applauded works such as the moody landscape 'Cronulla', painted in 1945. His by now trademark cloudy sky lowers towards a tumultuous sea; a dozen houses lie on the remote point. In 'The Train to the Mountains' (1943) he gives us a study on the behaviour of smoke and vanishing perspective. A whispier plume rises in the distance, mimicking the greater one. Another 1945 work, 'Ploughing at Hinton', may barely be recognised as Australian with its unidentifiable trees, church tower, white farmhouse and man in shirtsleeves labouring behind two horses. The work is old-fashioned, particularly when contrasted with that of the new Australian artists. Painters such as William Dobell, Russell Drysdale and Sidney Nolan were intent on what would rapidly become an iconography of gums, harsh light, austerity – a kind of post-colonial identity-seeking.

During the last decades of his life, Wakelin painted still-life works featuring domestic objects, and domestic scenes featuring his wife and children. They are gentle, inoffensive, and possibly painted in the full knowledge that they would appeal to the more conservative art-buying

'The Bridge Under Constuction' by Roland Wakelin, c. 1928–29. The building of the Sydney Harbour Bridge was a popular subject at the time. This painting shares a wall in the Federation Square Gallery with Grace Cossington Smith's 'The Bridge In-curve', 1930. *National Gallery of Victoria, Melbourne, reproduced courtesy of the artist's estate*

public. The most arresting and beautiful aspect of all of them is his use of colour. His earlier rebelliousness and flag-waving had been about that more than anything else, and it never deserted him.

In an interview conducted with John Hetherington during his seventies, Wakelin stated that the harsh criticism he endured in his early career did him no lasting harm. 'Good art can't be produced in tranquillity ... If the young painters of today had more conflict they'd perhaps paint better pictures.'[17] It is perhaps the statement of an old man astonished and disappointed by the work of younger artists. The Wordsworthian sentiment also betrays weariness. It is far more true of the artist Wakelin to remember Paul Cézanne's dictum, which Wakelin kept close to his heart: 'Penetrate what is before you and persevere in expressing yourself as logically as possible.' Wakelin continued: '[T]he world has gone on pretty fast and today I'm considered a bit old fashioned. I don't mind that. I follow my own bent. I always have ... In my time I've seen a lot of gods rise, then fall from their pedestals. I've an open mind about abstract expressionism, let me say, but I don't see where it will lead ... I feel there is a limit to what can be achieved with it.'[18]

Wakelin, self-effacing and blessed with a widely appreciated sense of humour, never saw himself as a god. He knew he had been eclipsed not only by the great upswelling of twentieth-century Australian art but also by those who had been his less successful contemporaries. Ignored in her youth, Grace Cossington Smith is now regarded as the more prominent painter of the period.

In his native land, Wakelin is all but forgotten. As Hetherington comments: '[M]any Australian connoisseurs of painting do not know he is a New Zealander. Many New Zealanders are also unaware of it ... About twenty years ago the New Zealand Government ... published a book listing the names and achievements of New Zealand artists. Roland Wakelin was not mentioned. Perhaps New Zealand's indifference is understandable. Wakelin has lived in Australia for fifty years, and has only once been back to New Zealand ... when he and his wife went over on a short visit.'[19] So common was it for New Zealand-born painters never to return that Olaf Ruhen, writing of Wakelin's compatriot Robert Johnson, pointed out: 'He loved New Zealand as a New Zealander, and still saw it without prejudice ... Johnson is perhaps the only New Zealand artist who returned ... again and again, to paint it from a home in another country.'[20] This quote appears in Christopher Johnstone's *Landscape Paintings of New Zealand: A journey from north to south*, a definitive volume that includes 210 New Zealand painters. Wakelin is not among them.

The Auckland Art Gallery Research Library holds a folder of material on our lost painter. Among the papers is a letter dated 26 April 1985, 14 years after Wakelin's death. It is from Charles Nodrum of Charles Nodrum Gallery in Richmond, Victoria, and includes a photograph of 'New Zealand Landscape' (1947). This work springs from that one short return to the North Island, and was exhibited at the Art Gallery of South

Australia during a loan exhibition of Australian paintings for the Royal Visit of 1954. Nodrum wanted to sell it to the director of Auckland Art Gallery for $4,750. He asked if the director knew where the picture was painted.

Attached to the letter is a reply from Roger Blackley, who then held the position of Curator, Historical New Zealand Art. He declined the offer, writing that the painting is a 'beautiful, albeit conventional work. It would be nice to add a New Zealand Wakelin to the collection, but I don't think this is the one. I'm sorry, but I can't suggest a location for the picture.'

The gallery was in possession of only one other Wakelin. Almost 20 years earlier Air New Zealand had gifted 'Blues Point' (1933) as part of an endeavour to create an Australian collection. To date, the only other painting the gallery holds is 'Auckland Landscape', a bright geometric painting of gabled roofs that could be Mount Eden, or Ponsonby, or one of the other older suburbs. The painting is undated.

Wakelin filled in a form in response to the purchase of 'Blues Point' in 1966, and interestingly listed his nationality as British. Many New Zealanders of English extraction of his generation would have done the same. But I can't help wondering if Wakelin's statement is to some extent obfuscation. Far less confronting, in this instance, perhaps, for this exile to say he was British rather than Australian.

1925

In this year, plumb in the middle of the 20s, there is a glorious freedom in the air. People are starting to forget the war and the world is full of dreams and possibilities. Broadcast radio is a new and constant connection with the outside world, an outside real-time voice intruding for the first time into the domestic realm. Listeners pay a licence fee to the station of their choice – in Sydney they can choose from 2SB and 2FC, both of which will become part of the new ABC in a few years' time. Books are more freely available, ideas are spreading, school is compulsory. Many lucky women are finding themselves liberated by new labour-saving devices such as vacuum cleaners, refrigerators and wringer washing machines. Their clothes are less cumbersome and they have access to higher education. And they can have fun – kick up their heels to the Charleston, smoke and drink, travel at a speed suited to the jazz age: motorcars are now common-place enough for laws to have been passed in Australia and New Zealand requiring drivers' licences. The world is moving faster, shifting, changed forever by the blood bath of the Great War and anger at the conditions of the working class. On either side of the Tasman labour movements are forming; in both countries these are dominated by Australian men. The revolution is in sight.

Far away in the Taranaki, young Douglas Stewart is 12 and enjoying an idyllic childhood in the village of Eltham. Bright, happy, healthy, adventurous and well loved, in 1925 he wins a scholarship to New Plymouth Boys' where he will board for the next five years.

Jean Devanny is 29. She has been living in Wellington since 1922, running the boarding house in Knigges Street, writing around the breakfast dishes, conducting fierce political arguments, loving Hal and possibly other men – and, if John A. Lee is to be believed, turning the odd trick. *The Butcher Shop* is on the way to being published. She is a keen and vocal member of the local women's branch of the Labour Party. Six years ago her little daughter Erin died from septicaemia and Jean is still, occasionally, overcome with paralysing grief. She's better than she was – for a number of years she stopped playing the piano or writing. This year will bring a source of great anxiety: her son Karl will be diagnosed with a serious heart condition. In her political life she is surrounded by Australian unionists, men she admires and perhaps comes to emulate. Strident, tall and hatchet-faced she strides about, it is often remarked, like a man. Clever, self-educated and tough as nails, with many friends and admirers and just as many enemies, Jean is having the time of her life.

Wise and calm Roland Wakelin's three life-changing years in Europe are behind him and he is living in a cottage at Dee Why with his wife and son. Estelle is about to fall pregnant with their beloved daughter Judy. An exhibition of his recent work opens at Macquarie Galleries on 15 April with a catalogue introduction by painter Margaret Preston. This year is the first of his supposed Cézanne period – though surely that influence is evident long before. He is 38 years old and has another two years' hard yakka before he paints 'The Red House'. 'By then,' he will say in retrospect, 'the tide was beginning to turn.'[1]

Eric Baume is three years into the helter-skelter life of a journalist in Sydney, working on the *Guardian*. The newspaper is the brainchild of Sir Joynton Smith, ex-Lord Mayor of Sydney; Robert Packer, the first of the Packer dynasty; and Claude McKay. It is one of the city's proliferation of newspapers: six dailies and four on Sundays. Baume covers stories from the underworld: gangs, drug-running and corruption. His wife has been with him for over a year and their second child Diana is due. Mary is often unwell but Baume is seldom home. He's out gambling, drinking, womanising or chasing stories. He's also a blushing and titillated occasional attendee of fellow New Zealander Dulcie Deamer's bohemian set.

In 1925 Dulcie Deamer is 35 years old and enraptured with her first experience of adventurous single-womanhood.

The Party Girl

Home sweet home for Dulcie Deamer, after 14 years of world travel with husband Albert, is a one-quid-a-week room in Barcom Street, Kings Cross. Since 1923 she has rented a series of rooms around the Cross, all shabbily furnished, mostly infested with cockroaches, but usually including the welcome luxuries of a gas ring and a single window. Dulcie loves her new life.

The area is beginning to see some changes. It is slowly becoming more like the Cross we would recognise today with its hotels, clubs and restaurants. Along Williams Street old residential buildings and tenements are being demolished, and taller blocks rise in the city beyond St Mary's Cathedral on the next hill. Deamer would describe Sydney of the 20s as a 'small town ... [with] pot-holed tracks for the tradesmen's carts ... no washing machines, no radio, no refrigerators – everybody had a leaky icebox ...'[2]

When she had first seen Sydney as a young bride, met off the boat by an aunt, she had seen it as a huge city. 'Sydney overwhelmed me. I wrote back to the family, trying to convey how staggered I was by this metropolis. Hansom cabs everywhere – and *motor cars*. We had only seen one, drowned in its own dust ... People dashed out of their Featherston cottages to stare as if something apocalyptic had appeared.'[3]

In 1925 there are two pubs at the top of William Street, both of which she regards as 'respectable', and a big Chinese caff. If she doesn't fancy chop suey she can buy 'ambiguous rissoles at the ham-and-beef shop opposite the tram stop'. Or if that doesn't appeal, she can put her feet under a table at one of the 'William Street rough-and-ready eateries where Irish stew or sausage-and-mash cost 18d'. If there's a party to go to, she can wander down to one of a number of discreetly presented wardrobe shops (as second-hand clothes stores were called then), and find a 'gay if slightly tarnished party frock for 10 shillings', or splash out as much as £1 for something in better condition.[4]

Three years into life as a single woman, Dulcie is making the most of it, having never really been single before. Albert Goldie, actor, theatre manager and writer, short, big-talking and usually insolvent, has been summarily dumped. Their four surviving children have been handed over to Dulcie's widowed mother Mabel, who has been living in Sydney since Dr Deamer's death from Spanish flu in Auckland. She is 53 and, as her granddaughter Rosemary will one day say, 'weary of life'.⁵ Dulcie's parents had only been back in New Zealand for 18 months when he died. For several years prior, they had shared flats in Sydney with Dulcie and Albert, caring for the children while the couple travelled, worked and played. Now Grannie has returned, found a flat in Coogee, rescued the older boys from boarding school in Bowral and taken on the younger two. Money is tight, but she is caring for the children as best she can, relying on Providence and prayer, which she finds usually works. A Roman Catholic convert from Low Church Anglicanism, she is sustained by her new faith. Horrified by many of Dulcie's much-publicised activities, she is nevertheless always welcoming and loving should 'Duss', as the children called their mother, call in on her way home from a swim.

Perhaps, as Dulcie waltzes down Woolcott Street (next year the name will be changed to Darlinghurst Road) towards her favourite bohemian wardrobe shop, she thinks about her mother, whom she has on a pedestal – a pedestal she has no interest in attaining herself. Poor Mother! Dulcie would be lost without her, although there is some luck in the fact that not all of the six arrivals during the first seven years of her marriage survived. Two died in infancy. In interviews she refers sentimentally to her 'six children', which her daughter will remember became a family joke. Often she referred to her children as her 'young', as if they were a litter. As Louis Nowra remarks, she displayed 'a chilly indifference to her children all her life'.⁶ By now Deamer has published four novels, three of them serialised by William Randolph Hearst's newspaper chain in America, and writes regularly for hugely popular *Australian Women's Mirror*. How else is she to pursue her career as a writer and indulge her love of late nights, parties and showing off? You can't do that when you have three sons and a little daughter to care for, talk to and empathise with. It takes up too much time and energy more fascinatingly spent on oneself. Much better by far to hand them over to Mother, who understands children. She has what

Deamer calls a 'super gift' for it.[7] Mabel also understands that if her grand-children were to stay in Dulcie's care they could be hungry, sad, dirty and possibly in danger. They would certainly be ignored while their mother spent time with her friends, who would seem to Mabel to be variously famous, infamous, insolvent, dyspeptic, dandified, and/or sensualists dabbling in the occult. Poets, writers, actors, journalists, artists – this is the company Deamer prefers to that of her 'young'.

Grannie's heart aches for the children, but also for her errant daughter. Her passionate embrace of Catholicism with all the fervour of the newly converted has passed to the next generations – one of Dulcie's sisters is a nun, and Dulcie's children will all strive to maintain, with varying degrees of success, living faiths. Very often, throughout her long life, attempts will be made by well-meaning relatives to bring Deamer back to Christ from the edge of the bohemian vortex. None will succeed.

Bohemianism is Deamer's religion, its main tenet being freedom: sexual, artistic and intellectual. The abandonment of her children seems cold-hearted, but we can say, in an attempt to understand, that she was a young bride at only 17, impatient for life experience and adventure. Early on, most likely, she discovered she loved sex and the babies kept on coming, one after the other, as an irksome side-effect.

Father of the brood, Albert Goldie, disappeared too, and nobody is judging him. For a short period after their separation he lived with Dulcie and his new blonde girlfriend in a flat, but Dulcie appears to have had nothing to do with him after this. Grannie always maintained a soft spot for him, so that he had some ongoing contact with the children. Albert will die in hospital in 1934, having been found utterly drunk on a Melbourne street. Son Edwin will also later suffer from alcoholism but be redeemed by the Church.

Right now, Albert's death is nine years away and Deamer is delighted to be separated from him. Perhaps as she goes singly along the street she ponders how, as with any dissolution of a marriage, there are always many reasons why people cannot continue to live together. The years of trav-elling were not blissful. Deamer describes them as 'step-by-step marital disillusionment'.[8] Even so, Dulcie and Albert may have been better travel companions than they were at the domestic, day-to-day existence of peeling the potatoes, paying the rent and getting the kids off to school.

The clue for their decision to finally divorce could lie in the shared credit for a film shot in Sydney in 1922, the same year as their separation. This was *A Daughter of Australia*, produced by and starring the American Lawson Harris. The story of this now lost film follows the fortunes of a young Englishman accused of a murder he didn't commit. He escapes arrest by emigrating to Australia, where he works on a cattle station and forms a relationship with the squatter's daughter. A silent movie, it starred some minor American and Australian actors and earned a degree of notoriety when a shootout was filmed in Martin Place. Passers-by were alarmed and two extras were injured. Dulcie and Albert's shared credit is as the screenwriters – i.e. they wrote the film *together*. If their marriage was already in trouble after years of penury, travel and unwanted children, then writing in tandem, as countless writer couples have also discovered, could have been untenable, the final nail in the coffin. Deamer may also have resented Goldie's earlier attempt at writing.

Perhaps, on Woolcott in 1925, before she reaches the wardrobe shop, Deamer stops in at the book exchange and peruses the shelves, and among the westerns and romances, classics and penny dreadfuls comes across a battered copy of *A Corner in the Water* by Bert Mudge and Albert Goldie, and thinks again how dare her husband write a book! Well, co-write. In 1909 he and his friend Bert published the novel with the Sydney Worker Trustees. Perhaps she is comforted by the fact that the trustees are hardly reputable publishers. And already the book is sinking like a stone, just as *A Daughter of Australia* will soon do.

Does Deamer hide the book behind another on the shelf and go on her way, pleased it was so unsuccessful? She is the author in the family, always will be, even though, after her early wild success, she didn't publish her own first novel until 1913. Better if Goldie had contented himself with all the things he already was – writer, director and actor. Hadn't she allowed him to attend, in the privilege of her company, the lively inaugural meeting of the Australian Writers' and Artists' Union? This precursor to the Fellowship of Australian Writers was launched on 20 April 1911.

The launch is one of her favourite hoolies to remember, since she was the only woman. It was a 'stag party'.[9] Among entertainment provided by others, she and Albert performed a thought-reading act for the all-male

audience. Telepathy was all the rage, care of Madam Blavatsky's Theoso-
phists, and was regarded as one of the new paranormal sciences. Deamer is
interested in the occult. Although she doesn't know it in 1925, the young
New Zealander who will become one of her closest (and most infamous)
friends has arrived in Sydney. Rosaleen Norton, future Witch of Kings
Cross, is only nine years old and has shifted with her family from Dunedin
to the North Shore suburb of Lindfield.

People who knew Deamer through the 1920s and 30s marvelled at her
voracious appetite for parties and attention. Could it be that her frenetic
behaviour was somehow motivated by the barely perceived guilt of abandoning her children, as well as by a desire for life to move just as quickly as
it had throughout her marriage? She was not a woman given to examining
her conscience or mulling over the past. The writing of her autobiography
took her four years and it lay unpublished – along with at least six unpublished novels – until long after her death.

It could be, as Deamer heads towards the Kings Cross wardrobe shop,
that she is assailed by memories of other streets in other cities during those
travelling decades. She and Goldie moved between America, England and
France three times, as well as voyaging to South Africa, Canada, Belgium,
Switzerland, Italy and the South Sea Islands. 'I crossed the equator eight
times!' she would boast. In every place her husband chased his fortune.
Deamer, with her proud reputation as an author of stories about sexy,
scantily clad stone-age men and women, did not like being left holding
the baby. Sometimes the children would be put in private nurseries. Sometimes, as Marjorie Quinn suspected, they would be left alone in the hotel.
Deamer certainly suffered from homesickness: 'A postcard of a Sydney
beach was enough to give one a violent heart-wrench'.[10]

Thank heavens, again, for Mother.

If Deamer, as she opens the wardrobe-shop door and breathes in the
musty smell of all these alluring costumes to be worn and returned for
the tiniest of outlays, finds herself thinking of that inaugural meeting of
the writers' and artists' union in 1911, she might also think of how later
in that same year she and her husband embarked on the first journey for
America. There were no pretty things then. The Goldies had been poor
in Sydney and poorer in New York, as more of their unwanted children
arrived. Motivation to write her novel, *The Suttee of Saffa*, could have

sprung partly from the need to make money. Highly sexualised, and in purple, melodramatic prose, it was the first of her historical works. They could be seen, in some ways, as precursors to today's *Game of Thrones* and other historical fantasies. If Deamer had been born a century later she may well have written for television.

Let's imagine that folded over a coat hanger in that wardrobe shop is an Indian silk shawl, once part of a sari, and that it sets Deamer thinking about that first novel.

The story owes its genesis to her thrilling experiences in India during the first year of her marriage, when Albert was managing the doomed London Comedy Company and nationalism was taking hold across the country. In Calcutta, Deamer got caught up in a riot at the Temple of Kali and was given refuge by a Brahmin priest. In Bombay she witnessed a burning ghat that held the body of a 12-year-old wife, and never forgot the horrific sight of a small, burning foot. On another occasion a bomb was thrown into her carriage. And, more relevantly, a fat Bengalese millionaire had the gall to attempt abduction with the idea of adding her to his harem. It is this idea that is central to the novel. She will say, later in her life, that she is embarrassed by the heroine's willing subordination to a dominant man.

'Either you love India, or you don't. No middle way. I've had to devote some space to it. Remember I stepped straight into it from a New Zealand village,' she will write.[11] From India she and Albert went on to Rangoon, China and Hong Kong. In Canton she was pregnant. 'It hadn't made the slightest difference. Morning sickness or any other qualms were simply not written in my book of words.'[12]

Later on this day in 1925 she has returned to her grotty first-floor back, as bedsits were called then. As she chews on an ambiguous rissole, Deamer might wonder if this is the moment she will ingest a qualm. She might reflect on how many times she has escaped death: lucky that the Indian carriage bomb did not explode, lucky that she changed her travel plans at the last moment in 1912 to ensure that she embarked on the *Olympic*, rather than use her booking on the *Titanic*. Or at least this is what she told a journalist in 1933, when her Golden Decade was drawing to a close. In the manner of a true narcissist Deamer believes she is untouchable – she can survive anything.

It is this period of sausage-and-mash, second-hand clothes, constant parties (she would boast she'd been to more than two thousand of them), tatty costumes and near penury that she will come to regard as golden, more than any other in her life. She tells people this, and also that she weathered a nervous breakdown in 1922, the year she finally left Albert for good, so desperate was she for constant freedom. A cynic might come to the conclusion that this is an expedient tale to justify the abandonment of her children. She was certainly exhausted and conflicted, and relieved to be away from Goldie and his boom-and-bust schemes. 'I haven't the business instincts of a rabbit, and Albert, overweighted with ideas and drive, and underweighted with judgement and stability was more often than not semi-broke.'[13]

Ambiguous rissole weighing heavily on her stomach, Deamer takes in the view from the single window and contemplates her costume for this evening. From her back room she can see dustbins, clotheslines, tenements, incinerators and rubbish heaps, chooks, skinny cats and grubby kids, but she barely takes any of it in, so intent is she on the night's great excitement. She turns away, opens her cupboard and takes out the leopard-skin costume. Should she wear it again? She has to make her way over to Haymarket, and it's a very special occasion. More than any of her novels, articles or plays, tonight's honour will define her place in history. Deamer will be crowned Queen of Bohemia.

The leopardskin had its debut in 1923, worn over the top of a body stocking at the first Artists' Ball, an event Deamer will attend every year until 1953. These Sydney events are based on the English Artists' Balls, where guests attend in fancy dress – as Indian princes, pirates, princesses, policemen, ghosts, skeletons, cannibals, witches and clowns. They are about the only occasion when men can polish their tiaras, pop them on their heads, squeeze themselves into ballgowns and get away with it. Deamer's leopardskin costume will not be seen at every ball, but it is certainly destined to more than its fair share of outings. One of Norman Lindsay's daughters-in-law will remember, 'We would groan every time Dulcie came out to do her party piece splits in her leopard skin, and we'd think, "Oh, Christ, not again."'[14]

Tonight the costume is only two years old, still fresh enough, with none of the tears and smirches it will acquire after a decade or so of the high life. While Deamer brushes her hair, powders her nose and applies her dark lipstick she plans her performance and thinks fondly of her dear friends.

They are the I Felici, Letterati, Conoscenti e Lunatici – The Happy, Literary, Wise and Mad, a group of bohemians who want nothing more than to entertain each other loudly, laugh, play games, argue and drink gallons of wine: a kind of party club. This year is Deamer's third as Grand Initiator. Sam Rosa, a socialist journalist and writer, is the Grand Master. When Deamer first met him he was on the staff of the *Worker*, having earlier written for and edited *Truth*. Like Deamer, he's a kind of outsider – probably born in Australia but spent his childhood and youth in London. Also like Deamer, he writes fiction – or did. His novel *The Coming Terror; or the Australian Revolution: A romance of the 20th century* was published in 1894.

Usually the group meet at the Roma Café in Pitt Street, but tonight the activities will take place at Theo's Club in Campbell Street. It is the Grand Master's job to encourage attendees to 'sing, chant or play-act for the benefit of the whole company … [It was] informal, collective private theatre and it suited Deamer perfectly.'[15] Louis Nowra goes further than this, stating: 'Plain and vain, Deamer loved attention and was a relentless flirt whose wild sex life existed more in the minds of others than in reality. She treated parties with more reverence than her plays and novels and spent much time writing skits for them.'[16]

What of the Grand Initiator? Deamer herself explains her role, step by step:

> I rise in my place, so the accepted candidate is in no doubt as to his next move. He and I embrace, and there is a hearty kiss with no nonsense about it.
>
> Applause. Mock-serious protests if the new initiate exhibits more than average ardour, or tends to make it a marathon even. He then gets his membership card, which he must guard with his life, finds his place at the table, and is one of us.
>
> The number of times I may rise to the occasion on a Saturday varies from once or twice to five or six embraces. Reckon the number of Saturdays in a year, multiply that by a decade and you'll have some idea of the procession of gents, young, old or middle-aged, I have ceremoniously kissed … And I like kissing. I could keep on liking it because I'm basically impersonal … Thank heaven I was born with an aptitude for being impersonal joie de vivre.[17]

To
Olive –
with love, &.
every best wish
for happiness –   *from Dulcie 1924*

Dulcie Deamer in leopardskin costume in 1923. *Swiss Studios*

And there we have it, a gift for impersonal *joie de vivre*, the signpost to her road away from domestic slavery.

To our twenty-first-century eyes, the silly titles of Grand Initiator and Grand Master suggest childhood games, or, if grown-ups are involved, organisations like the Freemasons at best or the Ku Klux Klan at worst. Deamer's behaviour, the 'hearty' kissing, also seems silly, until we recall that the sexual revolution, so called, is at least 40 years away. To her contemporaries, and particularly to those of an older generation, her behaviour would have been titillating and shocking.

You may remember that Deamer's poor mother, who might have been a free thinker but was nonetheless informed by the Victorian age, had taught her daughter that 'if a man says he loves you and doesn't ask you to marry him, it's an insult'.[18] This is a variation on the theme also familiar to young women of the period: 'If a man kisses you and doesn't ask you to marry him, etc, etc'. Deamer is, as always, pushing the boundaries. Later in the year she will publish an article 'The Compleat Kisser: A handbook yet to be written', to demonstrate her prowess.[19]

There are no photographs to illustrate Deamer's crowning this night in the Haymarket, which abounds with free spirits as much as does the Cross, but we can be assured it was a bravura performance complete with costume and script. Deamer was from that night, henceforth and forever until her dying breath, the Queen of Bohemia.

*

Others of our New Zealanders came into contact with Deamer through this period. She recalls her brush with Eric Baume:

> He was on his way up in the writing game, and was later, as a broadcaster, to become as well known as the GPO clock or any other Sydney landmark. I had had to join issue with him once in the matter of a novel of his dealing with Maoris, he and I both being New Zealanders, and he knowing as well as I that his facts weren't right. But there were no hard feelings between us. I admit that the Noble Order was 'good copy' but Eric, journalist or not, was a member. And he gave way to temptation, and wrote us up in a daily. His treatment of the Grand Master was not exactly respectful. And the GM, extremely wroth, pronounced the equivalent of excommunication against him, in absentia, as a betrayer of the Order … the traitor suddenly appeared

... like the boy on the burning deck, pale but determined. And he was pale
... Looking straight at the GM he made a formal and abject apology for
'unforgivable behaviour'.[20]

Jean Devanny knew her too, and would recall meeting the bohemians
at the Roma Café:

The writers and journalists were kindness and generosity personified;
especially that section known as 'the Bohemian bunch'. The 'queen' of this
group, Dulcie Deamer, poet, novelist, and freelance journalist, was a compatriot of mine. My first luncheon with this group, as their guest, astonished
me no end: their hilarity in a public restaurant; Dulcie's sparkle and gush.
I was inducted into their circle by a ceremony in which, blindfolded, I was
made to promise that, while in Australia, I would cast my prohibition prin-
ciples to the four winds, think of the poor sheep, eschew water and drink
wine ... But the atmosphere of Bohemia made no appeal to me.[21]

It is no surprise, given what we know already of Devanny's character,
and Deamer's, that there was no mutual attraction. Deamer lived for
parties and persiflage, Devanny lived to stand on soapboxes and change the
world. Also, despite growing up believing the lie of what Vincent O'Sullivan calls New Zealand's 'egalitarian flourish', the women would have
been well aware they came from different social classes.[22] Dulcie's father
was a Christ's College-educated doctor, Jean's a boilermaker. Dulcie's
governess mother had educated her at home; Jean briefly had gone to the
local school. Both Mrs Crook and Mrs Deamer had given their daughters
lessons – Jean learned to play the piano, while Dulcie learned about ghosts
and the joy of nudity. Dulcie was a debutante in Dunedin and sent to
elocution classes, while Jean was sent out as a housemaid at 13.

Perhaps on that first meeting they would have seen more of what they
had in common, apart from their nationality. There was only four years'
difference in age, and they both lived in near penury, though earned what
they could from writing. Deamer recalled how she could 'dash into the
Bulletin with a poem, a par, or an article on the day and collect your few
bob or a guinea. It was a life-saver.'[23] Devanny would have received some
paltry royalties from her novels – but most likely next to nothing.

Neither women gives a date for this encounter, but it would have been
in the months between the Devannys' arrival in 1929 and Jean's departure

for a disastrous job cooking for a squatter in the outback. The Depression was climbing to full roar and she had been living in a series of slum tenements in Surry Hills and the Cross. Deamer and Devanny would also have met at meetings of the Fellowship of Australian Writers. Proof of this comes from none other than a New South Wales police officer. In a report on 'Other Malcontent and Dissident Organisations', record is made of a fellowship meeting on 23 June 1942, when the women proposed a resolution to keep Australia free of fascism. It was carried unanimously.[24]

Deamer did not share Devanny's political concerns, though she had one over her compatriot. At one of the Artists' Balls in the 1940s the *Bulletin* table was layered in posters with the legend: 'Make Dulcie Deamer Prime Minister'. No one ever suggested that for Devanny, not even jokingly.

Although the two women were never to be friends, in the late 20s and early 30s they were neighbours in a part of town that was changing dramatically. As Deamer notes: 'It was on the edge of the incoming Depression that the Cross became, quite suddenly, a hang-out of the underworld … almost overnight the papers were full of razor gang vendettas and back lane dope peddlers, the locale of the lawlessness always being around the top of William Street'.[25] In an effort to solve the problem, the Sydney city commissioners decided to radically increase the street lighting. It made no difference – crime flourished in back-alley shadows. It did, however, make the Cross a destination for Sydneysiders who may never have ventured there before: in the early 30s it was a treat for children to be taken to see the bright lights of the Cross. Meanwhile Deamer's friends, one after another, got into financial trouble, if they weren't in it already. Her closest friends were often among those who found the bright bubble of bohemianism was all too easily pricked, the glitz and glitter falling away to reveal very real, grey poverty.

Douglas Stewart gives us a snapshot of Deamer in her middle age, describing her as 'sprightly … with her head held proudly high and a proud high-stepping walk'.[26] Recalling her leopardskin costume, he wonders whether her compulsion to wear it again and again arose from her cavewoman heroine in her prize-winning story of 1907. As late as 1954, in a letter to Miles Franklin, Jean Devanny refers to 'a certain woman writer we both know well', who enjoys 'nude parties and measuring the men's sexual organs'.[27]

Much as Deamer loved the limelight, and felt herself the centre of a social whirl, it is debatable whether some of the writers she knew socially and through the Fellowship of Australian Writers – among them, Henry Lawson, Banjo Paterson, Steele Rudd and Mary Gilmore – regarded her as a friend. But we do know that poet David McKee Wright was fond of her. He was another trans-Tasman identity, who had abandoned a wife and family in Scotland before emigrating to New Zealand. He had co-habited with another woman there, and worked as an editor on a local paper before coming to Sydney and writing for the *Bulletin*. Deamer put him in 'the great lover class'.[28] Another contemporary described him as having 'long silvery hair and thin, finely modelled face ... I knew him as the New Zealand poet, once a minister of religion, who had left the church and had a predilection for writing about the devil, for David Wright was not an ascetic. He loved life.'[29]

From this roll call of associates, and there are hundreds more, it could be assumed that Deamer did not easily make friends with other women. She loved men and desperately wanted them to love her. But she was to make one last very close friend in later life, when she was in her fifties: a woman she met in around 1945 through her friend Frank Bennett, who was a Sydney-based disciple of the mystic Aleister Crowley.

DEAMER'S NEW ZEALAND FRIEND ROSALEEN NORTON

If we leap ahead to the late 1940s, we will see that the little New Zealander who came to live in Lindfield 20 years ago is all grown up and in her thirties. She is living with her much younger poet boyfriend, Gavin Greenlees, at 179 Brougham Street in Kings Cross – not too far away from Deamer. The Queen of Bohemia is fascinated by this young woman with raven-black hair and naturally pointed ears, who dresses in wild colours and is already notorious for her paintings. Rosaleen Norton's subjects are luridly coloured women mating with panthers, flame and fire, horned Pans, snakes intertwined with giant penises, grinning toothy demons, hideous hobgoblins and well-endowed hermaphrodites. Norton would not describe her work as belonging to the surrealist school – for her they are paintings that hark back to the European pagan past. (From this distance they look like bad record covers from the 70s.) Norton believes she is a born witch because of an odd deformity, an extraneous strip of flesh that runs from her armpit to her waist which she regards as a third breast. She also has two blue dots on her knee, 'witch's marks', that appeared when she was seven years old: further proof, if she needs any, that she springs from the dark side. Since childhood she has been fascinated by magic and now practises the arts daily, with enthusiastic participation in sex rites, particularly those that involve cunnilingus.

Deamer may well have heard of Norton before she met her. Not only by reputation as the Witch of Kings Cross, but also because Norton had been publishing short pieces in the literary journal *Pertinent*, in which Dulcie Deamer, and well-known writers such as Kylie Tennant and George Farwell, had also published. Deamer would have heard of the paintings, which Norton made periodic attempts to sell. An exhibition in Melbourne in 1940 produced no sales but garnered national attention when the vice squad raided the gallery and took away four of the pictures. Norton became the first woman to face charges of obscenity in Victoria.

It is through Roie, as Norton's friends call her, that Deamer makes the acquaintance of 17-year-old New Zealander Anna Hoffmann, an enthusiastic acolyte. In 2009, towards the end of her life, Hoffmann will self-publish a volume of memoir, *Tales of Anna Hoffmann*. Some 40 pages are devoted to recollections of her beloved High Priestess, with the Queen of Bohemia featuring in some of the anecdotes. Hoffmann's first-hand experience gives a vivid picture of the scene that revolved around the New Zealand witch.

When Deamer – or any visitor – arrived at the tiny flat she would pass by the welcoming sign 'Welcome to ghosts, goblins, witches and warlocks', and once inside bear witness to the chaotic, dirty mess that Rosaleen cultivated. Dirt was part of her identity as a witch. Her live-in lover Gavin Greenlees would end up in a mental asylum. He was a gay poet from Adelaide and, like Hoffmann, utterly in Norton's thrall. He didn't like the young New Zealander hanging around, and probably did not like the older one either, since she too took up Norton's attention. Gavin's life was dismal, with periods of incarceration in Callan Park Hospital for the Insane in Rozelle, as well as a later jail sentence. He was schizophrenic, possibly epileptic and obsessed with sex. Despite his homosexuality he partook in various sex rites with Norton, who liked to shock anyone listening by announcing she preferred gay men because she could do what she liked with them in bed, which seems unlikely. Greenlees and Hoffmann competed for the witch's affections and were part of the inner circle in the wider coven. When Hoffmann first met Deamer at a night-club in the mid-50s she observed that Norton and Deamer were very good friends.

'Trying not to show my possessiveness I made friends with Dulcie as soon as possible,' she writes. 'This proved easier than expected because she had such an open and generous nature that it wasn't long before we were laughing together and calling each other by our first names.

'Filling her glass with a pale wine ... Dulcie Deamer raised her glass to declare, "Life is a matter of poetry."'[30]

Hoffmann didn't seem to know about Deamer's long-forgotten novels. Since World War II, racy historical novels like these had fallen well out of favour. But one of her poems demonstrated that Deamer had inti-mate knowledge of Norton's black masses and orgies in a cemetery 'in a very respectable suburb of Sydney.'[31] The poem is from *The Silver Branch*, a slim volume published in 1948, and includes the lines, 'Dream of the speckled fungus, dream of the asp,/Dream of the entranced stone, of pard, of witch;/Dream where the male and female mandrake grasp/Mad body-mating in a nettled ditch.' ('Pard', according to the *Shorter Oxford*, is a word of Indo-Iranian origin now used only by poets, and means leopard or panther.)

Hoffmann did not include Deamer in her recollections of the naked 'rituals of the Sabbath' she enthusiastically attended. Perhaps the older woman's initial fascination with Norton had worn off by the time they met. Nor does her memoir go into details about the 'act of communion ... with the entire congregation taking part', with Norton lying naked on a pile of stones that served as an altar in the respectable cemetery. After the 'communion' the coven would dance until they fell 'to the ground in an erotic trance.'[32]

Young Anna hung around the flat every spare minute she could, ignoring crazy, jealous Gavin, and whiffing up the hashish and opium that the witch smoked to open channels to the spirit world. She participated in rituals, having been sexually initiated into the coven by Norton herself.

Most likely she was an eye-witness to rites involving Sir Eugene Goossens, whom she knew from the Sydney Conservatorium of Music, where she had apparently been studying the violin. It was Goossens who introduced Roie and Anna, and it may well have been jealousy over their attachment that caused Anna to spill the beans.

Her allegations formed the case of an eagerly attended and sensational trial, but Norton did not go to prison. Instead Hoffmann was labelled 'mentally unstable', a 'menace', and did time in Long Bay for vagrancy before being deported while still only 17.[33] 'You came from New Zealand and New Zealand can have you', said the judge.[34] The much older Goossens was broken, destroyed by the New Zealand witch. To appreciate just how far he fell we must see how high he had climbed.

Sir Eugene Goossens was a protégé of Sir Thomas Beecham and earned Australia's affection by championing Joan Sutherland as she embarked on her stellar operatic career. He came to Australia to work with the Sydney Symphony Orchestra, a coup for the orchestra to have such a well-known conductor. So famous was he that Noël Coward wrote a song about him, and he counted among his friends Stravinsky and Picasso. Women loved him – he was married three times, and employed a valet whose partial duties were to keep away unwanted admirers. Drawn to Norton by her illustrations in a book of Greenlees' poetry, Goossens wrote to her in 1953 and cultivated a friendship. Like many people were, he was fascinated by her. It was his idea that Rosaleen and Gavin work with him on a composition inspired by *The Fall of the House of Usher*, by Edgar Allan Poe. Before long the famous conductor and the witch became lovers, and he joined in the satanic rituals, especially those that involved oral sex. His own beautiful wife filled her lonely months in Sydney by conducting various affairs. At night they were in separate bedrooms.

Three months after Anna was deported, Goossens was arrested on his way back into Australia after a holiday in Europe. On Norton's urging, he had gathered up a large quantity of printed and photographic material that Australian Customs deemed 'obscene'. There were also a number of alarming rubber masks for Norton to use in her rituals, and these were regarded as being just as offensive as the pornographic images. When the police raided the Kings Cross flat, they found letters from Goossens detailing their sexual connection, as well as incriminating photographs.

It was a wide-ranging scandal. Goossens' contract with the Sydney Symphony Orchestra was not renewed and he slunk back to Europe to try to pick up the pieces of his life.

What of Deamer in all this? Very mysteriously, despite Norton being such a good friend, Deamer doesn't mention her once in her autobiography. Neither does she mention famous Eugene Goossens, among all the other name-dropping. The smoking of hashish with her dangerous, hypersexual friend was also necessarily omitted, and we might perhaps not know about it all but for Anna Hoffman, who recalled visiting Norton's flat one evening and walking uninvited into the basement room where the smell of hashish was strong and '[a] number of people languished on the floor in various poses of lassitude. The Queen of Bohemia was there.'[35] The question arises – did Deamer's daughter edit out what she would have seen as an unhealthy relationship, much less the fascination with witchcraft? There was a period when Deamer referred to herself as the White Witch of Kings Cross as much as she did the Queen of Bohemia. Rosemary Goldie would have found this extremely alarming.

DEAMER'S DAUGHTER

Deamer died in August 1972 at the Little Sisters of the Poor in Randwick, two years after suffering a heart attack. There had been a flurry of attention in the 1960s: the ABC documentary *Stations of the Cross* of 1962, the interview with de Berg quoted above, and some possibly unwanted association with the scandal surrounding Rosaleen Norton. But by the 70s the Queen of Bohemia was forgotten. It is likely these last years of her life were fairly lonely, and would have been more so if it were not for her daughter.

In 1964, after the death of first-born Edwin with whom she had established a close friendship, Deamer received a sympathetic letter from her last-born, Rosemary Goldie. They had been estranged for many years and Rosemary, who was deeply religious, mended the bridge. Christopher had died in action during World War II; 'gentle and affectionate' Edwin was her second brother to die prematurely.[36] Edwin was, in Rosemary's opinion, the child who suffered the most from his mother's neglect.

Rosemary started to take her mother out for tea whenever she visited Sydney from Rome. On the surface, the lives of mother and daughter could not have been more different. Where they converge is that both were dominated by the opinions of wildly divergent groups of men, and both women in their own ways were trailblazers.

Raised by her beloved Grannie, Rosemary was bright and articulate. A photograph taken during her secondary school years at Our Lady of Mercy College in Parramatta shows a bespectacled, round-faced girl who bears little resemblance to her mother at that age. After school, with her grandmother's encouragement, Rosemary studied arts at the University of Sydney, and it was from there that she won a scholarship to attend the Sorbonne in Paris. Already a practising and devout Catholic, she was also a true academic, excelling in languages, and she may well have had a life in academia if she hadn't come into contact with inspirational Catholic philosopher Jacques Maritain. His influence led her towards a life completely devoted to the church.

When Rosemary Goldie returned to Sydney for further studies during the war years, she avoided her mother. She returned to Europe after the war, and spent most of her life there. Goldie was the first woman to have an executive role in the Roman Curia, serving for a decade as under-secretary in Pope Paul VI's newly established laity department, which worked towards implementing the changes wrought by Vatican II. She has been described as a 'champion of the Catholic laity', and she continued her influence after becoming a professor at the Pontifical Lateran University in Rome.[37] Some sources describe her as achieving the highest office a woman has ever held in the Catholic Church.

It was Goldie's desire to work towards Catholicism as an easily accessible faith, not one wrapped up in dogma and exercised only in Latin. Without this over-riding ambition, she may perhaps have deserted her post for the convent. She knew that her devotion to the Church could be expressed in the Vatican bureaucracy far more practically than it would have been had she taken up the more traditional role of a nun. During her 10 years in Rome she served under four popes, all of whom, it seems, were fond of her, giving her pet names and valuing her contribution. Like her mother she was tiny in stature, with a winning smile and keen intellect. We can assume that the church officials she worked alongside were also won over by the strength of her faith. In 1990 the Australian government also finally recognised her, and awarded her the Order of Australia for commitment to ecumenical relations.

Daughters very often take paths diametrically opposed to those taken by their mothers. We can look at Victorian or Edwardian mothers and their bewildering flapper daughters. We can estimate that the looser morals of the jazz age combined with the horrors of World War II to help consolidate the conservatism of the postwar generation of the 50s, who married young and championed the nuclear family, no matter how damaging it was to their happiness and the feminist cause. The generation that came after that, of the 1970s, pushed the boundaries in terms of women's liberation, sexuality, music, drugs and lifestyle.

It could be argued that young women coming of age now, in these first decades of the twenty-first century, display a social conservatism born of anxiety aroused by the blunt power of the corporate imperative and the uncertain survival of the very planet. The path taken by Goldie, who was well aware of her publicity-seeking mother's outrageous behaviour, no matter how much her grandmother may have tried to shield her from it, could be seen just as such an individual, opposing response.

However, 25 years after Deamer's death, it was Goldie who arranged for her mother's autobiography to be published in 1998, the same year as her own. *From a Roman Window* details the many changes Goldie had seen in the Catholic Church during her working life. It is not a personal memoir. Reluctance to write confessionally of her intimate life may well have sprung from antipathy to the narcissistic exhibitionism displayed by her mother. The closest she ever came to publicly criticising Deamer was to 'hint that she was not maternal and absent for much of her life'.[38] As a committed Christian, she forgave her mother for her abandonment.

Curiously, it may have been Deamer who planted the seed for Goldie's passionate Christianity. In 1921, when Rosemary was five years old, Deamer published her novel *Revelation*, which features Jesus as a character.

DEAMER'S NOVEL *REVELATION*

When Deamer wrote *The Golden Decade*, she wondered why her earlier novel *Revelation* (1921) had been so successful. 'I think perhaps our local

Press was thrown off-balance by a "local" abandoning the outback-and-blackened-billy tradition and daring – of all things! – to attempt the time of Tiberius and Christ.'[39]

One lonely copy of the novel survives in the Auckland Public Library. It has a red cloth cover, with the title and authoress's name positioned in a black frame. The pages are yellowed and fragile. On opening the worn volume, the reader is immediately returned to the 1920s by an advertisement for Dr J. Collis Browne's Chlorodyne, promoted as a remedy for everything. There are also ads for the Blackbird Fountainpen, for beef suet and baking powder.

In the first pages we are introduced to Astarte, a beautiful 15-year-old slave-girl who lives in Jerusalem during the reign of Tiberius Caesar. There are richly described animals, chambers, a 'many breasted' statuette of the Ephesian Diana and, unfortunately, a 'negress with a face like an old monkey'. At the end of Part I, soon after the entrance of Jesus of Nazareth, Astarte is sold by her owner to a eunuch who is buying on behalf of King Herod. She stands naked and 'very much excited', not understanding she will continue to be a slave in Herod's house. Soon after, she falls in love with David who has 'indescribable maleness' to match her 'virgin soil'. The only other person who has ever shown her love is the old Negress, Dido, and that was only when she was a child.

There are serpents, gazelles and leopards, and liberal employment of the term 'sex-consciousness', of which other women writers of the period were also fond. There is a villain, Valerius, who is a bad-to-the-bone soldier. Worse is Iris, Astarte's rival for David's love, who gives Astarte a ring poisoned with a substance used in African arrows. When Astarte dies a few chapters on, Jesus comes in handy to bring her back to life. Even after close contact with the Son of God, life for Astarte does not go smoothly. David's mother Naomi hates her and accuses her of adultery, so that she ends up in the 'house of Salome, the harlot', weeping for David. Meanwhile, David is looking for her, and goes to Jesus who is camping with his followers by a brook in the Valley of the Kidron. Jesus can't help him, and in any case is soon after arrested. Iris, whose breasts are like 'the low rose-foam swells of a summer sea', contracts leprosy around the same time. Astarte, whose 'low oval breasts, though full, were still firm', does not.

Both women vanish from the novel for most of Part III, which tells the story of the lead-up to the crucifixion from the point of view of David and his friend Cymon. When Jesus is finally nailed up, there is an earthquake that adds to the woes of the already drought-stricken land. For Astarte the earthquake is a blessing – it saves her from being 'whored to a stout man' by Salome's mother. David, walking 'like an automaton' despite there being no automatons in the ancient world, finds Astarte in the ruins of the earthquake, unconscious but breathing. He lays her on a bed of flowers in a grotto near Christ's tomb, but unfortunately Astarte has 'inward bleeding of the brain' from the quake and dies.

Stupefied by grief, David witnesses Jesus leaving the tomb. Deamer, whipping herself to a frenzy, describes his state of mind: 'Like an infinite cataract of jewels the sorrows of the world shone now – the million steps of that long stair by which the ever-growing spirit ascends towards eternal perfection; where all loves and aspirations and soul-hungers meet in the burning rose-heat of increased Love.' The novel ends as David, who has taken the name of Stephen, approaches martyrdom. The reader closes the novel knowing that our hero will be flogged to death.

Any sadness about his ghastly demise might be mitigated by a touch of nostalgia, especially if the reader is herself a writer. The endpapers bear a message from Mr T. Fisher Unwin, the publisher:

'The First Novel Library' is always willing to consider carefully MSS of Fiction, submitted by new writers.
1 Adelphi Terrace
London.

It is easy to make fun of the novel but salutary to remember how popular it was. *Revelation* was devoured around the world. It was one of only two of Deamer's books that Grannie had in the house. Perhaps little Rosemary, clever, listening and observant, first learned of Christ the Man at the knee of her mostly absent bohemian mother.

1939

Go out into the street in New Zealand or Australia and ask anyone under 30 about the significance of the year 1939 and chances are he/she won't know. In universities around the world history departments are shrinking. The subject is less and less popular even at high school, suffering the twin effects of the market imperative for vocation-driven courses and the narcissistic desires of the so-called 'selfie' generation. History is boring because someone else did it.

I begin this chapter early in 2017, two months after the election of President Donald Trump in the United States of America. I have no idea what will have come to pass in the time that will elapse between my writing these words and you reading them, but if the predictions are correct then the world may well be enduring another war of similar dimensions to the one that began at the end of 1939. History proves its value in times of upheaval. The word 'Orwellian' has recently been thrown around by journalists in the Western world, and sales of *1984* and *Animal Farm* have peaked. Young observers will also be learning the meaning of the word 'fascist', if they didn't already know, as well as newly coined terms such as 'alternative facts'. The internet will define these terms for them, rather than books. The *Guardian* website sees a massive increase in traffic whenever it runs an article on the lead-up to World War II and the way the politics of hatred are mimicking those that made it possible for Hitler to rise in Germany.

*

Early 1939 finds our New Zealanders only just beginning to suspect there could be another war. The closest conflict is in China, two years into the Japanese invasion. In faraway Europe the Italians are conquering Albania, Russia invades Finland and very soon the Germans will invade Czechoslovakia and Poland, signalling the beginning of the conflagration. Closer to home, the first Jewish refugees from German-occupied countries are beginning to arrive. In April, Australian Prime Minister Joseph Lyons dies and Earle Page succeeds him. His term lasts for less than three weeks before Robert Menzies is selected leader of the United Australia Party and begins his first term. Eventually, after serving a second term in the 40s and 50s, Menzies will become the longest-serving of Australian prime ministers, who traditionally have short periods of incumbency.

Fully established in Australia, Jean Devanny has added to her substantial list by publishing two books in two years: *Sugar Heaven* in 1936 and *Paradise Flow* in 1938. The year *Paradise Flow* is published, the Writers' Association – of which Devanny was first president – joins forces with the newly established Fellowship of Australian Writers. After a long and tumultuous affair with J.B. Miles, the general secretary of the Communist Party, she is separated from husband Hal and spending much of her time in Queensland. This year she will be expelled from the Communist Party, a tearing loss which upsets her – but not as much as the death of her son Karl five years earlier: 'For the second time in my life the sun went out.'[1]

Last year, in 1938, Roland Wakelin was represented in a highly prestigious exhibition, *150 Years of Australian Art*, at the New South Wales Art Gallery. He had three paintings included, his first in a museum exhibition. This year sees another solo show at the Macquarie Galleries and another shift in residence, this time to a flat on the corner of Challis Avenue and Victoria Street in Potts Point. He is 52 years old and assured of his place in contemporary Australian art.

Forty-nine-year-old Dulcie Deamer has also been in the limelight. Last year her play *Victory* was produced. This play, along with most of her others, is now lost. She is resident in the Cross and living life, as always, to the hilt.

Douglas Stewart is returned from a few months in England where he made the acquaintance of a long-admired poet, John Powys. Early in 1937, a year before he left for England, he proposed to painter Margaret Coen. This year they are halfway through their long engagement and he is in his first year of his long-coveted job as assistant to the literary editor for the *Bulletin*. A volume of his poetry, *The White Cry*, is published in London. After all the success and excitement, the year ends sadly. In October Stewart's mother, to whom he is very attached, passes away in New Zealand.

Of our five friends, 1939 is the most seminal for Eric Baume. This is the year he leaves for London to work as a war correspondent.

The Beast

We last spent time with Eric Baume when he was 23 and on his way to Australia. It was his first confessed experience of loneliness. He recalled that on the second day of the voyage he watched 'North Cape fade into the clouds, just after dawn when the decks were wet. I was alone. My eldest daughter, Nancy Jean, was far too young to travel. My wife's health would not permit an early trip for her.'[2]

Describing Baume's first night alone in Sydney in the Metropole pub, biographer Manning says 'loneliness hit him like a punch', before going on to remark how quickly the young man would, 'like so many migrants from New Zealand', fall in love with Sydney.[3] His New Zealand origins were not forgotten. Bill Olson comments in his 1967 biography, *Baume: Man and beast*: 'People who knew Baume well often wondered about his New Zealand birth. That such a green, quiet, pleasant place, where even the geysers are predictable and the inhabitants passive, could cradle a poor man's P.T. Barnum such as Baume seems incredible.'[4]

Among Baume's shipmates were some other newspapermen who were also going to work on the *Guardian*. The newspaper world of Sydney would neither welcome nor trust them, thinking there were far too many of them and that they were pushing Australians out of the birthright of their jobs in an already cut-throat environment. Most of these migrant ink-slingers found good jobs, early examples of successful New Zealand journalists who still abound in Australia today.

Packer's *Guardian* survived for six years, setting the low standards for the tabloid gutter press that would flourish later in the century. Crime was its main form of sustenance. 'Executions were meat for us,' Baume recalled. 'I remember featuring on the front page the death struggles of Williams, the violin-playing murderer who had killed his two little daughters.'⁵ His investigations were sometimes aided by the police, who had given him a blue press pass with 'New South Wales Police' embossed in gold letters. On one occasion he used it to wrest information out of a man who had transported a woman's body from a Coogee block of flats. The body was concealed in a trunk, and the man was unaware of what it contained. The *Daily Mail* quoted him: 'A tall, dark man looking like a policeman showed me a detective's card, and I was frightened and spilled my guts.'⁶ Voltaire Molesworth, the managing editor of the *Guardian*, stole photographs from the dead woman's flat and took copies before returning them to the police. This kind of activity, described by Baume as 'flashy', earned the newspaper many readers but also approbation.

Recalling his professional life during this time Baume believed he witnessed 'cynicism, brutality, even horror; so there were times in Sydney when I would have given the world to return to some tiny New Zealand town and write a paragraph in some dull, virtuous sheet about what a well-meaning pillar of municipal government had to say on mismanagement of the local pound'.⁷

The newspaper folded after six years, thanks to the advancing Depression and to New South Wales Premier Jack Lang. Managing editor Molesworth, who may well have been a member of the fascist organisation the New Guard, had never been sympathetic to the Labour Party and did his best to destroy Lang's reputation. On Packer's instructions Baume himself had joined the organisation so that he could watch its every move and report back.

When Lang became premier he had introduced what became known as the Packer Bill, which aimed at parliamentary control of aspects of reporting on political matters. Firmly in the centre of Lang's sights was Packer's popular newspaper the *Daily Telegraph*, which had run reports on Lang's preference for and support of the *Labor Daily*. The premier himself was a shareholder and director of that paper. Had the bill been passed, Packer believed, he would have lost everything. As it was, the bill was thrown out and Packer, whom most recall as an unpleasant man with very few friends and many enemies, escaped ruin. Not long afterwards he was injured on his yacht and was forced to give up work. He made a trip to England and died during the voyage back to Australia.

In the meantime, Baume was ambitious and energetic, finding time to write two books as well as working for a number of papers before being appointed editor of the *Sunday Sun*, the largest newspaper in Australia, in 1932. It was during this decade that he and his wife Mary moved to Gordon on the upper North Shore, having previously lived in Cremorne and Roseville. Baume had had a full year of freedom before Mary joined him. The birth of two more children and his wife's ongoing illness did not seem to alter his bachelor-like behaviour, aided by a large amount of money. He was one of the highest paid journalists in Australia, earning between £1500 and £2000 a year. The house was surrounded by a hectare of leafy grounds and the Baumes entertained lavishly, hosting parties of up to 40 guests. Mary, suffering unbearable pain from advancing rheumatoid arthritis, would at least have had him home on those occasions. Very often he was somewhere on the other side of the bridge, chasing stories or gambling and drinking, AWOL for 24 hours at a time. It was, understandably, a troubled marriage. There were periods when he lived away from the family and his role of comforter was taken over by a family friend, who came to live with them from New Zealand and stayed for many years.

Baume saw the pre-war period, once the Depression started to recede, as a kind of fool's paradise. He recalled: 'Australia least of all realized the German menace ... I can remember the doxologies ... sung at every cocktail party given by the Japanese in Sydney, attended by a slobbering bunch of socialites as well as a tail-coated assembly of minor German and Italian officials.'[8] He had something in common with Devanny in that a novel, his second, was banned at this time. This was *Burnt Sugar*, set in Queensland and abounding with Italian characters. In typically bombastic fashion Baume believed the banning came about because 'some of the statements against Fascism offended the Fascists'.[9]

Two years before the declaration of war, Baume left for America at the request of politician, philanthropist and newspaper magnate Sir Hugh Denison, who wanted Baume to buy features for a new weekly. As he headed across the Pacific aboard the liner *Monterey* he relished every moment of the slow voyage. Apart from half a dozen short trips to New Zealand, he had done 14 years' hard yakka in Australia, a period he described as 'unutterable turmoil'.[10] By this time he was the author of three books, various highflying jobs on newspapers had come and gone, and his arrogance and uncompromising nature had earned him many enemies. His nickname 'Baume the Bastard' had less to do with alliteration than his behaviour. More intimately, he had been swallowed by grief at the death of his beloved mother in 1934. As he followed the funeral cortège up to the Wellington cemetery he had vowed to become a better man, but hadn't quite managed it. Just as traumatic was the recent implosion of his once close friendship with Packer. Baume felt it keenly, stating that Packer had been like a father to him. Biographer Manning comments, 'I'd be prepared to say Packer's was the only regard Baume ever valued at all.'[11]

En route to America Baume filed stories from Fiji and Mexico. A whole chapter of his *I Have Lived These Years* is given over to his experiences in Suva, where he visited a hospital built with American money. He met young Fijians who were training as 'native practitioners' – that is, not as fully qualified doctors. This gave him the chance to expound his theories on race, which he would later attempt to express as fiction in his appalling 1950 novel *Half-Caste*:

> No native is ever happy completely in his associations, professional or otherwise, with those of the alien race who, by the glory of God and their great-grandfathers, regard themselves with a superb superiority. Even the New Zealand Maori, whose blood courses to-day throughout the veins of thousands of most prominent New Zealanders, is never completely at home in his full-blooded state with his white associates. The Australian black, more negroid, more strange and ancient, is never at ease with the white man ... The fact that the Maoris have had knights such as Sir Apirana Ngata or Sir James Carroll, or vivid politicians such as Tau Henare, does not suggest that within his own mental processes the native recipient of formal honours casts aside his own prejudices and ignores the prejudices of others.[12]

Much ink has been spilt on the idea that the two world wars of the twentieth century helped to unite indigenous people and colonists, in that soldiers were drawn from every race and all went off to fight a common enemy. The land wars of the nineteenth century, about which Baume's childhood gardener had poured stories into his eager ears, came well after the signing of the Treaty of Waitangi in 1840. The promise of equality, to many Māori, was proven to be a lie. Subjugation could not and would not ever be willing. At the time Baume was writing, the late nineteenth-century idea persisted in both Australia and New Zealand that the original inhabitants of both countries were dying out. I have already mentioned the memorial on Auckland's One Tree Hill, which was erected for that purpose – 'to smooth the pillow of dying race'. Māori, it was thought, would disappear through the effects of disease and poverty. It is a horrifying notion to us now, but as Michael King points out this was not necessarily a 'derogatory gesture' but an expression of 'respect and regret on the part of Pakeha who admired Maori'.[13] By Baume's time, intermarriage was marginally less frowned upon but seen as another cause of demise – the race would become diluted. In the 1980s Dame Whina Cooper was the last great exponent of intermarriage, and she was roundly criticised for it, even though it was her belief that it would save Māori.

After a period in Honolulu, where he had a Japanese secretary entirely unapologetic for Japanese actions in China, and who convinced him that a major war was imminent, Baume went on to San Francisco. He was back in the city where he had precociously come of age, but in the late 30s it held no fascination. His right-wing sensibilities were offended by what he saw as the 'modern American system of picketing' as people protested against late-Depression inequality.[14] He repaired to his uncle's ranch, and then to Hollywood, where he was guest speaker at the Authors' Club and made an ill-received joke about America being formed from the manure of Noah's ark.

The promise of a good story drew him down to Mexico. The high incidence of violence shocked him, but not as much as the extreme poverty, particularly the sight of homeless beggars shivering on doorsteps through the night. In Sydney he had been a 'street angel', and no doubt he was again here, forking out his loose change. It is often noted that people who espouse right-wing politics, and are particularly critical of state aid to the disadvantaged, will be personally generous. Throughout his life, Baume epitomised this dichotomy.

After an off-the-cuff remark to a Guadalajara newspaper that land reform, for some mysterious reason, reminded him of Australian legislation in respect of the allocation of farmland, he was written up as an 'Australian Communist'. This so earned the admiration of the administration that within his first day in Mexico City he was appointed Honorary

Consul for Australia and New Zealand. The Australian newspapers forbore to write this up, since it was seen as an example of Baume the Bastard-type behaviour and best ignored, but it was proudly reported in the *New Zealand Gazette*. Not surprisingly, anti-communist Baume didn't want the job. It took nine months to extricate himself – an irksome and time-consuming process, mitigated by his meetings with Leon Trotsky, who had been offered asylum in Mexico at the end of 1936. The articles that resulted from their conversations were syndicated in the United States and published in Australia. Jealous of Baume's access, and managing to express both anti-Semitism and loathing of communism in one breath, the *Bulletin* announced that Baume 'had been granted the interviews through the brotherhood of circumcision and had no right to print anything Trotsky had to say'.[15]

Indications that Germany would be an aggressor in a coming war were mounting. Trotsky himself predicted it during their conversations, and in Mexico City Baume met undercover Nazi airmen and soldiers working in menial and sales jobs. He was glad to get back to Sydney where he resumed his editorship of the *Sun*, and also began broadcasting on the 2GB network, a precursor of the ABC.

It must have been a conflicting time. Always proud of his German ancestry, he was now convinced that Germany would bring about another war. His commentary on the matter earned official complaints from Dr Asmis, German consul-general. The broadcasts were discontinued as a result. When Associated News introduced a new rule that editors were not allowed to broadcast, he lost his job. For the first time in many years, Baume had no income.

By the end of 1938 Mary was extremely ill and his three children were at boarding school, both factors that made life expensive. He needed a fairy godmother or, at the very least, a patron. His wish was granted but, as is often the case when wishes come true in fairy stories, with some unfortunate consequences.

The fairy godmother was the wealthy widow of a grazier, who wanted Baume to go into politics. Doubtless she had read his articles in various newspapers and perhaps listened to his broadcasts, and decided their politics were of the same deep blue. One of her first gifts was a gold cigarette case. Despite later admitting to his biographer that it made him feel like a gigolo, he didn't return it. Nor did he return the £2500 she slipped him one evening after he took her to dinner at the Australia Hotel. The gifts kept coming. Over the years he received from his admirer over £20,000, a phenomenal sum. It would come back to bite him.

In Europe war drew ever closer. When Ezra Norton, the managing director of the *Truth* group in Australia and New Zealand, offered Baume a job as foreign correspondent in England for £50 a week, he didn't hesitate, even though he would be leaving his grievously ill wife. The promise of adventure was irresistible, and so was the salary: an increase of £10 on his previous weekly income. On 15 September 1939, 12 days after the war began, he left for England.

At first, given his heartfelt identification as a wild colonial boy, the class system and snobbery of England intensely annoyed him. But in common with the experience of many colonials, he was soon just as intensely seduced by it, especially when the seduction later took the form of an actual lady willing to slide about with him on the black satin sheets he had especially made for his bed at the Ritz. He was 'duchessed', as the expression was: utterly won over by the baubles, fine living, good wine and country piles of the aristocracy. He made the acquaintance of T.S. Eliot, King Zog of Albania and the Marquess of Londonderry; he frequented the Casino, the Café de Paris, the Ritz and the Mirabelle, places he had previously only dreamed about. He must have felt he had achieved his rightful place at the centre of the world.

But he wasn't to hang around in England for long. Norton wanted him to go to France, to Arras, to be stationed among French troops. The Battle of Arras in 1917 had produced some of the bitterest fighting of World War I, and Baume, desperately keen to see active service – an ambition that had been with him since boyhood – was glad to accept. At long last, a real war. His own war. In preparation, and so that he looked the part, Baume had three diggers' hats made: one for himself and one each for the two Australian journalists who were to accompany him. Bizarrely, he was resentful that he hadn't been issued with an Australian uniform. Equally as odd were the manufactured hats that were not exactly diggers' hats, being slightly out in dimension and style.

Arras was a disappointment. This was the 'phoney war', soldiers marching up and down, doing target practice, playing cards, drinking and generally hanging around through the snowy winter, waiting for action. There was a brothel, of which all made full use. Ronald Monson, one of the Australian journalists obligingly wearing a pseudo-digger hat, remembered that Baume made their time there more interesting. Opinionated, brash and militaristic, he would have been in a fervour, and never so much as when Englishwoman Unity Mitford, whom Hitler had been romancing, was shot and injured in a Munich park and arrangements were made to fly her to London. Baume conceived the idea that she had with her the terms of a peace agreement. It was a total fabrication, his novelist's brain at war with his instincts as a journalist. He wrote up the story and sent it back to Australia, where it duly appeared in *Truth*.

His Australian colleagues stuck alongside him in Arras must have been dismayed. Monson certainly remembered being appalled when Baume gave a lecture, airing his opinions on what swines the Germans were and how the Australian Aborigine should be exterminated.

*

And here we will pause for a moment because many readers, justifiably offended, will either flick ahead to the next chapter or put this book down entirely. They could ask – why should a man like this be remembered at all? What possible benefit is there in remembering his life and his opinions? The man was an amoral, puffed-up, violently racist liar.

Racial prejudice, one of the greatest cruelties perpetuated by humanity, has the quality of gathering prisoners as it goes. As a boy, growing up in a society that was already fairly secular at the turn of the twentieth century, Baume was subject to anti-Semitic taunts. His German ancestry drew fire during World War I, not aided by his frequent trumpeting about the Ehrenfrieds of Hamburg, his maternal grandmother's family, who had once been exceedingly rich and in possession of a fleet of ships that they used for cargoes of leeches among other goods. Some of the epithets accorded him in Australia, inspired by his dark complexion and black curly hair, were purely racist. The rumour that his family was of Middle Eastern origins spawned nicknames that riffed on Baume the Bastard – the Black Bastard, the Syrian Bastard, the Afghan Bastard.

Those who are subject to racism will very often exercise it themselves in a subconscious attempt to elevate their perceived low standing. All antennae are primed to pick up the smallest slight; skins are thickened; the judgements made by others are internalised and expressed in the worst ways possible. We could argue that Baume's pronouncements put him on a parallel with those who had discriminated against him. They made him feel that he was up there with the big guys, that he was one of the winners.

I am not excusing Baume for his genocidal racial discrimination. There have been times, working on this book, when I considered jettisoning him altogether from the narrative. If Baume and I had co-existed, and if we had ever met, it is highly likely we would have despised one another. He'd have seen me as a soft pinko nincompoop with unfortunate feminist tendencies, and I'd be cowering from his overblown, aggressive misanthropy.

But as I work on it here in Auckland in early 2017, when the world seems to be on the brink of a rise of a new, corporate species of fascism, I find myself thinking about how biographers and historians are themselves more often of left-wing leanings than of right, and subsequently are attracted to subjects that reflect that. And yet, if we are not reminded of how people of all persuasions lived, the opinions they held, their relationships, careers and the long-reaching decisions they made, then the breadth of our understanding is narrowed.

It would be extremely naïve to suggest that men of Baume's political persuasions do not still exist. In fact, we could say that there are more of them than ever and that they are enjoying renewed influence. They may not openly suggest the extermination of an entire race, but the motivation is still there. Witness the response of the American government to the events surrounding the Dakota pipeline. It is more vital than ever that all of us extend tolerance and empathy to people of different political persuasions so that we can demonstrate another way of being. If Baume was still alive, and if he was reading this, he would likely snort with disgust and accuse me of high handedness, or a sense of moral superiority. He was a man who did not enjoy arguing with women, even though his last burst of fame was predicated on exactly that.

His wife argued with him, when she was well enough. He recalled an incident, while they were driving across the Sydney Harbour Bridge some time before the war, when Mary punched him hard on the nose, twice. He had said 'a filthy thing' to her, and the poor woman, who did not appear to possess a shred of violence, found this to be her only possible response.[16]

He owned that the punishment improved him, doubtless because it was the kind of punishment he understood.

*

Soon after Christmas 1939 Baume returned to London, where Mary joined him briefly. He escorted her back to Sydney by air, but within 24 hours of landing was on his way back, since in his absence the war had properly begun. On arrival, his German surname caused consternation among the customs officials. He was held up for three hours before convincing them that he was a New Zealander and an upstanding member of the press corps.

Now that the war had reached England, Baume was vindicated. He had raised ire in the months before by criticising British imperviousness, their seeming conviction that London was safe from the bombs. Now that the Blitzkrieg had begun he was in his element, wandering around the city in a tin hat and carrying a sleeping bag, so that he could kip in between gathering stories. He travelled around England giving lectures for the minister of information, apparently to audiences that numbered in their thousands. He embarked on an affair with Lady Margaret Stewart, who added to the excitement by convincing him that his phone was tapped. When his accommodation suffered in a raid he moved to the Savoy, where he took on a suite. The bedroom was his private domain; the sitting room he turned over to become his news office. The desks were pushed to the centre of the room, and Baume, wearing one of the fake uniforms he had had run up to his own design, strode about, dictating his stories in a loud voice. He had a cable service installed and bought typewriters. Telephones rang at all hours. Teleprinter machines spewed cables; maps and photographs were glued to the Savoy's pristine walls. There were piles of dirty plates and cups pushed into the corners. Once word got out that Baume basically kept an open door, allied servicemen on leave, as well as correspondents from other newspapers, thronged in and out. Noël Coward kept a room upstairs and would sometimes visit. New Zealand pilot Jimmy Ward, who would later win the Victoria Cross at the age of 22, poked his nose in. Lady Oxford, widow of ex-Prime Minister Asquith, was a regular visitor.

Baume built his little empire. A story circulated about how he had paid £80 to have his uniforms run up and those black satin sheets sewn for his bed. Tongues wagged about Lady Margaret, whom he had put on the news team. He appointed an old school friend from Waitaki Boys as his chief of staff. This was Dr Angus Harrop, who after the war would establish the weekly *New Zealand News UK* paper: it survived for 79 years before losing its life to the internet. Some of the younger journalists who cut their teeth in the Savoy newsroom went on to have brilliant Australian careers. New Zealand-born Keith Hooper was one of them, but not until after his incarceration in a German prisoner-of-war camp. Robert Raymond, who would later become producer on the famous and much-loved *Four Corners* weekly television programme, started work for Baume when he was only 19. New Zealand-born Elizabeth Riddell, who would garner fame not only as a journalist but also as a poet, was also on the staff.

The working day began at four o'clock in the afternoon and Baume would be up and down from the bars and restaurant downstairs. Often he would drink with the American correspondents who had far bigger expense accounts than he did. Besides, he needed his own lesser one to entertain his mysterious sources. Raymond, looking back on that period of his life, could only marvel that despite the fact many of Baume's bulletins had to be altered, being 'sensational, inflammatory and false, his predictions about the next stage of the war were so often proved to be correct'.[17] His biggest scoop was his correct prediction of the date Russia would enter the war. He wrote it up and cabled it away to Australia days in advance of its happening. Lady Oxford was likely the source of this top-secret military information, and she in turn would have got it from Prime Minister Churchill, who was not fond of Baume. The antipathy was mutual: Baume thought the PM was soft, and couldn't understand why full-scale bombing of German civilians had not yet commenced. He had other criticisms of Churchill, to do with 'drink sodden officers' and poor security at the Savoy. In his turn, Churchill would have liked to expel Baume for being 'unwise and disloyal and treacherous'.[18]

Further smuts adhered to his character when the Australian *Smith's Weekly* uncovered the story about the wealthy widow's gifts of thousands of pounds. Baume wanted to sue the magazine from London, and would have done so, probably unsuccessfully, if it hadn't been for editor Ezra Norton talking him out of it. Another black spot was Mary's receipt of an anonymous letter telling her about her husband's hanky-panky with Lady Stewart. There is no record of how Baume smoothed that one over.

Perhaps Mary, knowing her husband as well as she did, was not surprised. Baume was not the kind of man to think faithfulness to a wife was important. And because of her painful illness, their intimate life – on the rare occasion he was actually home – had ceased.

Poor character reports, the Savoy newsroom, the war and Lady Stewart may have combined to become an irksome burden. Whatever, Baume decided he was in need of a personal outlet and that he would revive his career as a novelist. By 1941 he had already published two novels and a volume of memoir. The novels *Half-Caste* (1933) and *Burnt Sugar* (1934) had earned him few accolades. He thus treasured a letter from no less than famous writer and journalist Dame Mary Gilmore, who had read *Burnt Sugar*, set in the sugar plantations of Queensland, and told him, 'it is a sculpture and it is a memorial, and it is a very fine thing to have done it'. Even better, poet Kenneth Slessor reviewed the novel and mentioned 'Mr Baume's astonishing power'.[19]

Half-Caste is the novel about which Dulcie Deamer took him to task at a meeting of I Felici. We'll take a closer look at that later.

Baume was very proud of the fact that he could, he thought, write effortlessly. He dictated his books to a harried typist, boasting that he could turn out 100,000 words a day, and that he never rewrote anything. Waving his arms, he would act out the scenes. In this manner he amused himself through the war years by writing four more novels, one of which he declared later in life made him 'blush with shame' and another he thought 'the worst book in the English language'.[20] This latter, *Sydney Duck*, sold an astonishing 800,000 copies and was translated into German and Dutch, a success deemed by its creator to relate only to the fact that few books were being published at the time.

At the end of 1943 Baume made a trip back to Australia, having not seen his wife and children for four years. During his absence war began on the Second Front, a development he'd predicted. He was devastated to have missed it, and got on a ship back to England as quickly as he could. He then travelled across the channel to France for what he would remember as the most important nine days of his life. It must have seemed to him that everything up until then had been a rehearsal.

In Paris he joined the Second Army, got hold of a jeep and a Mexican driver, and made his way to Brussels. A high point was witnessing the battle of Arnhem, actual front-line conflict, which meant that he was forever able to refute accusations that he spent the entire war at the Savoy. It was a vicious fight with huge losses on either side. Afterwards he and journalist Monson went on ahead of the army into Holland, passing dead American paratroopers on the way, some of whom he recalled had died with their hands clasped in a plea for mercy. Both he and Monson were subjected to shelling, though neither of them was hit.

Inspiration for his novella *Five Graves at Nijmegen* came from a battle over a bridge. After the Allies' victory, the Germans were made to pick up the British dead and bury them in the grounds of a hotel. The experience made an enormous impression on Baume. Many men, when they returned, would think of war as state-sanctioned murder. Baume would always be a militarist. He was sure that had Hitler not committed suicide, the Germans would have gone on fighting until the end.

Back in the comfort of the Savoy, Baume continued to file reports and to field accusations that he got all his information from brothels and pubs. After his nine-day Boy's True War Adventure, those criticisms meant nothing to him. He had his blue-blooded mistress, he had his best-selling novel *Sydney Duck*, he had seen real fighting. On VE Day he took Lady Margaret out for dinner – the woman who, after her death, he would describe as plain and dumpy and only ever a friend.

After VJ Day he went to Norway, where he attended the trial of the fascist politician and collaborator Vidkun Quisling. So famous was this trial that it bequeathed to us the word 'quisling', meaning traitor. When Quisling was found guilty, Baume paid various people off in order to get, in true tabloid style, a photograph of the execution. He would have got it, and it would have been a scoop almost as big as the Russian offensive, but the camera was faulty and he missed the money shot.

Baume would have been one of few people mourning the end of the war. He certainly didn't hurry back to Sydney, travelling in the immediate postwar months to America, Germany and around Britain, filing stories for *Truth*. When at last he was called back to Australia, it was to take over as editor-in-chief for the *Truth* group. Rather than returning to live with his wife and children, he took a flat in Kirribilli. Many men found it difficult to readjust to domestic life after the war, but usually because they were traumatised by their horrific experiences in the battlefield. Getting about

Eric Baume in the 1950s.

From the illustrative file on New Zealand writers (A–L), ref. 86-105-052, Alexander Turnbull Library, Wellington

in his individual uniform adorned with a Croix de Guerre given to him by an inebriated French general in Arras, Baume was extending his bachelor lifestyle. In the same manner as he had retained the widow's thousands of pounds, he kept the medal, though he did consider giving it to a museum.

These immediate years after the war were, Baume said, the worst in his life. Mary was sicker than ever and he was fighting constantly with Ezra Norton. Finally, just before Christmas 1952, he was sacked. While he continued to fight Norton, this time for compensation, there followed a brief period of working with his brother, who had established the Baume Advertising Agency in Sydney. By his own admission Baume was 'the most hopeless advertising man Australia had produced', having few social graces and an inability to sweet-talk clients.[21] The uniform was dispensed with and instead Baume wore a bowler hat, sported a moustache and carried a cane, believing this would help people believe he was the right man for the job. He wasn't. He was miserable, subsisting on the £20 a week his brother paid him, and waiting for a lucky break.

It came in the shape of broadcasting, a medium in which Baume was not only to find his niche but also to pioneer the radio shock jock in Australasia. By the mid-1950s he was on air regularly on 2GB, filling two Monday to Friday programmes *This I Believe* and *I'm on Your Side*. He was abrasive as ever and often as ill-informed, offering his conservative opinions on politicians and current events. These were happy years: his fame grew, he earned good money, and Mary's health improved marginally. He continued to write for *Truth* and various other papers, and became Australia's first television news commentator on ATN7. Tapes of *This I Believe* were flown to the United States and broadcast to millions of people.

Fame and fortune. But despite his many admirers and detractors, and Baume's happy conviction that he was forming opinions all over Australia and further afield, Ezra Norton lured him back to work for the *Truth* group, this time as director. They fought again, bitterly, particularly over the retirement of *Truth* newspaper in favour of the new *Sunday Mirror*. Even though the older, salacious newspaper had loyal readers and a history stretching back to the last decades of the nineteenth century, Norton believed he would do better with the new one. The paper, as Baume predicted, was a failure. Soon after, Norton's health declined and the paper was sold to Rupert Murdoch. After yet another long, protracted battle with management, Baume received a lump sum to pay him out of his contract.

It was the end of his newspaper career. He had made himself into a kind of legend, not so much for his skill as a journalist or news gatherer but because of how much he had been paid. The 50s were boom times and many people were earning more than ever before, but Baume set a kind of record, earning between £12,000 and £15,000 a year.

Back on radio, Baume tried to re-establish himself with listeners. 2GB and other radio stations broadcast *I'm On Your Side*, but it wasn't as popular as before. After a bout of ill health, he set himself up with a microphone in his own study at home, employing a secretary to help him with the day-to-day running of his enterprise. Audiences continued to flag, and his racist, misogynistic opinions garnered more enemies than they did supporters.

Further controversy erupted in 1963 when he was invited to West Germany and expressed praise for various aspects of the Nazi regime, particularly the Afrika Corps, whom he believed, somehow, had not been brutal. He had, in his heart, absolved them from guilt because they were not SS, the guards who manned the concentration camps. On his return Baume announced that he had experienced no anti-Semitism at all in postwar Germany.

The Jewish response was one of disgust and surprise. Wasn't the man a Jew himself? Didn't he care about the millions of Jews who had been murdered? Biographer Manning tries to cast some light: 'The explanation for these apparent contradictions is that Baume is an Australian (or a New Zealander, because he refuses to make any distinction between the two countries), a monarchist, a militarist, and a Jew in roughly that order.'[22] Surely sympathy for those who lost their lives in the Final Solution should not hinge particularly on whether one is or is not a Jew. It is a matter of abhorrence and horror at this extreme of institutionalised cruelty. In a restaurant in New Zealand during a 1966 tour in which he was accompanied by Manning, Baume told him that had he been born in Germany he would have been a Nazi. Perhaps he was drunk when he said this, so drunk that he forgot he was Jewish. All through his life he had a fascination with Catholicism, and would never pass up the opportunity to talk to a priest or a nun. Perhaps he longed to be able to convert, just as his mother did before her second marriage. Perhaps he wished, in some way, to be rescued from his Jewish-ness, and by expressing praise for West Germany and its recent history was experiencing again the schizoid loyalties of the cowardly bully as he had so often before.

Baume's popularity was at an all-time low and attacks were coming from all sides. In the same year as his trip to Germany he received a phone call from James Oswin, general manager of ATN7, asking him if he would compere a new television agony/chat show, *Beauty and the Beast*. Baume did not hesitate. He would be the beastliest of all beasts. After a slow start, the show became enormously popular, winning large audiences in every state and city except genteel Melbourne.

New Zealand had its own version of *Beauty and the Beast*, with the mild-mannered and suave Selwyn Toogood as our 'beast'. Baume was the antithesis, sometimes reducing his co-panellists to tears. These women were no shrinking violets; among them were film producer Pat Lovell (*Picnic at Hanging Rock, Gallipoli*), brilliant writer and broadcaster Anne Deveson, and journalist and media personality Maggie Tabberer. Baume was abusive, rude and cantankerous, but also aware that he had become in some ways a pastiche of himself, a kind of court jester. People loved to hate him.

The show ran with Baume as the beast for three years. At age 66 he received an OBE for services to journalism, which we could cynically assume he would not have received without his re-invention as a television personality. Then, as now, an identity on the box makes all the difference.

Only a year after his award, and his journey to New Zealand with his biographer – 'Rather you than me,' colleagues told Manning – Baume suffered another serious bout of illness. He died in April 1967.

In an obituary for Baume in the *Canberra Times*, Alan Fitzgerald wrote: 'He was the strident voice in the vacuum, he was the histrionic sage dealing with the ephemeral parish pump issues of the day', and further, he 'doggedly echoed the prejudices of that section of the population amounting to 51%'. This could be the last word on Eric Baume, except to examine more closely the opinion he held about the differences between Australia and New Zealand. He repeatedly refused to make any distinction between the two. He saw them as the same country, despite their individual indigenous populations and vastly different colonial histories, though he often spoke 'wistfully' of New Zealand. It seems Aotearoa occupied a romantic place in his bifurcated heart, but his feelings were never strong enough to bring him home permanently.

Baume is perhaps not a son of New Zealand whom we'd like to reclaim, though he had his fans. On his tour with Manning he'd been frequently stopped by people who listened to him on long-range radio. A West Coast barman recognised him purely from the sound of his voice. Still, he is a colourful figure who went west and prospered. It is important to remember that he engendered love as well as fury in his many listeners and readers in both countries. Along with his more unpleasant attributes, he was generous and charismatic. Australian war correspondent Ronald Monson said of him that he 'put his arm around the world'.[23]

BAUME'S NOVEL *HALF-CASTE*

First, a digression.

In 2014 I was invited to London to take part in a literary festival with participants drawn exclusively from New Zealand and Australia. It was a strange experience, not least because the organisers had not had the funds to run a decent publicity campaign. Audiences were small and mostly made up of expatriates. As one Australian writer remarked, we had come a very long way to talk to one another.

I was the only New Zealander in a panel discussion on 'Lost Classics' from our part of the world. My colleagues were impassioned and erudite – a literary critic and a publisher. Both of them had lists of books they considered Australian classics by writers such as Miles Franklin, Katharine Susannah Prichard, Henry Lawson and others. There had been a recent series of Australian classics published as 'lost', though surely they were all rediscovered if not really lost in the first place.

As the sole Kiwi I had thought long and hard about which books to discuss. The three I selected were *The Witch's Thorn* by Ruth Park, published in 1951; *Maori Girl* by Noel Hilliard (1960) and *Mackenzie* by James McNeish, first published in 1970. Of these three, *Mackenzie* is possibly the least lost. It tells the story of the famous nineteenth-century

Copies of Ruth Park's
forgotten novel may still
surface in second-hand
bookshops and op shops.
This is the Horwitz edition
of 1966. The rather lurid
illustration shows hero Wi
carrying the child Bethany.

Scottish sheep rustler and his dog in Otago. It is true to the period, has
a big cast, and also pays tribute to the original inhabitants of the land.
Writer Martin Edmond deftly describes it as 'a work as idiosyncratic,
obdurate and strange as the man it is about'.[24] A television series was based
on the book, which increased its popularity at the time.

Maori Girl and *The Witch's Thorn* are very much North Island books.
Both tell stories of Māori–Pākehā relationships. *Maori Girl* is set in
Wellington in the 1950s, and is beautifully written, with liberal use of idio-
matic speech. Its author Noel Hilliard was a left-wing journalist, novelist
and short-story writer. Much of his work was published in Russian. His
wife, Kiriwai Mete, was introduced to him by revered poet Hone Tuwhare,
and it is probably because of Hilliard's love for her that his novel has an
autobiographical, truthful feel. He went on to write sequels – *Power of Joy*

(1965), *Maori Woman* (1974) and *The Glory and the Dream* (1978) – but they were not so well known or appreciated.

Hilliard takes as his main character Netta Samuel, one of nine children growing up in relative poverty in the Taranaki district. In her teens Netta goes to Wellington to look for work. At first she lives in a boarding house, working as the cook. It is there that she falls into bad company and has a relationship with a greasy Pākehā called Eric, who takes advantage of her innocence and naivety. Later she has a much more loving relationship with another Pākehā, Arthur, who does love her, until he finds out she's pregnant with Eric's child and deserts her. The novel has a tragic ending – a long time after Eric abandons her, he sees Netta drunk in a Wellington pub.

New Zealander Ruth Park was adopted by Australian literature as one of theirs. She was a famous and much-loved writer on both sides of the Tasman and further afield. Novels, children's books and, later in life, her three volumes of autobiography were all well received. *The Witch's Thorn*, written after she emigrated to Australia, is almost entirely forgotten. It has some Australian references – Kingsford Smith's flight across the globe, and a nun called Sister Eucalyptus (Egypt). When I found a battered copy in a second-hand bookshop, it was the first I knew of it, though I was a Ruth Park fan. There are some salient reasons for its virtual disappearance.

The story is set between the wars in a small fictitious King Country town called Te Kano, mostly populated by Irish Catholics and Māori. Central in the narrative is illegitimate child Bethell Jury, and what becomes of her after the death of her grandmother and the disappearance of her promiscuous mother. Although written in a realist style, the novel is dreamlike, nightmarish. There is grinding poverty and disastrous family relationships. People endure appalling cruelties, especially the children. Neighbour Ellen Gow lives with her husband and many children in a hovel in a sump, which is freezing cold and abounding with hellish vapours. Her main source of misery is the endless pregnancies that result from being repeatedly raped by her brutal husband. There is a German publican with incestuous desire for his daughters. A widowed Pākehā with eight children to support has turned to prostitution. Casual and deliberate racism proliferates not only among the townspeople but also authorially.

Hero Georgie Wi is so vast that when he goes to the cinema he needs two seats. Uncle Pihopa has a full moko, a cannibal past, no trousers and, it is repeated several times, lest we forget, he stinks. He believes strongly in the colour bar, not being keen on 'Hinamen', including Jim Joe the Chinese fruiterer. To keep warm at night, the old man sleeps in ashes from the fire. Princey, one of his relatives, worries that he'll snack on his buttocks. There is a scene revolving around the slapstick comedy of Pihopa coming to life at his own tangi and then being killed by the shock of being dead.

It's unfair, perhaps, to go on so much about Uncle Pihopa, when really he is a peripheral character. Mostly we move between Bethell's miserable time staying with the Gows, her brief period given shelter by the prostitute, and her final homecoming to her loving, newly adopted father Wi, who regards her as being 'just as good as a Maori'. In order to adopt her Wi spins a story to the local priest: he is her real father, Bethell's mother went with Māori men, and he was one of them.

In the meantime Hoot, a Māori boy not much older than Bethell, falls in love with her. He takes her on an outing to some disused burial caves and reference is made to a tangi and the new laws introduced to stop the ceremonies going on for more than three days. There is added detail: in the past, farewells would last for so long that the deceased would start to melt through the floorboards.

Hoot knows he will have to wait until Bethell is a little older before he can court her properly. He steals one kiss and announces:

'Now I shall be a white man.'
'I'm not white people,' cried Bethell passionately. 'Aren't we all the same underneath?'

And that, I suppose, is the nub. That is what the author wants us to take away with us, the wisdom of that time, which is that fundamentally all human beings are the same. It was a comforting notion that endured for much of the twentieth century: all peoples of the world could live in peace and harmony, the past could be forgotten and we could sense a deep human connection – the colonised absolving the manifold sins of the colonisers, the colonised offering true equality and lack of discrimination in return. The ideal was to search for what made us the same, to let bygones be bygones and look to the future, the brave new world.

The Witch's Thorn is written with great feeling and has all of Ruth Park's characteristic love and empathy for every character. It is an important story about the parallel suffering of second-generation Irish New Zealanders and Māori and how they got along, or didn't. The metaphor of the title, that a person pricked by a witch's thorn will carry the poison along to the next person, illustrates heredity and teases the notion of escape from it. Do we have to remain the people we are born to be? Can we escape deprivation and poverty?

And yes, of course, the story is racist. For a Pākehā author to create a character like Uncle Pihopa would now be unthinkable. Further, any author gaining traction in the literary world by writing about a culture not her own would be censured for cultural appropriation, viewed in some quarters as theft.

The amnesia that has banished *Maori Girl* and *The Witch's Thorn* from our literary memories is partially the result of a well-intentioned and widespread cultural norm that discouraged non-Māori from writing about Māori. Consequently there were rafts of novels published set in New Zealand that had no Māori characters and so presented a very warped, thin notion of how we live. The few writers who attempted to write about New Zealand as we saw it, myself included, could be censured as racist for the mere fact that we included Māori characters. As recently as 2016 Waikato University history professor Nepia Mahuika told my historical fiction students that if they were not Māori then they should not create Māori characters. The students, mostly in their early twenties, accepted this cultural edict. When I responded mildly that most of my books have Māori characters, it sparked no discussion in the classroom, only an uncomfortable silence. It is as if, so many years on from the freedom that allowed Park, writing from the distance of West Island, to create a slapstick clown like Uncle Pihopa, we are not allowed to consider, create, deliberate or love Māori characters if we are not ourselves Māori. Surely this extreme position is not only ridiculous but dangerous. It is a form of mutual oppression.

In the nineteenth century, European writers could believe that they were giving voices to people who had none. Throughout the twentieth century indigenous writers around the world published excellent novels, and arising alongside that great upswelling of voices was this notion that we could only write about who we were. Imagination, like God, lost its vigour.

It was a dangerous idea for a man to imagine how a woman thought or for a heterosexual to imagine homosexuality, even though the practice of writing from opposing points of view had long been a method of fostering understanding.

I suggested, in that talk in London, that these lost classics should not remain lost. I wondered if we would at last reach a stage of cultural maturity where we could look back at these very flawed mid-century Pākehā attempts to spin stories that expressed love and respect for Māori, and if in the process we could forgive those novels for their ham-fisted, often inadvertent prejudice. In the audience was a young woman who tweeted: 'Stephanie Johnson says we should read racist books.'

What a dangerous thing is instant publication. I did not suggest that we should read 'racist books' but rather books from our heritage that do not necessarily fit with current sensitivities. There is much in both novels to upset us, it is true, but also much to delight and fill us with pride. Ruth Park and Noel Hilliard were remembered by those who knew them as people of principle. They did their best. We could not say that, with any conscience, of Eric Baume.

*

Half-Caste, written in Sydney in 1932–33, precedes the others by around 20 years. It wrestles clumsily with the idea of racial inheritance.

The novel opens by introducing us to a newly arrived Scotsman in Auckland, Peter Wade, who is getting ready to go to the opera. 'He rather hoped to find Maori in a primitive state.'[25] At this early point of his arrival he has not met any. The invitation to the opera has come from a mysterious older woman, who is attending the theatre with her young companion Ngaire Trevithick, who has dark brown eyes and golden hair. When Wade later dines with benefactor Helene and Ngaire at their home in Mount Albert, he meets their Persian-cross cat. He holds forth: 'Marvellous thing about animals – you put two breeds together and form a third breed which may be more valuable than either of the original strains. The superiority is often recognized. Now if only man were so perceptive where different breeds of humans were concerned, it might end a lot of the world's troubles, what? But we're all so dense. Must keep to our pure strains. Can't let the master race get contaminated ...'[26]

Ngaire's appetite for her dinner evaporates and Wade, because he doesn't understand that she is the half-caste of the title, is confused. She becomes quiet and sad, and when Helene hears her crying alone in her bed that night she mutters to herself, 'Damn the girl. He's a fine man. Why can't she forget she's half-Maori?'[27] The implication is that Ngaire is so ashamed of her Māori blood she can't establish a relationship with a Scotsman, despite the fact that at this time in our history thousands of people claimed combined Caledonian and Māori heritage.

The third chapter abandons the established narrative and plunges into a history lesson: 'Over a century before the first Spanish galleons ventured westward from the Azores, Chief Marutuahu rolled his fleet of war canoes down to the Tahitian shores and set sail with his tribe across two thousand miles of the Pacific into the south-west towards New Zealand.'[28] A few pages later Baume arrives at the land wars of the 1860s:

> For twenty years the Maori courage held out against the British musket until the warriors were so decimated that further resistance was impossible. Their courage won them the right to a portion of their former lands and representation in the government established by the conquerors ... So to survive, the Maori withdrew to the lands that remained to them, clung tenaciously to the ways of their fathers, and the two peoples were divided. Such divisions do not last. Where a society as a unit draws a line, the individual member of the society will cross it.[29]

The individual member, in this case, is Ngaire Trevithick. The narrative then returns to her, rolling back the years to her mother Rewa and a sailor from Liverpool, and the conception of Ngaire on a beach. A German doctor visiting the mother and new baby finds 'Rewa reclining on her cot inside the shack surrounded by a group of pipe-smoking, babbling women. In the semi-darkness was the rancid smell of perspiration mixed with the fumes of the drying shark, which hung from the rafters. Women entering the room for the first time paused to rub noses with the mother before accepting a puff from the ceremonial pipe ... He smiled at Rewa, and her coffee-brown face smiled back, the tension of her full lips bringing the blue tattoo marks on her lips into bright relief.'[30]

It is possible that during his time on the *Waipa Post* Baume travelled to the Kawhia district, which is where he imagines Rewa lives. It is also possible that he was a guest in a kāinga and that his nose was offended by drying shark, but it is unlikely that the fish was dried inside a whare. Also, although Māori adopted tobacco use with tragic results, and would often share pipes, smoking was never 'ceremonial'.

Rewa tells the doctor of the conception, making the other women uncomfortable because she is the daughter of the chief, 'a descendant of Te Kooti'. But Rewa has had the benefit of an English-style education and 'mortifies tourists' by quoting Chaucer and Shakespeare: 'Her education was her captive, a thing she had wrung from a conquering race and she loved to parade it publicly. If she sometimes chanted lines of Shakespeare at a tribal celebration it wasn't so much from love of Shakespeare as from her joy at making England's greatest poet the servant of a Maori girl.'[31]

After the doctor leaves, Rewa looks at her pale baby: 'There is more in life than the dominance of a Maori bull. It is only the colour of the skin that makes the difference.'[32] Here again, appallingly expressed, is the sentiment Ruth Park approached – that we are all the same, that there is no cause for worry about the things that make us different. The aim is homogeneity.

When the narrative returns to Auckland in the early 30s, Ngaire and Peter Wade are driving out of town in Helene's Bentley, Ngaire behind the wheel. They put the roof down, smoke cigarettes, drive 'westward along the isthmus then north again through the rolling pasture lands until they were back along the coast'. Ngaire has gone to an Anglican school in Auckland, possibly based on Diocesan School for Girls. They talk about religion. Peter says:

> 'As soon as a man admits there may be more than one correct way to worship God, he weakens his own belief ... when you ask a man to be tolerant of other beliefs, you're merely asking him to give up his own.'
> 'Then you don't believe in tolerance?'
> He smiled at her, 'I hope I don't impress you that way. I believe in it very much, but I think people ought to know what it means.'[33]

This was the great Pākehā fear of the time. If you give an inch, you will lose a mile. Tolerance is all very well, but only one way – the way that maintains the status quo.

Back at the pā Ngaire has a close friend, Paul, who gave up studying for the ministry after three years because a night on the whisky made the page blur and he saw instead 'the beautiful brown faces of the girls at home, the girls who fall into your arms when you are ready for them. So I killed the Pakeha's god too lest he spoil the beautiful girls when I brought him among them.'[34]

This paragraph owes more to the author's smutty ideas about dusky maidens than anything else, ideas that may well have been urged on by American anthropologist Margaret Mead's 1928 book *Coming of Age in Samoa*. It's doubtful Baume would have read Mead's book, but he would have heard about her portrayal of Polynesian sexual behaviour, a portrayal later proved false by New Zealand anthropologist Derek Freeman.

Ngaire has rejected her faithful friend Paul thanks to the influences exerted by her private girls' school. She thinks he is dirty, whereas she recognises 'the value of clean clothing and a clean body, of polished nails and good manners'.[35] The reader is expected to accept her apparent opinion that no Māori has these attributes. She wonders how she can possibly tell her admirer, 'I'm a bastard, Peter. A half-breed bastard who was suckled by a woman with a tattooed face. My father was a drunken bum ...'[36]

She writes to the German doctor and asks him what to do. Doctor Sembach thinks '... you would love to go to Scotland where ze Maori do not live – there ze past would disappear and never trouble you again ... In Scotland ze gorse is yellow and like New Zealand smells ze same.'[37] The attempt at writing a German accent is mirrored throughout by an insulting idea of how Māori spoke.

Meanwhile, Paul is dying. He wants Ngaire never to visit the pā again – he loves her and hates seeing her suffer as she does there. He tells Sembach not to let her know he's dying and to keep her away from his tangi, so Sembach goes to visit Ngaire after not seeing her for four years. He delivers a letter from Paul saying her inheritance is all gone because he spent it. 'Thus the Maori take vengeance on strangers who spring up like parasites in our midst.'

Ngaire is aware that her failure to tell Peter about her heritage is wrong because if they have a child it could be 'dark-skinned, thick-lipped offspring [who] would suddenly make one or both of them subject to the cruel laughter and probably ostracism by the society in which they had been raised'.[38] To put some flesh on the bones of this idea, we learn in reportage about Ngaire's experiences when she left school. She tells Peter about how she went to live with a Pākehā family, the Mercers. The father is a judge and the mother cold-hearted. While she lived with them she met up again with Robert Treacy, a racist snob who had earlier tried to rape her. For some unfathomable reason they become friends and she falls half in love with him. Mrs Mercer tells Ngaire she has to leave the home and get a job, but when the judge won't help her find work she turns to Treacy, who gets his own back for not succeeding in raping her. He says he has only been taking her out to get in with the judge, that he'll only help her if she's his mistress. In true melodramatic fashion, she becomes Mercer's maid for four months, hiding in the house.

Peter is appalled and says, '… he treated you as though you were some native girl'. Still Ngaire cannot tell him the truth of her heritage. But Peter asks her to marry him, and she wonders if his earlier remark came because 'habitual domination has led to habitual contempt'.[39]

She accepts his proposal, and Helene, delighted, tells her that she's bequeathing Ngaire her entire estate. The wedding is arranged and takes place at 'a little vine-covered Methodist church'. All the guests are Pākehā – the German doctor has informed the Māori relatives, including long-suffering Bella, that they cannot come. Bella shows up anyway:

> There had been a gasp as an old woman started to her feet and tried to draw back out of sight. She was much too slow. She stood there not ten feet from them in a loose denim dress, her large eyes red-rimmed from weeping, her tattooed lips drooping open, and the whole head framed in the red handkerchief tied about it. It was Bella. Ngaire fainted.[40]

After the wedding reception Sembach tells Ngaire she's in good hands now and should not worry that Bella had come uninvited:

> Ngaire … laughed again and her eyes were hard and glistening. Sembach didn't like it, but there was nothing he could do in the short period of time left to him. Nothing at all … For the first time in his long active life he realized that racial problems were not racial problems at all. They were thousands of individual problems which looked like a single unit only because those who studied them insisted upon seeing them that way. But the solution remained an individual solution for each person concerned.[41]

The not very happy couple honeymoon in the South Island, then return to the north, where they stay in a Rotorua hotel. Who should be there at the same time but the dastardly Treacy. By unspoken mutual agreement Ngaire and Treacy pretend they've never met. Ngaire observes that the two men 'had a bond between them – the white man's bond which was so much of the white man's environment that most of them never knew of its existence'.[42] But the moment she is alone with Treacy he tells her, 'It seems you've married this very eligible young man without telling him that your children are apt to be piccaninnies.'[43]

Later, she goes to Treacy's hotel room to strike a bargain that he won't tell Peter about her Māori heritage. Of course he wants sex. Luckily, there is a conveniently loaded gun lying on the desk, so she shoots him. The body is not discovered before she and Peter leave for Auckland to board the ship to Scotland. Somewhere beyond the Gulf, Ngaire chucks the key to Treacy's room overboard. She is unhappy and suffering from nausea – she is expecting a baby.

When the ship docks in San Francisco Ngaire asks to wander about by herself. Straight away she goes to Pan-American Airways and buys a ticket back to New Zealand. She leaves a note in the hotel for Peter: 'If I bring you pain now, it is as nothing compared with the pain I would bring if I remained beside you.'[44] Back in Auckland Ngaire goes to Helene. She tells her, 'You think I've lost my mind but you don't want to say so to my face. But I haven't lost my mind, Helene. If anything, I've found it.'[45] She believes the only reason Helene ever loved her was because she could see that Ngaire was a criminal, and Helene had had practice at loving criminals, having once been married to one.

What, asks the bewildered reader, was her crime before she shot the would-be rapist? Is Baume suggesting that her crime is her mixed heritage, or her concealment of it? She explains to Helene: 'I'm just telling you why you loved me – because deep inside your white soul, so deep that even you have forgotten about it, is the feeling that it's morally and ethically wrong to be anything but white.'[46] To justify killing Treacy she says, 'He needed to be killed simply because he was a white man who thought he had rights over me because I was of another race. That is always sufficient reason for a Maori to kill a white man … but I killed him because I was a white woman trying to hide a criminal past. Now I'm not a white woman any more. I'm Maori. Only by being Maori can I excuse myself. It's the only way I'll find peace.'[47]

So saying, she returns to Bella and the village.

When the jilted Scotsman follows his wife's trail back to Auckland he is met by the German doctor, who tells him the truth of Ngaire's parentage. Peter is taken aback. 'Damn it, she's a Maori, not a negress!' Sembach asks him what he would say if she was a negress and Peter assures him he wouldn't care. Together they travel to Ngaire's village, only to find that she has committed suicide, leaving a note:

Darling Peter,

Sembach says you are coming, and if you come you will know why I went away from you. For a time I thought I might stay here until our child was born – hoping things would be different for me then. But now I know they will never change. I am not for the Maori. But I am not for your people either. I tried so hard and failed. Forgive me Peter, please, please forgive me. If you need to know more, talk to Helene. Only know that I could not have seen you without going away with you again, and to do that would be to kill us both ... I shall die with your name on my lips,

Ngaire[48]

Baume wrote two different endings for the book. In the 1933 edition, Ngaire does not commit suicide. When Peter arrives at the village the baby has been born and Ngaire greets him warmly because the baby has blue eyes! He forgives her for running away, and for the truth of her lineage.

The novel is still available today in rare-book sections of libraries and, more surprisingly, also as an ebook. On the Harlequin Romance website it is listed as general fiction, and described, with capitals, as 'Clean and Wholesome'.

As recently as 2015 *Half-Caste* received attention from Kirstine Moffatt in her essay 'What is in the blood will come out: Belonging, expulsion and the New Zealand settler home' in Jessie Weston's *Ko Meri*. Comparing Baume's novel to Weston's nineteenth-century novel, in which the bi-racial heroine also dies, Moffatt remarks that 'anxieties about the "taint" of Māori blood and the atavistic power of Māori heritage continued well into the twentieth century. In Eric Baume's *Half-Caste*, Ngaire Trevithick is alienated from her Maori community by virtue of her pale skin and European education ... The novelists who create these characters fear the Maori "other" so much that they reject assimilation in favour of expulsion and, in many cases, annihilation. The death of these heroines symbolizes the death of the race.'[49]

Tastes in novels change generation by generation, and we are seeing in our time a blurring between the once great divide between literary and commercial fiction. Broadly, commercial fiction relies heavily on story, whereas literary fiction may be more concerned with style and the manner of telling. Literary fiction may challenge contemporary mores and shibboleths, while commercial fiction may not. Clumsily told, *Half-Caste* is so rich in story that it verges on melodrama. Most certainly it reinforces the common prejudices and opinions of its time.

1951

1951 is the sixth year of peace following the end of World War II, and Australia is experiencing a boom time. Wool shorn from the backs of Australian sheep is manufactured into uniforms, mittens and balaclavas for American soldiers fighting in Korea, with the result that sheep farmers' yearly incomes have quintupled – they are buying cars and radios, fine clothes and furniture. Inflation is galloping and Prime Minister Menzies is trying to control it by introducing taxes. His budget this year will target Holden dealers, razor blades, shaving cream, ice cream and sweets, among other commodities deemed luxuries.

In view of growing international concern about communism, he introduces the Communist Party Dissolution Act. A referendum is held in September on the issue and Menzies is defeated by 50,000 votes.

The cost of the Snowy Mountains Scheme, designed to provide both hydroelectricity and irrigation from the Murray and Murrumbidgee rivers, has blown out from its original cost of £65 million to more than £200 million. Construction goes ahead, drawing men from all over Australia. Many of the workers are new immigrants, who may now become new citizens of the new nation. Two years ago, Australia Day 1949 marked the beginning of Australian citizenship.

Holden is in its third year of manufacturing on Australian soil what have rapidly become iconographic Australian cars; cricketer Don

Bradman is the most famous and revered sportsman ever; and shopping and consumption are the new norms. The beer keg has become a regular fixture at parties, a focal point for the men otherwise booted out of pubs at six o'clock. Parties are divided by gender: while the men honk back the beer, the women gather in the kitchen, in keeping with the widespread idea that women who willingly consort with the men are loose. Nonetheless, hems are up, bathing suits are smaller and beach-culture is taking hold.

*

Douglas Stewart is the father of a three-year-old daughter and in his second decade as editor of the *Bulletin*'s 'Red Page'. The magazine is enormously popular and he is besieged with copy for his small literary section. For business and pleasure he conducts correspondence with many writers on both sides of the Tasman. He will later remark that this period was a 'tremendously exciting time. We did feel that we were at the centre of the movement of Australian culture at that time. There wasn't much else ... *Southerly* and *Meanjin* were only just starting ... I had absolute freedom and because the writers too recognised it as the centre, the only place they could get published, we met everybody who was worth knowing and tremendous people just used to walk in the door. I remember seeing Miles Franklin and Mary Gilmore one day appear like a couple of giantesses or goddesses or something in the doorway.'[1]

Eric Baume is back in Sydney but possibly estranged from his long-suffering wife. There is a period soon after his return during which he lives alone in Kirribilli before going back to the family home in Gordon. Every day he travels into the city to the *Truth* office, where he writes, edits, and fights with manager Ezra Norton. It is a time of adjustment for him as he recovers from the great excitement of the war and intervening travel to Berlin, France and the United States.

For Roland Wakelin 1951 is a positive, productive and possibly nostalgic year. He takes a position teaching at the National Gallery School, Melbourne, and his work is represented in the prestigious *Jubilee Exhibition of Australian Art* with the inclusion of 'The Bridge from North Sydney, 1939'. In December he and his wife will travel to New Zealand, staying for three months and visiting his brother in Wellington. It is the only visit he makes to the land of his birth.

Dulcie Deamer is 51 years old but living life with the enthusiasm of a teenager looking forward always to the next party. It is 11 years since she had a novel published, which is not to say that her output has slowed. She writes on with fervour, surviving on next to nothing. As her daughter Rosemary will recall, Dulcie stays in bed until late each day, 'writing for her own pleasure'. She is also spending a lot of time delving into the occult with her exciting new New Zealand friend Rosaleen Norton.

For Jean Devanny, 1951 is the year she consolidates her attachment to Queensland, a part of Australia in which she has travelled and worked since the 1930s. Not only does she publish her popular *Travels in North Queensland* but she also buys a cottage at 2 Castling Street, Townsville, for £650. It will be her first true home, the only house she ever owns, and she will live there until her death in 1962.

The Communist

'In human and animal alike only tameness bores.'[2]

When reading Jean Devanny's novels or non-fiction, her autobiography, Carole Ferrier's excellent biography, or commentary from other sources, it is easy to experience a surprising, niggling envy for her life and times. Surprising, also, because Devanny's life was in many respects tragic.

The first source of this envy is for the conviction, passion and energy that fuelled Devanny's position at the vanguard of twentieth-century feminism and left-wing thought. The second is for the articulate love and knowledge she movingly expresses for the natural world. Her non-fiction works *By Tropic Sea and Jungle* and *Travels in North Queensland* are much neglected and deserve a renaissance, if only to remind us of what we have so far lost and stand to lose in the near future.

Of the five West Islanders, Devanny was the only one to eventually make her home outside Sydney. Many New Zealanders fall in love with that city and never go further afield. Others, like Devanny, formed a more ambivalent relationship with it. Her connection with Queensland began in the 1930s when she travelled far and wide throughout the state on exhausting speaking tours for the Communist Party of Australia, the

CPA. She had grown up in rural, verdant Golden Bay at the tip of the South Island and her affection sprang partly from what she perceives as a similarity: 'I was greatly taken with the type and calibre of these people. The mountainous country resembled my homeland, and developed like characteristics in the natives. North Queenslanders were soft of mien; and in general they were kind and generous.'[3] She was to retain this love for the north of Queensland all her life.

*

By 1951 the Devannys had been in New South Wales for 22 years. It was August 1929 when the family first arrived in Sydney, at the end of a decade in which newspaper *Truth* described the city as a 'mecca for magsmen'. Depression was biting and crime was rife.

Devanny was to recall not only how the 'midday heat had us in a lather of perspiration' but also how she and her family

> 'marvelled to find Sydneysiders so "foreign" ... Many of the social aspects of Sydney shocked us. For instance, the ramifications of the White Australia Policy. All enlightened New Zealanders of my generation detested the White Australia Policy. The teaching of pride in, and respect for, our native people the Maoris was part of the school curriculum ... the New Zealand Labour Movement had reflected this feeling. It had officially pronounced the WAP to be a nefarious and reactionary doctrine ... [we were] shocked and confounded ... to find the theory expanded to include South Europeans!'[4]

New Zealanders are often accused of propagating the utopian myth that eulogises New Zealand race relations. In that light, Devanny has been roundly criticised for this statement, sometimes unfairly. While it is true that many New Zealanders had no understanding of Māori culture, let alone respect for or pride in their indigenous people, it is also true that a superficial identification with tangata whenua was common. In rural areas, such as the one Devanny knew, Māori were more integrated with new populations than they were in the cities, where they were almost invisible. It is important to note that by the time of her arrival in Sydney, Devanny had earned applause for her treatment of Māori characters in her novels, in particular Jimmy Tutaki in *The Butcher Shop* and Rangi Fell in *Bushman Burke*.

Jean Devanny, c. late 1920s.
S.P. Andrew photographer, Box-074-002, Hocken Collections – Uare Taoka o Hākena,
University of Otago

But although in many ways a successful and sympathetic character, Jimmy Tutaki illustrates Devanny's confusion about Māori, particularly when it comes to sex. He is as knowledgeable about English literature as his Pākehā employers and attended the same school as his Pākehā contemporary Barry Messenger. He has high standing in his own community and seems to be well versed in Māoritanga. However, once Miette begins pursuing him, Devanny tells us he is 'only a few decades removed from the savage' and so is unable to resist a white woman of low character who makes herself available.

Bushman Burke was also known as *Taipo*, the nickname Devanny gives her central character. Devanny believed the word meant wētā, an insect native to New Zealand, but it is also a transliteration of 'typoid', and may mean a kind of supernatural being. Whatever, the novel is less about him than it is about Flo, the flapper who marries him for his inheritance. Flo's father Wallace is a well-off divorce lawyer with a reputation for being on the side of wronged wives. Taipo is caught in Flo's glittering thrall despite his preference for women who don't smoke, drink or wear cosmetics. He is fully aware that she does not love him and is marrying him for his money. Flo has an ongoing affair with Rangi Fell, whose mother is Māori. Unlike Taipo, Rangi can recite poetry, jazz (i.e. dance) beautifully, and sing. Rangi functions as the villain of the novel, interested in Flo only for sex and a good time.

Flo treats Taipo very badly. While she tries and fails to turn him into a city man, she is rude, cold and hypercritical. On her insistence he has tennis lessons and learns to dance, but disaster looms: he finds out about her affair with Rangi. Immediately he returns to his bush home on the West Coast. Flo follows him, and in keeping with many of Devanny's heroines, undergoes an epiphany and becomes the woman she should be. The novel ends as Flo falls in love with Taipo properly.

Bushman Burke was Devanny's seventh book, and the second to last novel she would set in New Zealand. The people and landscape of Queensland would forever replace the southern country as the landscape of her imagination.

*

Within the first year of their arrival in Sydney, the Devannys had joined the Communist Party. The party had by now aligned itself firmly with the Soviet Union, which meant that it was more concerned with policies that would suit that faraway monolith, rather than any vision of a communist Australia. Jean Devanny embraced the party with all the fervour of the newly converted. Neither the New Zealand Labour Party nor the Australian Labor Party was left leaning enough for her; both had been a source of disappointment.

The Devannys' misconception that the Depression was less severe in Australia than it was at home was very quickly corrected. The family moved from slum dwelling to slum dwelling between Surry Hills and Wolloomooloo. Work was hard to come by. Karl was deadly ill and Hal was unemployed. Jean had no choice but to forget about her writing. In 1930, desperate to support her family, she left the city far behind to work on a sheep station in the northwest of New South Wales. She had been offered a job as a 'general' for a squatter. She was paid £2 a week and lasted only a few months – as long as she could stand. She recalled, 'The train journey out shook me badly. The consuming and over-all impression I gained was that here was a land at once in its forming time and decayed, worn out.'[5] It was her first journey into the bush, so different from the countryside of her homeland, and it served to whet her appetite for it. The people too fascinated her. The hard lives endured by the tough inhabitants of this part of her new land inspired her first Australian novel, *Out of Such Fires*, which was published in New York in 1934. It was never to be published in England, banned for its outspoken disregard for organised religion.

It is perhaps worth remembering here that the banning of *The Butcher Shop* in Australia in 1929, the year of Devanny's arrival, may have been less due to its content than to Devanny's readiness to invite trouble. Not long in Sydney, she gave a talk at the Aeolian Hall on 'Literature and Morality' and the perils of government-sanctioned censorship. She had 'put her head above the parapet, where it was noticed by authorities'.[6]

Back in Sydney she continued her political work. The Communist Party found the means to provide her with a small stipend, enough to meet her costs and a little left over for the family. One of her first actions was to help organise a mass meeting of unemployed women at the town hall. When the throng, led by men and containing all of the Devannys, marched to Parliament House, they were met by the police, who promptly arrested them all. 'That my whole family were in jail together was reckoned a record for the revolutionary Labour Movement,' noted Devanny dryly.[7]

One of the aims of the meeting was to involve more women in the movement: 'Significant of the difference in cultural standards between Australia and New Zealand was the complete absence of women at many of my meetings,' she wrote. 'In my homeland, women were the half of every political gathering. Here – a sprinkling appeared in the halls of the FOSU [Friends of the Soviet Union] and the Party ... gradually the women turned up. We were soon getting meetings of women only.'[8] Although Devanny was never to call herself a feminist, women's issues consumed her more than any other. In 1930 she worked also for Mrs Piddington's birth control clinic in Martin Place, an association that has led to her being accused of eugenicism.

It is true that early feminist movements advocating reliable birth control, which improved the lives of women, were linked with eugenics, but not all women espoused the most extreme aspects of the theory. Women from the left and right of the political spectrum are often uncomfortable bedmates on feminist issues. Devanny's writing displays great compassion and understanding for those who would be persecuted or dispensed with under a eugenicist regime, as would be demonstrated in the near future by the persecution of non-Aryans in Nazi Germany.

Political conviction and a newly contracted travel bug combined to send Devanny off to the world congress of Workers International Relief (WIR) scheduled to take place in October 1931 in Berlin. She left Sydney in August, all expenses paid by the Australian Communist Party, on the Nordeutscher-Lloyd freighter *Murla*. When the ship stopped at Fremantle she travelled up to Greenmount, an hour and a half by train from Perth, to meet Katharine Susannah Prichard, an author she hugely admired and a founding member of the Australian Communist Party. Jean would undoubtedly have read Prichard's most enduring novel, *Coonardoo: The well in the shadow* (1929), which centres on an Aboriginal woman on a farm in Western Australia.

To read *Coonardoo* now is to marvel not only at the quality of the writing but also at Prichard's empathy and understanding of Aboriginal people at a time that was, after all, only a year after the Coniston massacre in the Northern Territory. This was the last recorded officially sanctioned mass murder of indigenous Australians – men, women and children. Few people of European descent felt or expressed concern for Aboriginals' continued survival, let alone their wellbeing. But just as Eleanor Dark's *The Timeless Land* did in 1941, *Coonardoo* answered an overdue curiosity. We may quibble and disparage these attempts now, in the twenty-first century, while a renaissance of true Aboriginal literature, written and performed by indigenous authors and playwrights, is flowering. Lawyer, writer and academic Professor Larissa Behrendt deems *Coonardoo* to be 'about white sorrow, not black empowerment. The book leaves out any possibility that Coonardoo and her community could benefit from the assertion of their own authority or autonomy.'[9] But if we are to judge these books by the standards of the time, Katharine Susannah Prichard and Eleanor Dark, and particularly the former, were trailblazers.

Devanny and Prichard spent two pleasurable days together walking in the country and talking about literature and politics. They differed in their opinions of D.H. Lawrence's *Lady Chatterley's Lover*. Prichard, whose work was greatly influenced by Lawrence, loved it; Devanny did not. She commented later that Prichard's 'personality I found to be in marked contrast with my own. Her manner was quiet and serene, her expression deeply thoughtful, if not grave ... I joyed in the literary discussion and interchange of opinion and ideas.'[10] Years later, Prichard wrote in a letter to a friend: 'Jean Devanny is wonderful. No one I know is so vital, magnetic, absolutely devoted and disinterested. She is a great woman, really. I wish I could give all my time to Party work as she does.'[11] She and Devanny were to become firm friends, though the relationship was tested, wavered and crashed, never to recover, in the late 1940s.

Devanny set sail for Europe. To pass the time on the voyage she wrote what would be her last novel set in New Zealand, *Poor Swine*. The story is set in Granity, a mining village on the West Coast of the South Island. By now her literary style was well established into her trademark combination of romance, sometimes cloying and even histrionic, combined with socialism, sometimes didactic. It was not a particularly winning formula, and *Poor Swine* had a hard time of it, published only after deliberation by the authorities on whether it should be banned. There was a moral

concern: the central character is a married woman who enjoys the attention of more than one lover without any detectable authorial censure.

Sex appears to have been on Devanny's mind in Europe too. From
Berlin she was invited to travel to the Soviet Union, and on her return
to Australia she would regale her audiences with the vision of a muscle-
bound agricultural worker she had seen in a wheat field. On one famous
occasion, having described this Adonis, she informed her astonished
listeners that 'sex was a delightful experience in the Soviet Union'.[12] At a
Waterside Workers' Federation meeting, where we can assume that most
of the attendees were men, she repeated the sentiment. A voice from the
back called out, 'It's not too bloody bad here either, lady.'[13]

It seems that back in Australia more jokes were told about her possible
sexual exploits in the Soviet Union than her political activities. Despite
Hal's revolutionary ideas, he must have been embarrassed by these stories of
Jean's Red Guards and Russians with rippling muscles. The couple had been
miserable for some time. Jean dates their first separation – there would be
several – to the day of her arrival back in Sydney. 'From [that] day ... my relationship with my husband was fundamentally changed. By mutual agreement, each from then on was absolved from marital obligations.'[14] They may
have ceased their sexual relationship, but for almost all of their lives they
remained financially and emotionally dependent on one another.

Devanny's work for the party redoubled on her return. The visit to the
Soviet Union inspired the establishment of WIR art and theatre clubs in
Sydney. Artists who were not necessarily sympathetic to communism but
interested in social realism formed a splinter group, which they named the
Workers' Art Club. Devanny remained associated with the group, seeing it
as a broad-front organisation and a way to garner interest and support for
workers' rights. This did not please the party, which wanted the working
class to be united inside the Communist Party only. She was forced to
leave the WIR, and endured further criticism from the entirely male secre-
tariat for her publicly expressed views on birth control and the party's lack
of regard for the contribution made by women. Her daughter Pat Hurd
believed that Devanny was so upset by this that in March 1933 she was
dangerously 'close to having a breakdown'.[15]

Drusilla Modjeska comments that Devanny 'never called herself a
feminist with its bourgeois connotations and accepted without question

that under socialism the "woman question" would cease to exist'.[16] She was
to discover, as many women have since, that if a man has left-leaning politics it will not necessarily make him a champion of women's causes. As late
as 1985 New Zealand feminist scholar Lynley Cvitanovich was asking:
'What does it mean in the nineteen eighties to be a man and a socialist
and what might commitment to socialist politics mean for personal relationships with women? Do men continue to fit women unproblematically
into the categories of Marxist analysis and how might we deal with this as
socialist women?' Cvitanovich remarks, 'Jean Devanny was one of the first
in New Zealand to begin grappling with these kinds of issues.'[17] She then
goes on to describe a 'national gathering of socialist activists' in the 1980s
which is ripe for satire:

> In the background the cooking and the kitchen jobs still get done. There
> is a man in charge and there are no complaints. His helpers are both men
> and women. You need to look especially closely though to see how things
> are running. It is the men who wander in and chop and slice 'real' political
> issues and a few onions. Shortly they meander off. The women wander in
> too. They chop and slice and peel and stir. Hours later they are still there.
> Not such an easy thing for them to simply pass in and out and consider
> they have done their bit. Like Val Devoy in the novel (*Dawn Beloved*) these
> men give women's needs only lip service. Ultimately domestic concerns are
> assumed to be inseparable from women's concerns.[18]

Had Devanny witnessed the scene above, it is probable that she would
have seen nothing amiss. It was normal then, as it mostly continues to be,
for women to bear the domestic burden. Women of the early twentieth
century who managed, as Virginia Woolf famously said, to 'kill the angel
in the house', were the ones most likely to achieve 'a room of one's own', as
Katherine Mansfield did. These women were rarely from the working class.
In Devanny's circle of women writer friends, all were better cushioned
than she was. Katharine Susannah Prichard, whose husband had tragically
committed suicide, was middle class, and had her own home. Eleanor
Dark's husband was a doctor. Miles Franklin, although she endured
poverty at the end of her life, was a successful writer with an income for
most of it. Marjorie Barnard was university educated, held various white-
collar jobs and maintained a sense of security by remaining in the family
home with her elderly mother, whom she looked after. Devanny was

dependent on a stipend from the Communist Party of Australia which, despite its many criticisms of her, certainly got its money's worth.

Devanny's long-running affair with J.B. Miles, the party's general secretary, began on her return from the Soviet Union. She never names him in her autobiography; instead she calls him Leader. In keeping with all of her relationships, the affair was extremely tumultuous. She was a woman of great, stormy, conflicting emotions, who had the knack of annoying even her closest friends, but once she had made a decision to pledge her allegiance, that loyalty was set in stone. For the most part she writes of Leader with worshipful respect, at least until he turned against her, as many in the party would later do. But for now he was as thrilled as she was to be engaging in a secret love affair.

Physically, Miles was unprepossessing. Probably shorter than Devanny, who was tall and thin, he had a noticeably big head and short limbs. He was also married, with five children. There was a level of delusion in the couple's conviction that nobody knew about the affair. Gossip was rife, and as Devanny herself was never blessed with any degree of discretion, more people knew about the relationship than the lovers thought. She and Miles would talk and argue deep into the night. And of course, among the many things they disagreed on were women's issues, or at least the degree to which women should be liberated, or even listened to.

Devanny's love for Miles was inextricably tied up with her devotion to communist ideals. Communism for many thinkers and writers of the time had the fire and soul of a religion. It was embraced with righteous fervour. For Devanny, sleeping with Miles could have been a little like sleeping with the high priest. Through him came all communications from the Soviet Union; through him came the invitation to attend the world congress of Workers International Relief in the first place. He had recognised Devanny's power as a public speaker; he had heard her argue with many of the members of the party on various issues. Early in their association, at least, he had great respect for her and recognised her as a valuable asset to the party.

In the two years following the trip to Europe and the USSR, Devanny worked tirelessly for the party, travelling to Melbourne on a speaking tour and addressing crowds of tens of thousands in the Sydney Domain. On one occasion the police lifted the platform and tipped it up to get her off.

When a riot erupted she was dragged away and put into a nearby lock-up.
Hal Devanny took her place and carried on speaking over the turmoil.
Consequently Jean was sentenced to three months jail or a fine of £30 for
resisting arrest and assaulting the police. With her characteristic fiery lack
of self-control she told the court, 'I don't deny that I kicked him! I'd do it
again!'[19] Fortunately, International Class-War Prisoners' Aid paid up, as a
fine that size could have broken the family finances. The Devannys were
barely staying afloat, moving from one miserable slum to another, and all
the time anxious about Karl's health.

Somehow, with the prodigious energy that so many people who knew
her would comment on, Devanny managed in 1932 and 33 to write two
more novels, *The Ghost Wife* and *The Virtuous Courtesan*. Neither book
has much literary merit. Each in its way caused a scandal. Just as Devanny
was forced by her circumstances to work harder than anyone else, she was
also forced to write for what she imagined was the marketplace. Her good
friend Kay Brown, whom Devanny would later say was closer to her than
a daughter, remembered her buying two cartons of cigarettes and hiding
out in a secret room in the Cross so she could bang out these steamy tales.
Brown would bring her food and not divulge the address to a living soul.

So scandalous was *The Virtuous Courtesan*, it was not allowed into
Australia until 1958, 23 years after its New York publication in 1935.
Not only does it contain gay and lesbian characters, it also portrays heavy
drinking among the middle class and a working-class girl who is sold into
prostitution at the age of 10. Another character carries out a do-it-your-
self abortion with a knitting needle. The question Devanny seems to ask
is whether marriage is a form of legalised prostitution no better or worse
than the illegal version. This is an issue that dominated feminist discussion
well into the late twentieth century.

SUGAR HEAVEN

In 1934 Devanny travelled to Queensland for the first time, little realising
that the northeastern state would become not only the setting for some
of her most successful novels, but also, eventually, her home. There were
many trials and tribulations to be got through in the interim, as well as a
bereavement from which she never quite recovered.

For a long time Devanny had suffered from a gynaecological problem, which would worsen with the onset of menopause. In her correspondence with Miles Franklin she recalls an operation that she had in the 1940s to remove 'ten pounds of malignant growth' and treatment for an 'ulcerated vagina'.[20] Diagnosis was still sometime in the future. Now, she was 40 years of age, extremely anxious about her son's health, exhausted, thin and frantic. On the one hand the party was happy to release her from her punishing schedule for a period of convalescence, but on the other charged her with setting up a branch in Cairns. She was a stroppy, unwell woman travelling alone, with little idea of how to look after herself. At least for part of the time she had Kay Brown with her. Pat Hurd, in her contribution to her mother's autobiography, recalls that a Mount Isa audience on that first tour was antagonistic because both women were wearing slacks and Devanny was known to be from New Zealand: 'Someone called out "What can you know about Australia? We don't want to listen to you." Devanny replied: "I know this much about Australians, they all wear wrist watches and call each other bastard." When the laughter died down, she had them eating out of her hand.'[21] The observation about wristwatches would have pleased the crowd. Wristwatches were a status symbol and still relatively expensive.

Miners, farm workers, mill hands, plantation labourers and people of small towns would have felt familiar to Devanny. From her affection and commitment to Queensland, she would write four novels set there: *Sugar Heaven* (1936), *Paradise Flow* (1938), *Roll Back the Night* (1945) and *Cindie* (1949), and two non-fiction works, *By Tropic Sea and Jungle* (1948) and *Travels in North Queensland* (1951).

The inspiration for *Sugar Heaven* came during this first trip. At the time of her visit there was a push from the cane cutters to improve their pay and long hours. Added complexities, which Jean wove into the story, came about from the influx of non-unionised Italians working in the area and the incidence of Weil's disease, a very unpleasant and painful skin condition that afflicted the cane cutters. Interestingly, Drusilla Modjeska names it as her favourite of Devanny's work. Other commentators have harshly criticised it, and Devanny herself saw that her desire to proselytise and preach on workers' rights and conditions had overwhelmed the narrative.

The edition I borrow from the Auckland Library is a beautiful modern antique, published in 1936 by Modern Publishers, 191 Hay Street, Sydney. Long ago it was lovingly covered by a librarian in the same thick pale-green and white flecked wallpaper I remember from childhood visits to the houses of elderly relatives. Two lending record slips have come loose in the front. They are headed TIME ALLOWED FOR READING, followed by a stern warning that the time must not be exceeded or the reader will be charged THREE PENCE FOR THE FIRST WEEK OF PART THEREOF and ONE PENNY PER DAY thereafter. The novel is over 300 pages long. How many readers had to part with their pennies, or were forced to return it before they'd finished? The first borrowing was on 5 May 1937, and the book was issued fairly frequently after that until 1948, when it fell very much out of favour, or perhaps for a period it was lost. The next time a reader wanted it was October 1967. Somebody else may have tried to borrow it in 1976 but the date has been scratched out. To hold this book in my hands is to be transported back to the war years.

On the inside cover, which has at some point come adrift and been glued to the frontispiece, Jean Devanny is described as 'a well known Australian publicist and author'. In 1935 the word publicist retained some of its old meaning. Over the course of a century it had gone from describing a writer on the law of nations to what the *Shorter Oxford Dictionary* calls 'a writer on current public topics'. It was only five years earlier, in 1930, that 'publicist' had entered the dictionary in its current meaning of 'publicity agent'. It is probable that Devanny and her publishers leaned further towards the older meaning of the word. The use of the word here, then, is to announce to the reader that this is a valid contemporary novel by a writer who knows what she's talking about.

Sugar Heaven is in some ways a Queensland version of *Dawn Beloved*, set a decade or so later, in 1935. It too is about a young woman coming to terms with the restrictions and true nature of marriage. Dulcie, like Dawn, is learning about life from a more worldly husband. Dawn's husband Val was a miner; Dulcie's husband Hefty is a cane cutter. Just as Dawn was, the young wife in *Sugar Heaven* is occasionally overwhelmed by conflicting urges: 'Her cheeks flamed now, with shame. Hate and desire had intermingled in the ancient inscrutable way and Dulcie was totally unprepared for such a manifestation.'[22]

The couple are newly married. Each of them has a secret past. Hefty has been married to livewire Eileen, who is now married to his brother Bill and conducting a clandestine affair with one of the Italian workers. Dulcie's secret is that she was a scab during an industrial dispute in Sydney. When Hefty finds out about this, he sees it as evening things up between them, since he had neglected to tell her about the existence of his first wife. Husband and wife barely know one another, and Dulcie does all she can to avoid sex with Hefty, just as Dawn did for a time with Val, until both wives discover they enjoy it.

In this novel Jean Devanny concerns herself not only with sex, marriage, workers' rights and conditions, but also with the Aboriginal predicament, a tragedy that would distress her throughout her years in West Island. Hefty's brother Bill tells Dulcie about the hunting parties:

> 'I'm sorry if I've hurt you, Dulcie, but you must face facts. It is true that our early settlers used to hunt the abos as they now hunt kangaroos and walla-bies. It was particularly abominable up on the Tablelands. They used to drive the blacks into trees, fire the trees and shoot them as they dropped from the branches to avoid the fire. They drove them into rivers and picked them off that way. They poisoned their food. They commonly left abo babies to die after killing off their parents. They used to boast about their day's bag of blacks as they now boast about their bag of birds or kangaroos …'[23]

Bill's lesson arises out of a discussion about the treatment of Kanakas on the cane fields after the introduction of the White Australia Policy. Kanakas, hailing from Melanesia – and in many cases blackbirded – were also starved, their wells and food supplies poisoned, since it was cheaper and easier for some of their employers to do this than to pay for their workers' repatriation.

Closer to Devanny's personal experience is the Communist Party's treatment of Eileen, who decides she would like to join the organisation after the sugar-cane workers' strike. She is refused membership because of her affair with the Italian. Her husband tells her, 'You're a fool to think you can play around like this and at the same time attain membership of the Party.'[24] When she and Dulcie eventually become friends, Eileen confides, 'Then the strike came. It made me want to join the Party. But they won't have me. Party women have to be conventionally pure it seems.'[25] This is nothing less than a cry from the author's own heart.

When the men go back to work not much progress has been made, and there is infighting within the Australian Workers' Union and other labour organisations. Throughout the novel Devanny is critical of the monolith sugar corporations but goes easy on the small farmers, explaining that they are just as much at the mercy of the big companies as anyone. This sympathy, along with her criticisms of the CPA's attitude towards women, did not endear her to party officials.

Towards the end of *Sugar Heaven*, Devanny tries to weave together Dulcie's personal life and the political environment. The result is clumsy, almost risible:

> The strike situation had thrown up out of obscurity more issues than the bare one of class. She was led to think, deeply and almost with fear, of the need of a man for a woman. Her old conception of sex repelled her now. She glimpsed sex as a real force, apart from love; as a physical necessitous urge like food hunger, satisfaction of which meant clearer action for the class, clear heads, quiet bodies, better men. With inward love tremors she visioned Hefty's eyes at certain times when he had emerged from her embrace. How clean and pure they had been! And once, when he had been terribly worried about the strike, and she had loved him in her dainty, yielding and yet withholding way, he had murmured: 'How you have helped me! Good comrade!'[26]

Dale Spender, however, is apposite on this typically Devanny-ish, uncomfortable shackling together of sex and politics. She writes, 'I am critical of *The Butcher Shop*, for example, which in its brave and bold assertion of women's right to sexuality, seems to give sex and satisfaction too much significance as a solution. But some of her political novels ... such as *Sugar Heaven* and *Cindie* ... were for me a salutary introduction to the political/social/racial – and misogynist – history of Australia. I would recommend Jean Devanny's fiction to all alert, intellectually active individuals who cherish the dream of a just world.'[27]

Of *Sugar Heaven*'s genesis Devanny herself wrote: 'I collected up all the facts of the struggle and organised them into a book, fact in the form of fiction ... This book went far beyond the new vogue in writing at that time: the creative reporting (reportage, it was called), invented by Austrian/Czech Egon Kisch and popularised by him throughout the literary world.'[28] Egon Kisch was a communist literary celebrity whom

Devanny was to meet when she returned to Sydney. He had been refused entry to Australia, being forced to sit a language test in Gaelic as a ham-fisted means of keeping him out of the country. Language tests were a weapon of the White Australia Policy, and usually conducted in English. Perhaps, when the authorities really wanted to keep someone out, they hit them with Gaelic. Kisch could speak several languages but Gaelic wasn't one of them. Undeterred, he jumped ship in Melbourne, breaking his leg in the process. The injury did not prevent him from speaking to rallies of thousands in Victoria and New South Wales. He also influenced the writing of social realism in Australia, including Devanny's novels.

DISUNITY AND LOSS

It could be that Devanny's friendship with Kisch, by whom she seems to have been entirely captivated, went a little way to assuaging the next tragedy in her life. It was heartbreak of the kind that only the strong survive, and one she had already endured: the death of a child. There is no record of who made the decision to keep her in the dark about it until she returned to Sydney, but that is what happened. She was told on arrival that her son Karl had passed away.

Biographer Carole Ferrier maintains that Karl had Tb, not a heart and thyroid problem, which is what the Devannys believed. He was often bedridden, with the added complication of what doctors thought was a type of rheumatism. At the time of his death he was only 22 years old.

'For the second time in my life the sun went out,' wrote Devanny.[29] She was plunged into a deep depression, part of which was caused by guilt. Would Karl have died if she had stayed at his bedside to nurse and care for him, to make sure he ate well and to keep his spirits up? She had left a very sick young man to fend for himself. Not only had she killed the angel in the house, but she'd possibly hastened the death of her own son.

Point of Departure contains very little about Karl's death, an omission that Miles Franklin questioned. In the late 40s and early 50s Franklin read and re-read the manuscript, and carried out a lengthy correspondence with Devanny throughout the writing of many drafts. In one of Devanny's letters, obviously in relation to Franklin's inquiry about Karl's passing, Devanny replied, 'My son, Miles. I *can't* write about his death ...'[30]

Jean Devanny with
Katharine Susannah
Prichard sometime in the
1930s. The two women had
much in common – their
careers as writers and their
communism – but their
friendship was tested and
wavered.

In her grief, she threw herself into her work. Early in 1935, she and
Katharine Susannah Prichard set up the Writers' League with help from
Egon Kisch. This is perhaps Devanny's most lasting legacy, since by a fairly
convoluted process the league combined with a later organisation, the
Writers' Association (of which Devanny was president), which would
eventually become the Fellowship of Australian Writers, and then the
Australian Society of Authors.

Devanny and her husband saw little of each other through this period
– it is Kisch she writes about the most. When he left Australia she was
bereft. Perhaps they had become lovers, or perhaps it was just – although
'just' in these circumstances is rarely descriptive – an affair of the mind.

In April 1935 Devanny went back to Queensland for eight months.
She spoke openly about the possible war looming on the horizon. The
Communist Party's official line was that the USSR was at risk of invasion
given the rise of fascism in Europe, the Japanese invasion of Manchuria
and the continuing Depression. In Queensland there were large, peaceful
public meetings, with none of the riots that often erupted at meetings of
similar size in Sydney. It was during this eight months away that Devanny

formed a sustaining friendship with two members of the party in Brisbane, Isaiah (Ike) and Anne Askew. She also caught the attention of Joe McCarthy, who was the organiser for the Cairns party branch. He was attracted to her, but she maintained that attraction was not reciprocal: 'Joe was devoid of imagination – and having said that, one has said everything.'[31] Of all the men in the CPA, including J.P. Miles, McCarthy was one of the most damaging to Devanny. He fell in love with her but in the way an unimaginative man will fall in love: the woman must be his, or she is nothing. When Devanny later needed his support he actively sabotaged her reputation.

Health and money were serious concerns for Devanny throughout the late 1930s. Despite two physical breakdowns she found the funds to contribute to the publication of *Sugar Heaven* and to write another novel, *Paradise Flow*. When the latter was published in 1938, Devanny was once again in Cairns, apparently conducting an affair with Charlie Sailor, a married Torres Strait Islander. In North Queensland and in Sydney, her preoccupation with sexual matters was often given vent on the podium. Not only did she express herself frankly on the matter, she was far ahead of her time. The party men, judgemental and sexually conservative, were horrified. Devanny was in some respects their poster girl. She was a famous writer and a popular speaker off the political circuit as well as on it. In January 1939, for example, she was one of the speakers at a dinner held for H.G. Wells, attended by many prominent Sydney-siders. But for all her fame, these party men wanted to control her.

At the end of that year, once again exhausted and wrung out, Devanny came to the end of a longer stay in Sydney. She had been living in a rented room in the Cross, so tiny that she had to keep her suitcases elsewhere. They were stolen, which was a terrible blow, since she possessed so little. She had also suffered two bouts of serious illness. During the first she was given refuge by Miles Franklin at her house in Carlton; during the second she went to stay with a woman doctor friend in Melbourne, who found her a difficult patient. She described Devanny's 'unfailing rejoinder: 'But you see, dear, you don't understand. That's not correct thinking.' And went on: 'I'm fond of her, but her vanity is colossal. There's no argument, she's simply right. Marx knew everything from the dawn of civilisation to the end of time ...'[32]

Devanny's departure to Queensland in 1939 was a sad farewell. 'My husband accompanied me to the train,' she recalled. 'And as he stood beside the carriage window, a wave of regret for the disunity between us swept over me. I fell to weeping.'[33] Worse was to come. Within the next 12 months she would be expelled from the Communist Party, an organisation for which she had made the most enormous sacrifices.

By September of 1940, Devanny was living near Emuford, a small mining town near Cairns. She was the only female member of the camp, occupying a tin shelter built for her by fellow members of the party who were working the mine. It was here that she wrote *By Tropic Sea and Jungle*, the first of her natural history books on Queensland.

Reading it now, it is obvious it is written for a market. The book consists of sketches written in a bright, chatty and intimate manner. Many of them finish very abruptly, as if they were intended for magazine publication rather than to be gathered together in a volume. The book is divided into two parts, the first consisting of short pieces on fishermen and lugger boys, flora and fauna, and life in the sugar towns. Her descriptions of the natural world are vivid, almost photographic. Of a visit to Babinda, she writes: 'Tree-ferns leaned from the banks; white water rippled over golden stones; great round boulders, banded with fawn, mauve and purple, were mirrored in flat waters against the background of jungle scrub.'[34] She describes a python digesting freshly killed wallaby with 'a hump as high as a chairback'.[35] She also listens to men talking about damper, good and bad. One of them says: 'My experiences with cooks are too numerous to mention. If the cook's bad it's summed up in camp by the question, "Who called the cook a bastard?" and the reply "Who called the bastard a cook?" There are cooks and cuckoos. The cuckoo's the bastard.'[36]

She relates a story told her by an old man about the half a dozen tribes of Aborigines who once inhabited the area:

It was the influx of Chinese that wiped them out. The Chinese grew bananas on the Tully River and employed Abos almost entirely. They paid them a small wage, and got it back by selling opium to them after they themselves had smoked it. This, together with venereal disease and influenza, wiped them out by the hundred. The poor devils would soak the opium charcoal in hot water and drink it. In the 'nineties I've gone into camps and found the whole bunch – men, women and children – dead to the world. Couldn't kick a grunt out of them.[37]

Devanny has the ear of an oral historian. We can almost hear the old man's voice telling this shocking, tragic tale, clear down the years, as if it was recorded.

The second section of the book finds the author camped at Emuford. It seems the men with whom she shares her camp are kind and generous. At one point she is given a native cat, or quoll, as a pet. It escapes, but not before she has delighted in its 'upheld white paw, its defiant but wild gaze'.[38] She is fascinated by the insect life, making careful observation of various species of ants and a terrifying sounding creature called a fish-killer, a three- to four-inch insect that kills small fish and frogs with its strong forelegs, and can both swim and fly. At one point she refers to herself as a 'collector', since she is sending much of what she finds down to Cairns.[39] In the early 40s there was still much to be discovered and understood, and amateur collectors such as Devanny would often do as much damage as good. She describes killing snakes, and accompanying loggers to take out the last of the red cedar. On another occasion she shoots a rat-kangaroo, having described how the marsupial gives out simultaneous sounds of a 'blurt and thud … what is described in vulgar terms as a "raspberry" every time his hind legs hit the ground'.[40] She is, of course, mistaken. An animal would require a peculiar anatomy to allow it to fart on every leap.

So taken is she with the gassy kangaroo-rat that she tries to trap one. When this is unsuccessful, she and her companions shoot him: 'We found that the bullet had blown off the lower jaw and gone through the bottom of the heart. He was a buck, well grown, as big as a large hare. His thick fur was very soft and white near the skin, red-tipped on the back and less so on the sides. His hard tail was practically the same length as his body'.[41]

As the ravages of pollution, climate change and overpopulation wipe out much of what wildlife we have left, it will become increasingly difficult for us to imagine how this jolly account could be given by a woman of intelligence and compassion. People who kill endangered animals in our world are pilloried, loathed, and suffer the ignominy of their triumphal photographs going viral. In the 1940s the ancient paradigm of man at the mercy of nature prevailed: there were far more of them than there were of us, and we had every right to kill whatever animal we liked. The supply was seemingly inexhaustible.

The authorial presence in *By Tropic Sea and Jungle* is bubbly, curious and optimistic, and gives no hint of the horrifying event that would happen at Emuford. The communists who had invited Devanny to join them, all men, grew tired of her lecturing. As it was, they were all under some degree of police surveillance thanks to Devanny's reputation as a rabble-rouser. Then a local woman spread a rumour that she had seen Devanny having sex in the open air with one of the men, Murdoch Macdonald. When the rumour reached Devanny she was furious and asked Macdonald to do something about it. Instead he struck her, and refused to talk to the local woman and others who were convinced of the story's veracity.

Many women, in this situation, would keep their own counsel and take some sort of cold comfort from the knowledge that the rumour was lies. They might wait for the story to die down and for the truth to out. More sensibly, they might disappear from the area, never to return. Not Devanny. She made the journey northeast to Cairns and asked Joe McCarthy for help. He gave her his assurance that he would help her, but then made himself scarce. When she couldn't find him, Devanny returned to Emuford alone. This was a serious mistake.

It is certain that the men in the camp assaulted her, and probable that she was also raped by more than one of them. Sometime afterwards she was taken to hospital by ambulance and the men, in time-proven fashion, let it be known that Devanny had been willing, and that she had been working for them as a cook and general dogsbody. And so insult was added to injury: not only did they assault her, but they demeaned and devalued the work she had been doing there.

Charges were not laid against these men, and Devanny herself kept quiet. She repaired to her old friends, the Askews, with whom she was still staying when Ike Askew died in early March. Around this time she had the operation mentioned in her letter to Miles Franklin. It was a radical hysterectomy. The only person who ever knew the truth of what happened at Emuford, aside from Devanny and her assailants, was Anne Askew. A loyal and true friend, she kept Devanny's experience to herself and the secret died with her.

Inevitably, stories of Devanny's supposed sexual activities at the mining camp reached Sydney. They resulted in her expulsion from the party. Some of these stories were trite: she had, for example, been seen swimming in the nude. Some of it was pure, vindictive gossip: a trade union official's wife told her she was a homewrecker. Her moral conduct, so called, was the major reason for her expulsion, the news of which came to her while she was convalescing in Brisbane. Men will believe other men, something that Devanny knew only too well. She did not protest her innocence, although there is evidence she did write a statement about the event and its aftermath and sent it to J.B. Miles in Sydney, where it was destroyed.

Much of Devanny's conduct during the following year was so deranged and destructive that a modern psychologist would likely diagnose her as suffering from post-traumatic stress disorder. There were attempted reunions with Hal in Sydney, even though he apparently beat her when he learned of her expulsion from the CPA. She demanded that he ditch his girlfriend and support her, despite the fact that he had had a mild stroke. Hal, whom she always criticised for his mild manners and lack of spunk, agreed to her demands, and for some time they battled on together in a house in Neutral Bay. There were also ongoing skirmishes with various members of the Communist Party who were, it is easy to see with hindsight, terrified of what Devanny could publicly say about her treatment at their hands. J.B. Miles, devoid of any residual affection from their long-running affair, had no sympathy for her, as was demonstrated in 1942 when Devanny made a special trip to Sydney on his instigation. Perhaps she hoped he would apologise, or go some way to recompense her for her injuries. Instead, he warned her not to write or say anything negative about the party. Even Katharine Susannah Prichard failed to stand by her. In Pat Hurd's addendum to her mother's autobiography, she writes that despite Prichard's supposed friendship, when Devanny was 'hard-pressed and suffering, KSP does nothing to help; she lines herself up with the prosecution!'[42]

In the early 1950s, while Miles Franklin was assisting Devanny in her efforts to find a publisher for *Point of Departure*, the manuscript was given to an anonymous journalist to read. The journalist was a man with connections to the Australian Labor Party. His response, which Franklin sent to Devanny, must have gone a little way to assuage these old hurts:

> The hatred of the intelligent – the writer – and intellectual is a hangover from the old Labor party ... If we weren't so hopeless in the Labor Party there would be a proud place in it for the Jean Devannys of this world. Instead, we let them go over to the Commos who turn them into working

cattle. Read the itinerary handed out to Jean year after year. It would kill an ox. What courage – integrity and fundamental decency. She threw her husband, her children, herself and finally her health into this Cause – only to be finally and contemptuously rejected.[43]

Although the expulsion from the Communist Party was difficult to bear, in the long run it did Devanny a lot of good. She healed slowly, and she returned to Queensland where she spent time on Magnetic Island and on the Barrier Reef. *By Tropic Sea and Jungle* was published in 1944, and *Cindie*, her last and, to my mind, best novel, in 1949. Separated once again from Hal, she conducted an affair with an older man whose identity she guards throughout her memoir, but he may well have been Dr Hugh Flecker, a natural scientist who had been encouraging of her efforts in that direction. A whole chapter of *Travels in North Queensland* is devoted to a trip she makes with him to Low Island Reef to collect coral and shells and discover species of mollusc, starfish, algae and rare coastal plants. He had no affiliation whatsoever with the CPA, and was indeed antipathetic to it. At one stage he asked her to marry him, but only if she had relinquished all connections. She had not, and would not, until 1950, by which stage she was living peacefully enough with Hal in a rented house in Townsville.

Devanny, perhaps, had contracted some version of Stockholm syndrome to go alongside the possible PTS: she wanted, throughout much of the 40s, to be reinstated as a member of the party that had treated her so badly. When they did finally re-admit her it was only a brief contre-temps. At the point she was able finally to turn her back on the party, she labelled them all 'liars, cheats and miscreants' – an opinion that held until five years before her death, when she mysteriously re-joined.[44] It was the party's response to her historical novel *Cindie*, rather than the scandalous lies they had disseminated about her personal conduct, that forced her resignation. The Communist Party newspaper, *Tribune*, refused to review it. The official line was that Devanny's portrayal of the mistreatment of Kanaka labour in the Queensland sugar fields at the turn of the century was incorrect. It was not: Devanny had done her research and believed that the 'the cruelty [to the Kanakas] lay chiefly in the recruiting' – that is, blackbirding. Further, she held that their conditions on the plantations were the same as those handed out to white men after the White Australia Policy came into play and Kanaka labour was ended.

'There was a picture in their minds, I fancy, of the "noble savage", a picture as far removed from reality as anything well could be,' wrote Devanny.

> Impossible for them to envisage the conditions in most of the islands from which the Kanakas were recruited or 'blackbirded': the hunger, the filth, the cannibalism, the fear of primitive magic, the deadly internecine feuds incessantly raging between the tribes – and the comparison presented by their Queensland mode of life ... Not that I am attempting here to excuse the cruelties and abominations of blackbirding. Or to minimise them one jot. Why should I? My whole life-work and outlook, my ingrained acceptance as a New Zealander of the coloured man as equal with white, my studies in anthropology, my cultivation of coloured persons as personal friends, my writings – all together, these establish that a tolerant attitude towards injustice perpetrated upon coloured peoples is not to be numbered among my many faults ... many Kanakas were opposed to enforced repatriation.[45]

J.B. Miles, whose opinion she still valued, refused not only to read the novel but to discuss it with her. Perhaps he knew that he would be on the receiving end of such high-handed statements as the one above – a typically New Zealand response to accusations of racism. As far as Prichard's desertion of Devanny goes, it probably had more to do with this issue surrounding the portrayal of the Kanakas rather than those surrounding her friend's apparently scandalous behaviour.

Many of us, having had doses of Christianity in our childhoods, will return to the church in our senior years. Devanny's devotion to the party was so devout that the loss of it in late midlife left a great gaping hole in her heart and mind not easily filled by anything else. Perhaps the motivation to rejoin was more spiritual and emotional than intellectual, particularly as the party was at that time trying to persuade her not to publish her autobiography. Her long letters to Miles Franklin regarding the manuscript demonstrate that she herself had grave doubts about the book, not so much from anxiety about who or what she might expose but about its structure and pace, its value as literature. When the book was rejected by a publisher in 1953, Devanny had one sad sleepless night, but wrote to Franklin the next day: 'this morning my irrepressible optimism is once more flying the flag'.[46] Publication of the memoir during her lifetime would doubtless have resulted in much argument and accusation. It was not until 1986, long after her death, that it finally broke into the world.

In the same letter to Miles Franklin, Devanny expressed her sorrow at a letter from a 'loved sister in New Zealand' who told her about the family's pride in her early career as a writer, but also 'how disappointed and shocked they were when I gave it all up for "notorious" politics'.[47] Part of her distress, perhaps, was her sister's ignorance of the work that had come later, despite the 'notorious' politics. The sister must have missed the reviews. In a 1950 letter to Franklin, Devanny mentions some critical response to *Cindie*: 'I have had some good reviews of my last book from NZ, where it seems to have caused a stir in the literary world, which pleased me greatly. One critic suggested that I should return home and devote myself to my own country.'[48]

The intimate correspondence between these two very different but important writers was sustaining to both of them in their later years. It is shocking that Miles Franklin, a scion of Australian letters, was at the end of her life often lonely and in relative penury. In 1954 Devanny wrote to her: 'I can't bear to think of you desolate, as you state, sitting alone in that house from which you can't look out ... The only thing I dread in life is loneliness. While working hard I did not know the meaning of the word, but now I absolutely refuse to have Hal leave me alone. He knows. He had his day – the twenty years in Sydney while I was on the loose, scrounging a crust for him, and now he will meet my needs. I am finished with being a doormat for any worthless creature.'[49]

Such bitterness! No wonder Hal told a visitor that he thought Devanny was frequently quite unhinged, and that he often did his best to avoid her. Fourteen years earlier Devanny had written to Prichard: 'Hal is tremendously useful to me politically, but otherwise I have to count him out. He has been trying to get to NZ for a long time, but he would have to be born again to achieve any dynamic at all ... He is no good to me, as a husband, as a provider, or anything else, yet he stands between me and any sort of happiness at all, since the eyes of the workers are on me. The P[arty] provides me with a pittance, otherwise I would starve.'[50] We often lash out at the people closest to us, and Devanny, plagued by frequent ill-health, rattling with self-doubt while giving every appearance of being convinced of her own correct thinking – a zealot in many ways – lashed out more than most.

A HOME OF HER OWN

Devanny's daughter Pat, who also had periods of estrangement from her mother, believed that her mother's last years in Townsville were predominantly happy ones. She had a couple of close friends, a productive and beautiful garden, and a great curiosity and love for the animals and insects that shared it, including a pet python. She went swimming in a tidal creek near her home without fear of crocodiles or sharks, rode her bicycle everywhere, and watched two movies a week at the local cinemas. Aside from her correspondence with Miles Franklin, she also exchanged letters with many others, including natural scientists and aspiring writers to whom she was always encouraging.

And, despite everything, she had Hal, who would outlive her by two years. After almost two decades of hard slog in New Zealand, together they had crossed the Tasman in search of a new and better life, by which stage they were in their thirties. The life they had in West Island was certainly new, and different in ways they could never have imagined. Had Devanny joined the Communist Party in New Zealand and fallen in love with the leader; if she had informally dissolved her marriage and conducted affairs with other men; if she had gone on to write more novels set in the land of her birth that questioned that status quo and said hard things about her own colonial history – what then? It is possible she would have ended up a pariah, more isolated than she ever felt in her little house in Townsville. Devanny had a big, abrasive personality, more suited perhaps to stereotypical notions of the Australian national character than the supposedly more sombre, private, quiet Pākehā.

The departure from the homeland often affords the traveller or emigrant an opportunity to re-invent themselves, to become someone else. Devanny's friend Kay Brown apparently stated that 'Devanny found New Zealand social conditions had not offered sufficiently fertile ground for the socialist project to which she was committed.'[51] That may or may not have been true, had it been put to the test. What can be stated with some degree of certainty, is that Devanny would not have become the woman she was if she had stayed at home in a smaller country, with all the strictures and restraints placed on her by the demands and expectations of relatives and long-term friends.

Perhaps the penultimate word on Devanny's longstanding reputation in New Zealand could be from John A. Lee, who wrote in his 1977 letter to Andrée Lévesque Olssen, 'Jean Devanny, strange how completely she vanished. There is no grave as deep as the Commo party.'[52] But she didn't so much vanish into the party as disappear behind the iron curtain that hangs across the watery border between our two nations. It seems that the curtain may have opened a chink to allow Devanny's work to slowly regain ground in the years since her death, ground that could metaphorically be thought of as a small island. This fictional island, the one we imagine her happily inhabiting, is not a tropical cay of the kind she was so fond of and wrote of so winningly in *Travels in North Queensland*. Instead it lies fittingly in the middle of the turbulent, stormy Tasman Sea, and so allows both sides of the ditch to lay claim to this extraordinary, brilliant, highly sexed, maddening, ferocious, inexhaustible woman called Jean Devanny.

Of my five West Islanders she is the one I would most like to have met.

1972

By 1972 most of our West Islanders have passed away: Jean Devanny in 1962, Eric Baume in 1967 and Roland Wakelin in 1971.

This is the year the parties end for Dulcie Deamer – though, who knows, perhaps she's still conducting kissing competitions and doing the splits in her leopardskin suit in whatever wild wine-soaked heaven bohemians go to when they die.

Nationally, there are many changes. Some are far reaching and begin to define the Australia we know today. On 26 January the famous Aboriginal Tent Embassy is set up in Canberra. Among its co-founders are activists who will become household names, among them Gary Foley, Roberta Sykes and Mum Shirl. This year pastor, activist, sportsman and governor Douglas Nicholls will make history as the first Aboriginal to be knighted.

At the end of the year Prime Minister William McMahon will be replaced by Gough Whitlam. It is the first Labor government after 23 years of a Liberal Country Party coalition regime. Their slogan 'It's Time' is mirrored on the other side of the Tasman when the New Zealand Labour Party comes to power under Norman Kirk, ending a 12-year reign by the National Party.

Two Australian women triumph on two wildly divergent international competitive platforms. In the sporting world swimmer Shane Gould excels at the Munich Olympics, winning three gold medals, one silver and a bronze. In recognition of her achievement she is made Australian of the Year. In Puerto Rico Kerry Anne Wells is crowned as the first Australian Miss Universe. As the decade wears on, feminist opposition to beauty pageants will become more strident.

After decades of smoking as a social norm, 'Smoking is a health hazard' is introduced as a warning in advertising for cigarettes and tobacco products. Next year, 1973, the warning will be printed on the packets themselves. Australians continue to puff away as if there's no tomorrow.

In the world of books, Thea Astley wins the Miles Franklin Award with her novel *The Acolyte*. It is the third time since 1962 she has won the prize, which is an extraordinary achievement in a literary environment dominated by men. Thomas Keneally's novel *The Chant of Jimmie Blacksmith* is nominated for the Booker Prize. The story is based on the life of Aboriginal bushranger Jimmy Governor and told from his perspective. In his later life Keneally will say he would not now attempt that point of view. In six years a film based on the novel will be made.

The theatre world is thriving. Playwright Alex Buzo wins the Australian Literary Society Medal for *Macquarie: A play*, and also for *Tom*. David Williamson's iconographic play *Don's Party* is produced in Sydney for the first time, to mixed reviews.

Commercial radio is dominated by the band Led Zeppelin (which is this year touring Australia and New Zealand), along with Cat Stevens, Jethro Tull, Don McLean, Neil Young, Slade, Deep Purple, John Lennon, Elton John, Rod Stewart, The Rolling Stones, America, Paul Simon, Wings. Australian Helen Reddy will record her anthem of the moment, 'I Am Woman'.

The Adventures of Barry McKenzie, which could be seen as a kind of precursor to the more famous *Crocodile Dundee* (1986), is the film of the year. It's a story of an Australian yobbo on his travels to the UK. Among the cast is Barry Humphries, who has several roles including that of Aunt Edna Everage from Moonee Ponds. This character will later become world famous as Dame Edna.

And although we may think the terrorist threat is recent, Sydney suffers on 16 September a bombing in Haymarket by Croatian separatists. The target is the Yugoslav General Trade and Tourist Agency and 16 people are injured.

What, then, of our only surviving West Islander? Douglas Stewart is 59 years old and living in the suburb of St Ives, Sydney. Three years ago his friend and colleague Nancy Keesing published her lengthy essay, 'Douglas Stewart', as part of the series *Australian Writers & Their Work*. He is one of the most famous Australian writers of his era, having written across genres – plays, poetry, short stories and criticism – for nearly 30 years. He is also a long-term gatekeeper for Australian letters, having been for 14 years the literary editor of the *Bulletin*, then editor for publishers Angus & Robertson.

On Boxing Day 1972, biographer Doctor Clement Semmler arrives with his reel-to-reel tape machine to interview Stewart about his life and work.

The Man of Letters

The week I begin this chapter both Australia and New Zealand are in mourning for much-loved comedian and satirist John Clarke, who has died suddenly in Victoria at the age of 68. Such an outpouring of grief for a trans-Tasman identity, missed equally on either side of the ocean, is a rare and precious thing. In the *New Zealand Herald* a satirist who stayed home pays tribute, recalling an interview he did with Clarke in 1997. 'He loved poetry and all its magic tricks; some of his best and most closely observed satires were of poets whose work he loved,' writes Steve Braunias. 'He thought of New Zealand as a kind of distant aunt. There simply wasn't the work and there was also the obstacle of New Zealand television programmers and executives, many of whom he regarded affectionately as vermin.'[1]

Douglas Stewart died in 1985. The deaths of these two famous New Zealanders who made their homes in Australia are separated by some 30 years, but there are some similarities. Stewart was a writer and editor, not a comedian. Even so, he may well have espoused his dear friend Norman Lindsay's theory that all artists are entertainers. He may not have thought that the authorities in the New Zealand literary scene (his equivalent to Clarke's chosen medium of television) were vermin, but he did feel unjustly abandoned by them. He said as much to Vincent O'Sullivan, who visited him in Sydney in 1984 and recalled that he 'liked him very much.'[2] For the young O'Sullivan, visiting Stewart was a kind of pilgrimage: 'Stewart's "Ned Kelly" was one of the first professional plays I saw – a brilliant production with the Campions' NZ Players, and I definitely owe my later interest in Australian writing to the start that play gave me ... I think Douglas was touched that a younger NZ writer made the effort to call on him, as I very much felt that he thought our literary "establishment", by which he meant mainly Curnow and Glover, had condescended to him, and resented his opting to live in Australia, and become so successfully part of its literary world.'[3]

This sentiment expresses the peculiar phenomenon we have already witnessed with Devanny. If a New Zealand writer goes to Australia and fails, he/she is forgotten. If a New Zealand writer goes to Australia and succeeds, he/she is even more forgotten. The amnesia becomes aggressively conscious. Writer and activist Rosie Scott (1948–2017), a more recent and very successful West Island import, had the same experience, even though the novel published four years before she left, *Glory Days* (1984), was clasped to the collective bosom and became an international bestseller.

Among Stewart's papers in the Mitchell Library is a 1980 letter from another New Zealander, academic and writer Peter Simpson, who was then researching for his 1982 book on New Zealand novelist Ronald Hugh Morrieson. Morrieson's *The Scarecrow* and *Came a Hot Friday* had been published during Douglas Stewart's time at Angus & Robertson.

'I have often wondered how it came about that Morrieson was first published in Australia instead of in New Zealand,' writes Simpson:

Did he attempt to place his novels with NZ publishers first and only turn to Australia after his MSS were rejected here? Or did he immediately send his MSS to Australia? Perhaps you might be able to throw some light on these questions for me? It has always seemed to me that there was a certain rightness in RHM's first being published in Australia and meeting there greater acceptance than he has still (except for a growing minority) found at home. An easy relationship with his native environment is perhaps more typical of Australian writers than New Zealanders and Morrieson brought into New Zealand writing certain qualities which had been present in Australian writing for decades. Some Australian reviewers of the novels ... have seen affinities between Morrieson's books and Norman Lindsay's *Saturdee* and *Redheap* ... Do you think RHM might have been directly influenced by Lindsay or other Australian writers?'[4]

There are other questions in the letter. Simpson is especially curious as to why Stewart had rejected Morrieson's third and last novel, *Predicament*, then called *Is X Real?* Stewart's answer is simply that he hadn't liked it as much as the others. He explains that two years after the rejection, Morrieson sent 'a strange explosive letter' expressing the usual writers' anguish about poor sales and laying blame at the publisher's door.[5] Stewart invited him to submit another novel but Morrieson, by then in the throes of advanced alcoholism, only re-submitted the first one with a new title and a few minor changes. It could be that Morrieson felt he had an ally at Angus & Robertson in the shape of a fellow Taranakian, and the rejection of *Predicament* felt like a betrayal. In an email to me, Peter Simpson wrote, 'It's still surprising to me that they wouldn't publish *Predicament* which is not notably inferior to the first two in my opinion. I wonder if it would have made any difference to Ron's downward slide if they had?'[6] As any writer knows, rejections are especially painful. Simpson's suspicion that Morrieson would have been buoyed by an acceptance is very likely correct.

In a curious postscript to Stewart's and Morrieson's troubled association, a film was made in 2010 of the rejected novel. Despite starring the brilliant Jemaine Clement, it is a rather bad film and garnered poor reviews. For the *Dominion Post*, Graeme Tuckett wrote: '"Predicament" is adrift ... Poor casting and some underwhelming performances kill it stone dead.'[7] Rather eerily, the film was partially shot in Stewart's hometown of Eltham.

Neither Simpson nor O'Sullivan made contact with Stewart with the particular aim of talking about Stewart's own writing, although O'Sullivan could have told the grand old man of letters, as Stewart was by then, how much he had enjoyed the 'rich and vivid' language of *Ned Kelly*.[8] The year before O'Sullivan's visit, in 1983, Stewart received a letter from a fellow grand old man of letters who had stayed in Aotearoa but had briefly escaped to West Island. Historian Keith Sinclair had netted a writing fellowship at Australian National University in Canberra. In the letter he wonders if Stewart remembers him from about 1959, when Sinclair was writing a history of the Bank of New South Wales in New Zealand.

Stewart had written a piece about him in the *Bulletin* and someone had done a drawing of him. The purpose of his letter is to say how much he loved the newly published *Springtime in Taranaki*: 'Offhand I can't think of an NZ autobiography nearly as good. Both Brasch and Sargeson were so <u>evasive</u> about their love life, I mean. Your book reminds me a bit of Laurie Lee's *Cider with Rosie*: both books are lyrical ... I think your pic looks whimsical, sardonic, a bit uptight. My wife says "cheeky"'. In a casual postscript he adds, 'Oh – I shall be in Sydney 17–21 December, if you're going to be in the city', and gives Stewart the phone number.[9]

There is of course a very good reason why Stewart could be brazen about his youthful sexual adventures, and Charles Brasch and Frank Sargeson were not. Both were homosexual, Sargeson more openly than Brasch. To have written frankly about their love lives would have been tantamount to committing professional suicide. It seems odd that Sinclair would make this comparison, because he must have known about Sargeson, if not about Brasch. The literary scene in New Zealand was so small it was difficult to keep private lives altogether private.

During his years in West Island, Stewart received many other visits and letters from New Zealanders, whether resident in Australia or passing through. Two years before he left the *Bulletin*, Brasch, poet and founding editor of the literary journal *Landfall*, had called on him at his *Bulletin* office. Brasch kept journals throughout his writing life and left a vivid record of that 1956 meeting:

> He works in a dingy shabby badly lit partitioned-off little room by a window hard against a building & admitting only a grey half-light – he sat with his back to it so that I couldn't see him well. A spare dark-faced man with smooth dark hair & dark eyebrows, a little smaller than I am, speaking quietly & pleasantly. He was reserved & cautious, I felt, but I tried to be friendly & I think he thawed a little; I liked him almost at once. He had been to Canberra for a meeting of the Board of the Commonwealth Literary Fund. A romantic I suspect.[10]

Stewart himself recalled his working environment rather more favourably, as a romantic would: 'The *Bulletin* was one of those immensely civilised offices, now probably vanished from the earth, where you could do your own work in your own time and completely ignore everything and everybody if you happened to be taken by a ballad.'[11]

Brasch and Stewart talked about William Hart-Smith, a now almost forgotten poet who had arrived in Australia from New Zealand around the same time as Stewart. Stewart was so much an admirer of Hart-Smith's *Columbus Goes West*, published in 1948, that he was able to quote from it: 'two rather obvious romantic passages', commented Brasch, airily. They also discussed Denis Glover's *Arawata Bill*, which Stewart thought was Glover's best work. Their conversation turned to Dan Davin's choices for an important edition of New Zealand stories: Stewart was critical, since Davin had not selected any of the New Zealanders he had published in the *Bulletin*. They talked about Bill Oliver's positive review of Stewart's recent book, edited with Nancy Keesing, *Old Bush Songs*: Stewart approved. It may well have been through Keesing that Brasch had his introduction, since he and Keesing were cousins. Brasch's description of Stewart fits with Keesing's: he was a man whose 'physical presence would not turn heads', but who had many deep friendships and a formal, kindly way of conducting himself.[12]

Stewart obviously liked and respected Brasch. The journal entry concludes: 'He also invited me to contribute to *The Bulletin* – verse or stories, rather to my surprise; and asked that LF [*Landfall*] should be sent regularly for review, & Caxton and Pegasus books. So much friendly interest was unexpected.'[13] Brasch may well have found Stewart's bonhomie and curiosity fresh and unusual. He was likely steeped in the New Zealand literary culture, which very often may be steeped in mutual suspicion and toxic jealousy.

As a further demonstration of the insularity of this period, from Vincent O'Sullivan comes a story related to him by the Australian poet A.D. Hope, who met famous-in-New-Zealand poet Allen Curnow in Auckland. Hope expressed his regret that Australian and New Zealand writers knew so little of one another's work. Curnow replied, 'But you don't realise Alec, we don't need you.'[14]

I could fill a page or two here about what lies behind Curnow's remark: the provincialism, the stultifying isolation, the dominance of the literary scene by three generations of fairly talentless men when, as Australian critic Vance Palmer had remarked mid-century, the best New Zealand novels were being written by women.

Even now there is a sense, when one lives and works in New Zealand, of existing in a parallel universe. Books are published and fade away; they are not often championed by fellow writers, as was my experience as a young writer in Australia. Nothing has any impact unless it wins a prize overseas, no matter how unreadable the book, and nothing much has changed in relation to Curnow's 'we don't need you'. When novelist and university lecturer Paula Morris set up the Academy of New Zealand Letters in 2015 she was subjected to vitriol that arose from the same place. Why would you want to establish relationships between New Zealand writers and those of other countries? We don't need that. We are fine just as we are, thanks, talking to ourselves. When Peter Wells and I gathered together a group of enthusiasts in 1998 to establish the Auckland Writers' Festival, we encountered similar opposition from some quarters. At an early festival a leading Wellington literary identity said to me, 'This doesn't feel like New Zealand.' He meant, I think, the collegial atmosphere, the open discussion of ideas and sense of generosity, the fizz of excitement in the air.

What would Douglas Stewart think of how we are now? He certainly never wanted to live in New Zealand again, even though, as we shall see, much of the inspiration for his work throughout his life stemmed from the country of his birth.

REEL TO REEL

On Boxing Day 1972, Stewart receives a very important visitor at his North Shore home at 2 Banool Avenue, St Ives. This is his biographer Dr Clement Semmler, OBE, who arrives armed with a tape-recording machine. Stewart is flattered, I think, that Semmler has chosen him for his subject. He is one of Semmler's many admirers.

Already the biographer of poets Barcroft Boake (1965), Banjo Paterson (1966) and Kenneth Slessor (1966), Semmler has at this time worked 30 years at the Australian Broadcasting Commission, the last seven of these as deputy manager. Before that he was assistant controller of programming, a role he took very seriously. He is a jazz buff, and thanks to him Australian households in the 1940s heard some of the best jazz in the world. He had inspirational ideas for shows such as *The Sturt Report*, which he initiated in 1951. It was a popular programme voiced by two actors as they travelled down the Murrumbidgee and Murray rivers, reliving the journey made by Charles Sturt and George McLeary in 1829–30.

In 1969, three years prior to his arrival for this recording session, Semmler was awarded a Doctorate of Letters for his published work, all of it undertaken in his leisure time. One of these, *Broadcasting and the Australian Community*, was deemed to be so controversial that the ABC commissioner quashed it in 1955. Among other things, Semmler was critical of the legally required presence of two public servants on the commission, believing (as many people did) that it compromised the organisation's ability to make independent political commentary. The book was accepted by Oxford University Press on the proviso that the commission agreed to it. They did not, and the book was never published. More recently Semmler has been openly critical of the new broadcast medium of television, much of which he regards as frivolous and ill-informed. In five years' time when Semmler retires, he will fire off furious shots at his employer of 40 years. Not only is the ABC anti-intellectual, he will say, but he doubts 'if some senior executives had ever read a book'.[15] He believes that radio will find its niche as the more serious medium, an opinion that very likely endears him to famed radio dramatist Stewart.

Who is home at St Ives when Semmler arrives? Stewart's wife, painter Margaret Coen, is certainly there for some of the recording, because she helps her husband remember certain dates and years – for instance, when it was they were married.

'The fifth of December, 1945,' Margaret replies when Stewart calls for her help. Does she wonder why her husband can never remember, as married women have wondered for centuries? After all, their twenty-seventh anniversary was only a few weeks ago. Margaret could remember their courtship and marriage clearly, from the first time they met at the end of 1938. Many years later their daughter Meg, adopting her mother's voice in a loving and sensitive memoir of Coen's life, will write: 'I had never met such a dark, intense young man. Doug startled me by suggesting marriage almost as soon as we started going out.'[16] She held him off, well aware that married women usually struggle to continue as artists of any kind.

Neither can Stewart remember the year Meg was born, and Margaret supplies that as well. Meg, nearly 25, is in 1972 embarking on a career as a writer and filmmaker. She would have spent Christmas Day with her parents but is not home on the day of the interviews. She is flatting in Paddington and working at the Commonwealth Film Unit, which next year will become Film Australia.

The interviews begin conventionally enough with the subject of Stewart's childhood. The location of his father's birth escapes him too, and it seems that his wife can't help him with that. The *Bulletin* he describes as his childhood family bible, and he confesses that he had a poem a week rejected by the magazine for years. Eventually, he tells Semmler, a poem was accepted by the *Bulletin*'s 'rather disgraceful little sister the *Australian Women's Mirror*', edited by none other than Cecil Mann, who then went on to the *Bulletin*.[17] As we already know, Mann was instrumental in getting Stewart his start as his assistant on the 'Red Page'.

Why Stewart thinks of the *Mirror* as 'disgraceful' is curious. Dulcie Deamer wrote for it for years, and among the sillier pieces intended simply as entertainment are more thoughtful articles, such as the ones on women in Long Bay prison and women's refuges, which are well written and well researched. Perhaps his embarrassment about first publishing in the magazine has more to do with the fact it is a women's paper. It resonates with his response to his first published poem being in the children's pages of the *Taranaki News*.

When war broke out at the end of 1939, neither he nor Cecil Mann went to fight. Stewart explains to Semmler, 'I lasted one day [in the army] and was knocked out on medical grounds and Cecil lasted some weeks before he was bunged out as being too old, he was first world war vintage, and we were swapping jobs around and it became necessary for him to do much more political work and the Red Pages fell to me by accident, more or less.' It wasn't as if Stewart was inactive during the war years. As Meg recalls in her mother's biography, 'Doug went off to enlist in the AIF [Australian Imperial Force]. I was beside myself. He disappeared into Victoria Barracks for a whole weekend. I cried for two days. But he was rejected on medical grounds, for which I was most thankful ... it did seem incongruous that only the fittest specimens were accepted for the slaughter ... Doug became an air raid warden.'[18]

Stewart was rejected from service because of a stomach ulcer. Doctors provided him with a planned diet to help correct the problem. In the

Douglas and Meg Stewart in the Snowy Mountains, Australia, 1960s. Stewart loved fly fishing almost as much as he loved writing poetry and plays. The photograph was probably taken by his wife, painter Margaret Coen.
Meg Stewart collection

memoir of her mother, Meg expresses the opinion that the world was better served by his writing through the war, rather than fighting. They were productive years.

Elegy for an Airman, published in 1940, is dedicated to Stewart's childhood friend Desmond Carter, who was killed in action in 1939. It is Stewart's third book after *Green Lions* and *The White Cry*. The title poem celebrates the boys' idyllic childhoods, the neighbours and the changing seasons, the games of castles and princes, funerals for dead blackbirds. He writes of how he and his friend mapped the land around for what it offered them – mushrooms and blackberries, or the mud in the Ngaere swamp. In the last three stanzas the youthful poet faces the death of his friend with the statement, 'No one should die and not be wept by women'.[19] The verse ends with the assurance, 'The women have wept for you, comrade.' There is the sense of the young Stewart posturing, the poet taking up different stances. Letters from the period imply that he was voting left when his family voted the other way. Hence, perhaps, the use of 'comrade', a term in common use among communists as well as soldiers. But the poet's grief is genuine as he recalls, 'But I who remember/The childhood as far off as China.' Towards the end of the poem we are finally with the lost airman as an adult, and Stewart recalls the time they spent together in London before the war: '... the way we coughed and laughed in a London fog,/ Remember the way of a man, that you sang and were strong.'

There are 20 other poems in the book, all of them nature poems and fairly slight. Were it not for the one use of the word 'Maori' and the reference to the Ngaere swamp, a reader could think Stewart had spent his childhood in England. There are magnolias and pine trees, buttercups and thrushes. Some of the poems may well have been written during his short stay abroad, but it's likely most of the poems are juvenilia. The English trait was of course common in writing by Pākehā in the 1930s when, for most, New Zealand was little Britain. International readers of many books by Pākehā even now could be forgiven for thinking it is still viewed as such.

Elegy for an Airman shows us Stewart finding his feet two years into his new life in Australia. Illustrated by Norman Lindsay with his trademark naked nymphets looking startled among waterlilies, or naked tree-women with leaves for hair and hands arched over a fallen Icarus, the little book is an artefact of the period. The copy I borrow from the Auckland Library has a sticker affixed to the inside cover: 'The Churchill Auction 1942'. This was an initiative of Patrick Lawlor's in Wellington, where 'literary and art enthusiasts' were asked for donations from their collections for 'patriotic auctions in the four centres'. The desired outcome was not only 'to win the war but to strengthen our National culture'.[20]

*

Semmler is keen to discuss Norman Lindsay with Stewart, not just because of Lindsay's enormous influence on a generation of Australasian artists and writers but also because he was one of Stewart's closest friends. At the time of the interview, Lindsay has been dead for three years and it's likely Stewart is still grieving, but in the quiet way we learn later in life, when so many of our friends and relatives have died. It's also possible that he has had time to think about Lindsay in a more objective fashion.

'Well I have my doubts about the influence of Norman Lindsay,' he says, when his name is first mentioned. This would almost have been heresy at this time, but it is not something he says out of bitterness. They were very close, delighting in one another's company. Stewart, Margaret, Lindsay and his wife Rose spent most weekends together for a period of 14 years.

Lindsay and Stewart had met for the first time in 1938, at Lindsay's studio in Bridge Street near Circular Quay, then a kind of mecca for local artists. Many painters and sculptors had studios in the area. Stewart had been taken along by his friend and colleague, the poet Kenneth McKenzie, because he had had an idea for a cartoon Lindsay could draw for the *Bulletin*. It would depict 'Hitler taking a bath in the Mediterranean and annoying Musso'.[21] It was a successful proposition – the cartoon appeared in the *Bulletin* on 12 May 1938.

Stewart recalls that the first thing Lindsay asked him was what other art he practised. For Lindsay, renowned as a visual artist and a novelist, it was normal to excel at two art forms. 'I was a raw recruit from New Zealand with only the slightest knowledge of the fine arts picked up during six months in England,' Stewart wrote later.[22] He told him it was sculpture, a total fabrication.

'I used to be terrified of him,' Stewart tells Semmler. Lindsay 'had a very big reputation in New Zealand, but we would have read him only along with Bertrand Russell and D.H. Lawrence and other – Havelock Ellis – other sort of advance guard of the period'.

Stewart may also have been guarded and a little alarmed in Lindsay's company because it appears that his wife Margaret Coen and Lindsay had been lovers for a period before her marriage, and maintained a great affection for one another once the affair had run its course. Whether Stewart knew about the relationship is unknown. Margaret had a studio not far from Lindsay's, further along Pitt Street. She went there every day to paint but lived at home with her parents in Randwick. The two spent a lot of time together at Lindsay's studio, and Margaret would help him by 'cleaning up after he finished painting and also attended to what I guess you could call "household matters".'[23] Lindsay lived at his studio alone. He was married, but unhappily, and for a number of years he and his wife were informally separated. When the couple reunited for a time and lived together in the

Blue Mountains, the Stewarts left their flat in Crick Avenue, Kings Cross, and moved into Lindsay's studio. They were expecting a baby, and thought it would offer them a little more space. Stewart writes very amusingly of this time in his memoir on Norman Lindsay.

When Semmler presses him on the influence of Lindsay, refusing to accept Stewart's first pronouncement, Stewart demurs, pointing out the major distinction in their work. He sees himself as a nature poet, while Norman Lindsay's work was 'based in love or sex, whatever you like to call it – I was based in nature, and all my poetry starts there, I would think simply because I had a boyhood in the country in New Zealand, and this is where you form your outlook.' Stewart never really wrote about sex. He tells Semmler, 'The wonderful bit in *Tom Jones* – somebody's got one of the girls in the bedroom and Fielding says merely, "As nothing in the least out of the ordinary occurred, I shall not say anything more about it" – so bloody marvellous, you know – there's the whole of Lawrence, "Nothing out of the ordinary occurred", and this to me is the civilised mind.'

Through the years of Stewart's regular visits up to Lindsay's house, Springwood, the two men would often talk about nature. Lindsay loved it as much as he did, but not as actively. He was, as Stewart described him, a 'pedestrian', i.e. not keen on bush walking.[24] Stewart, on the other hand, was happy to spend hours in the bush, examining flora and fauna, and then writing his jewel-like nature poems that seem very often to distil the essence of whatever living being had taken his attention.

'Yeats laid down what's pretty well the perfect rule,' Stewart tells Semmler, 'and this is use the natural words in their natural order ...'

W.B. Yeats was an early hero, and Stewart's poetry, particularly his later, more lighthearted work, shows that this 'perfect rule' is one he adhered to. The poems may today seem old-fashioned, with their emphasis on rhythm and rhyme, but the language is always natural, with no poetic contractions or forced metaphor. Semmler calls it a 'catholic attitude to rhyme', and as a demonstration mentions the pairing of 'put his foot on' and 'mutton'. This is from Stewart's poem 'Reflections at a Parking Meter', a musing on how cars are not only taking over the world but irrevocably changing human nature. The words he refers to are in the verse:

> Some saw the true position quite reversed;
> The car, they said, was just a starter button

That loosed man's own fierce passions at their worst;
Fired with the chance it gave he stamped his foot on
His own accelerator in a burst
That knocked his fellows down like so much mutton.[25]

Another poem Semmler wants to discuss is a piece from Stewart's book *Rutherford* (1962). It is 'Fence', an ironical and humorous observation of suburban life, one of several observational poems that Semmler thinks are 'quite unique in Australian poetry, because they are somewhat odd in a Raleighian sense.'[26] By this he means they are lyrical, incisive and direct, with no obfuscation of meaning.

'Fence' is, it seems, about an actual broken fence that stood between the Stewarts' house and the neighbours, whom he calls the Hogans. The second and fourth verse of this nine-stanza poem read:

For fence is *defensa,* Latin; fence is old Roman
And heaven knows what wild tribes, rude and unknown,
It sprang from first, when man first took shelter with his woman;
Fence is no simple screen where Hogan may prune
His roses decently hidden by paling of lattice
Or sporting together some sunny afternoon
Be noticed with Mrs Hogan at nymphs and satyrs;
...
It is not wise to meet the Hogans in quarrel
They have a lawyer and he will issue writs:
Thieves and trespassers enter at deadly peril,
The brave dog bites the postman where he sits.
Just as they turn the hose against the summer's
Glare on the garden, so in far fiercer jets
Here they unleash the Hogans against all comers.

At the end of the poem, the neighbours nail up the broken fence 'so that Hogans are free to be Hogans/And Stewarts be Stewarts and no one shall watch us scorning ...'[27]

Douglas Stewart gives no indication of what he thinks of Semmler's comparison of his work to Sir Walter Raleigh's. Perhaps he knows that Raleigh ended his colourful, tobacco-championing life at the scaffold. Raleigh was not a man given to sitting alone in garrets writing verse – he was an explorer, spy and innovator – and, by today's terms, also a colonist and murderer. When he was hung, it was to appease the Spanish after a particularly bloody episode in South America.

There are other poets Semmler suggests as influences on Stewart's work, either in individual poems or more widely. He tries and fails to get Stewart's admission on the influence of John Donne or that of South African Roy Campbell, and, closer to home, of Stewart's close friend Kenneth Slessor. This may have irked Stewart a little, though he would have been well aware this is the bread and butter of the literary biographer. Once a connection is found, an influence confessed to, then riches are opened up, and the biographer can spend pages teasing them out.

Semmler is particularly interested in Stewart's ongoing fascination with New Zealand. Earlier biographer Nancy Keesing had seen Stewart's love for the country of his birth as a great strength. She wrote: 'In stressing Stewart's citizenship of two countries, it is also important to make it plain that in becoming a major interpreter of Australian landscape he has not rejected New Zealand: rather ... his continuing preoccupation with two landscapes enhances his interpretation of both.'[28] Semmler asks: 'The poem "Rutherford" – was this some sort of loyal New Zealand orientation, or you know, is it –'. Stewart interrupts: 'No that was by God's grace that he happened to live in my own part of Taranaki really. No, I was interested from that metaphysical period we've been talking about, which led inevitably to a study of evolution and to how much truth there could be in the theory of evolution, and was there not something more behind it which was worked out in the poem called "The Peahen".'

'The Peahen' explores the evolutionary theory that it is the dowdy female of the species that creates the splendid male. She does this by preferring the males that first begin to evolve the colourful feathers, and that as the generations spin around, the male becomes more and more glorious, and more desirable to the henbird, whose kind Stewart dubs 'that most poetical poultry'. This is natural selection. But the poet concludes:

> It could not be sufficient explanation;
> And if it were, what of the peahen's mind
> We'd proved responsible for his creation?
> Instinct or taste in her was so refined

That she who had made him perfect sought no sequel
Must deep within her clearly be his equal,

Her sensibility glorious as his plumage.
Could it be so? That dull, drab miserable bird?
We viewed her with new respect; we paid due homage;
But sometimes thought, whatever part she had played
In bringing that blazing splendour out of the dark,
Some utterly unknown principle was at work.[29]

The biographer is not distracted by the subject of natural selection and presses on with his question about Rutherford: 'It wasn't an act of New Zealand faith in other words.' Stewart replies, 'No not at all – it was just so useful that it all fell into my hands because I could do the New Zealand stuff without trouble.'

Semmler also pushes him on whether 'Worsley Enchanted' from *Sun Orchid* (1962) is part of an Antarctic fixation. Stewart interrupts him, but is seems Semmler is going to assume that this too is part of his subject's New Zealand loyalty.

Worsley was the New Zealand navigator of Shackleton's ill-fated voyage to Antarctica in 1914–16. The ship *Endurance* became frozen into the ice and the crew made a difficult and challenging trip overland, dragging their lifeboats after them. Eventually, under great duress, they sailed to Elephant Island and from there a small group made it to safety at Georgia. Both perilous voyages were navigated by Worsley. The men on Elephant Island were later collected, and all owed their survival to this extraordinary New Zealander. In recent years he has had a revival. He is the subject of Leanne Pooley's feature-length documentary *Shackleton's Captain* (2012), and is the subject of a dramatised mini-series *Shackleton* (2002), which stars Kenneth Branagh in the title role. In the 1920s and 30s, Worsley wrote books about his experiences on the *Endurance*. Stewart's generation, as boys, read these books and regarded Worsley as a hero. Semmler's sense that Stewart's initial curiosity about the story was seeded in his New Zealand childhood was probably right. Certainly the poem is a stellar work, almost filmic in its conception.

From boyhood heroes, acknowledged as such or not, Semmler moves on to humour and tolerance. He points out that the early poems had no humour at all, and that Stewart discovered it as he got older. He quotes Stewart as saying, 'Tolerance, the tolerance of maturity is not necessarily to be preferred to the romantic ardour of youth ...' As this interview is taking place, the so-called 'youth culture' that will come to dominate Western mainstream entertainment for decades is still in its infancy. The legacy of the 1968 Paris riots, of flower power, free love and long-haired hippies is daily more visible. Stewart, with his great curiosity for human behaviour and foibles, and with his ear to the ground for new writing by new writers, will be as aware of it as anybody. One of the last things he will ever say to his daughter Meg will be, 'The world is for you young people now.'[30] Perhaps his statement about tolerance and maturity is further bolstered by an awareness that many writers, composers and artists do their best work before the onset of middle age. At any rate, Stewart agrees with his biographer, and remarks, 'I think if you're going to continue writing at all you've got to become more tolerant and philosophical.'

Semmler returns to the influence of nationality, with regard to the Birdsville Track poems, which are without exception nature poems. He tells Stewart how much he has always admired them, and asks, '[I]s this a sort of gesture of the New Zealander to Australia, now becoming an Australian that you are going to write this sort of classic sequence with an Australian background?' Once again Stewart plays it down, impressing upon Semmler his long interest in his adopted country. 'No, it wasn't like that – I have always had a curiosity about Australia which you see in the first poems, just discovering bits of it.'

Elsewhere, Stewart is less guarded about his sense of displacement. There is a passage in *The Seven Rivers* where he describes coming for the first time to Duckmaloi, a place he would visit many times to fish. '[T]he first time I saw the place it gave me the horrors. The trouble was, I was a newcomer: doubly a newcomer, for I had not been long in Australia, and I had never before stayed at the guest house from which we fished. It takes a few years to learn to cherish the more formidable peculiarities of Australia; and it is a truly terrible experience to arrive for the first time at any guesthouse, even so kindly an abode as was the Richards.'[31] A little further on he writes about how, after some rain in the 'baked landscape, we saw, simultaneously, three snakes quietly weaving their way across our track. It was good weather for hunting frogs, I suppose; but they looked very much as if they were hunting fishermen. To a newcomer from New Zealand, these were quite an appalling sight.'[32]

The Seven Rivers has become a kind of classic in Australia, and could well herald a revival in Australian nature writing of the kind that is taking place around the world.

Fire on the Snow, Stewart's most famous verse play, one that garnered awards and was broadcast in many countries, is about Scott's famous expedition to the South Pole. Generations of Australian school children studied it, and a phrase from it became part of the lexicon in the way that few phrases from literature do today. Stewart had been told that when young lifesavers at the Sydney beaches go overboard from their surfboats, it is customary for them to say, 'I am just going outside ... I may be some time' – a line attributed to the doomed Captain Oates. Stewart maintains that he finds this appropriation 'a curious and unnerving thought'.[33] It must also have made his heart swell with pride.

The play had come to the attention of Leslie Rees, assistant director at the ABC, after he saw an excerpt in the *Bulletin*. He contacted Stewart, then 28 years old and working for the magazine, who told Rees he had 'no thought of having the work produced', and that his influences were Auden's 'The Ascent of F6' and T.S. Eliot's *Murder in the Cathedral*, which he may have heard broadcast as early as 1935. Rees championed the play, even though there was some debate as to whether 'a play by a New Zealand writer about Englishmen in Antarctica was truly Australian'.[34]

Despite the international success of *Fire on the Snow*, Semmler tells Stewart his favourite play is *The Golden Lover*. He asks him, 'Did you know Maoris well when you were a boy, did you get to know the Maori people at all, or did this come from reading or from firsthand association – I'd be interested to know something about that as a sort of background.'

Stewart replies, 'Well it is my own favourite play too – I think it's got more poetry and more laughter than any of the others, it's more natural to myself. And actually I loved writing it – which I usually don't.'

This sentiment resonates with one of Dorothy Parker's most quoted aphorisms about the writer's common experience of hating the process of writing but loving having written. Meg Stewart, writing as her mother, recalled, 'It wasn't the writing that took so much out of him, but the preparation, the intense effort of working it up beforehand, exhausted him. I don't know how he did it. Such concentration.'[35]

It is worth quoting at length from the tape transcripts on the subject of *The Golden Lover* because Stewart seems at once at ease and discomfited by Semmler's questioning him about his familiarity with kaupapa Māori:

Stewart: I did know the Maoris fairly well, but not en masse – they were not common and not frequent around Taranaki when I was there, but you saw them, they were the natural part of your life, just as you see migrants today, you saw Maoris then, they used to come round with kit bags selling white-bait at the door –

Semmler: – but your play seems to show a great knowledge about their mores, their customs, and their traditions and their folklore and so on.

Stewart: Well you grow up with all this in your bones, really. The Maori war, a lot of it, the Taranaki war, had been fought over ground where I went to school, and although I wasn't interested in those days in the history, you soaked it in. We had Maori boys at school with us and I got quite friendly with them, and when I was working on newspapers I had quite a bit to do with somebody who was about to start another Maori war – we had some amusing nights going out to report these dramatic things and I got friendly at that time with educated Maoris who were providing me with information for the paper and then I did go and live with them for only a short while, perhaps two or three weeks or a month or something, in North Auckland when I was carrying a swag up there for some ungodly reason. And a lot of the feeling I got from them, from living with these people, got into the play. But it's just a general feeling for New Zealand, the Maoris were part of the tradition, and from reading – I don't think I took Maoris and their culture up consciously in those days, but I'd been to Rotorua – everybody made a pilgrimage to Rotorua – they had dances and songs and Hakas, and you'd pick up something of their legend. Matter of fact when I wrote the play I was reading Cowan's fairy folk tales of New Zealand for the story of Hinemoa and Tutanekai which is an entirely different legend, much better known than the one I used ... And I just dropped onto this other one and, well it hit me like a blinding light, it was just the one I was ready to write.

If we are to cast a contemporary light on this, as opposed to Stewart's blinding light, we could truly get our collective knickers in a knot. Earlier I discussed Ruth Park's *The Witch's Thorn*, which suffers from the incipient and highly damaging racism of the time. Top-ranking New Zealand writers of that period had no cultural anxieties regarding the creation of Māori characters. In contemporary New Zealand, non-Māori writers are discouraged from writing about Māori. This is understandable, given the sometimes painful errors made by Pākehā writers, but it has resulted in the peculiar phenomenon of a raft of books over a period of decades that completely ignore the very presence of Māori. If there were to be a worldwide apocalypse and all that is left for future readers are literary works from the late twentieth-/early twenty-first century New Zealand, survivors could suspect us of an extreme, institutionalised racism – the opposite, in fact, of what we are trying to do.

In the interview, Semmler asks Stewart about the line from *The Golden Lover*, 'He is full of his importance and too many eels', and goes on to ask: 'Is this typical of the Maori, this sort of suddenly bringing things back to earth with a very prosaic sort of utterance you know, from flights of poetry down to the – well from the gor blimey to the ridiculous sort of thing?'

Stewart: Yes I think that would be right – they are people very like the Irish, they're an eloquent people ... they are a humorous, laughter loving people and like the Irish, capable of very quick changes of mood.

Semmler: ... There's a line where it says 'The dogs came to lick my shame with their tongues' – do the Maoris talk in images like this – is this their way of talking?

Stewart: I think they would have in Maori, I don't – never heard them today speak in, except in speeches – no, they just talk the most commonplace talk as far as I know.

And there we have it, the 'as far as I know'. In his finished biography, Semmler writes that Stewart 'had grown up with the customs and traditions of the Maoris well embedded in his consciousness'.[36] He is perhaps overstating the case.

I once heard the much-loved British writer David Lodge say that a novelist only needs to know enough about a subject to convince the reader that he/she is an expert. It's a matter of magic, of sleight of hand, of the right details put in the right places so that the narrative is not bogged down with unnecessary information, nor flying around with no roots in reality. How much Stewart knew of Māori culture before he went to live in Australia is debatable, but what he would have learned of speech patterns and idiom he would have learned directly from Māori friends and associates in Taranaki rather than from books.

His confidence in tackling Māori subjects may have been further bolstered by his friend, poet R.D. FitzGerald, who wrote to him from Rotorua when holidaying there with his young family in 1936:

> ... what amazed me was the tolerance of you New Zealanders and your lack of colour consciousness. I've no colour prejudices myself worth talking of, but I'm so used to them in other people that it almost shocks me to see white girls walking up the street in animated conversation with Maori girls or half-caste men. And when I walk along the road the Maori does not step out of the way of a white man; he expects me to step aside if anything. If they deserve, and I gather they do, this status, good luck to them ...[37]

Such sentiments were often expressed by Australians of the time. Even in the mid-1980s, when I lived in Australia, I would often find myself in conversations with Australians who were unhappy with the 'Aboriginal situation' and who would tell me New Zealanders were 'so lucky with the Maoris'. For FitzGerald, it was not only that appalling treatment of indigenous Australians that would have been on his mind, but the White Australia Policy which didn't come to an end until after World War II. New Zealanders are sometimes in danger of being unnecessarily smug during conversations of this kind. One glance at our current prison population, homelessness and substance abuse problems tells us that our 'colour prejudices' are alive and well.

*

The Golden Lover was Stewart's favourite of his dramatic works, equal with *Shipwreck*, which he completed in 1945. It is certainly one of his most successful, not only in the medium for which it was written but also as a live stage performance. In 1942 it won a national competition held by the ABC for a verse play, a genre that has all but died out. Perhaps the most recent attempt at a dramatic verse work of comparable exposure is British filmmaker Sally Potter's 2004 film *Yes*, which is entirely written in iambic pentameter. Viewers were either bored and infuriated, or totally captivated, which is a fairly predictable polarised response to the conceit and high artifice of a screenplay in verse.

A few years before Semmler's interview with Stewart, *The Golden Lover* was produced as a stage play across the Tasman. Among Stewart's papers in the Mitchell Library is a copy of *ACT*, a magazine published by Wellington's Downstage Theatre Society. It is the April–June edition of 1967 and cost 2/6. Playwright Bruce Mason is the editor and, it appears, writes most of the reviews. On the front cover is a captioned picture of Timoti te Heu Heu (sic) as Tiki and Shirley Duke as Tawhai, starring in the Maori Theatre Trust production that opened at Downstage, Wellington, on 3 April that year. Other cast members include Don Selwyn as 'a fine authoritative koro', Kuki Kaa, Thelma Grabmaier, Harata Solomon, Sue Hansen, Ada Rangiaho, Ray Henwood and Bob Hirini.

It is a phenomenal line-up. The names that leap out here are those of Don Selwyn, one of the most recognisable for mid-late century television audiences, starring in drama and directing film; and Timoti Te Heuheu, revered Ngāti Tūwharetoa leader and statesman. Harata Solomon was a well-known actress, singer, performer and cultural leader. Wi Kuki Kaa's career on stage and film spanned 30 years and included roles in Geoff Murphy's film *Utu* and Vincent Ward's *River Queen*. Welshman Ray Henwood, we may safely assume, played the golden lover himself, the patu paiarehe Whana, who tries to steal beautiful Tawhai away from her earthly (and, we are given to understand, fat and lazy) husband Ruarangi.

Mason writes:

> The problem is idiom. How to write a lyric comedy based on Maori legend, unable to use the language in which it originated, except for the odd chant, greeting or moan of distress? The lyric impulse of English has not been capable of quite this artless freshness since it was Anglo Saxon; how to

avoid an artificially poetic jargon? ... In 'The Golden Lover' written ... for radio, and now twenty years old, Douglas Stewart opts for a mixture of fern and bracken, striking an idiom somewhere between 'The Song of Solomon' and Alfred Domett's 'Ranolf and Amohia', redeemed by wit, some crisp comedy and appropriately earthy imagery ...

I hope this doesn't suggest that at Downstage, the play was anything but a fine success. It was and delighted the audience though I suspect that we all felt it to be half an hour too long. But Richard Campion has shown the town for the second time in a few weeks what he can do with a largely inexperienced Maori cast ... so an overlengthy but rewarding evening, suggesting new paths for New Zealand drama. For Richard Campion, another huia feather in his cap.

Alfred Domett was briefly the fourth New Zealand premier, a youthful friend of Robert Browning and a poet himself. His *Ranolf and Amohia, a South Sea Day Dream* was first published in 1872, following several earlier slim volumes of poetry. Encyclopaedia Britannica says of Domett that his 'idealization of the Maori in his writings contrasts with his support of the punitive control of Maori land'.[38] His reputation was not quite so damaged, or truthful, at the time Mason made the comparison. In Mason's view, Stewart's play fitted into an emerging subgenre of Pākehā telling Māori stories, among which Alfred Hill's Māori opera *Tapu* (1902) and famous cantata 'Hinemoa' left a lasting legacy. *Tapu* was produced in Sydney, complete with geysers and white cast in 'brown face'.

Mason neglects to mention that 'traditional Maori food' was served before the Downstage performance, most likely at the initiative of the Māori cast.[39] Not only would this help the audience to understand the most intrinsic tenet of Māori welcome, it would also have helped them enter the world conjured by the possibly homesick 29-year-old playwright burning the midnight oil in his Kings Cross flat.

*

I borrow a volume of Stewart's plays from the library. It has a handsome, restrained cover in yellowing white with a grey tile-like border. *Four Plays* contains *The Fire on the Snow*, *The Golden Lover*, *Ned Kelly* and *Shipwreck*, and was published in 1958. The copy was issued seven times from December 1958 to March 1959, the stamps filling half of one of the three columns on the glued-on due-date slip. After that, interest appears to have waned, certainly until the stamping system was abandoned and the computer system took over. Was it never borrowed again until I asked for it to be retrieved from the gulag reaches of the stacks? Leafed into the pages is a 2015 checkout item summary for a borrower with a Māori name. The name seems familiar – I look him up – and there, so is his face. He is an Auckland actor, director and writer, and I have seen him on stage. On the same day he borrowed another book – a volume of five plays by Māori playwrights. The slip marks a page about halfway through *The Golden Lover*. He might have given up on it, or read to the end. New Zealanders of his generation were taught to look for 'key words' in any text, an ill-advised idea possibly related to the fashion of moving away from linear narrative. The key words I imagine snagging his eye are, unfortunately, 'snoring', 'lazy', 'fat', 'smell' and 'shark oil'.

The play begins with the Announcer naming the source of the legend as James Cowan's *Faery Folk Tales of the Maori*, and toys with the idea that patu paiarehe really did exist 'as a fair-skinned red-haired people of different origin from the Maoris ... There are Maoris to-day who are proud of patu paiarehe blood in their veins, and who have light complexions and auburn hair to prove it.'[40]

Until relatively recently there were commonly accepted ideas that white-skinned people co-existed with Māori before British colonisation. Those theories have been rightfully tossed aside, along with even more far-fetched ideas that Māori originated in South America, India and even Greece. In 1947 Norwegian Thor Heyerdahl and his crew famously sailed across the Pacific in a papyrus raft, the *Kon Tiki*, in an attempt to prove that the Pacific was settled in successive migrations from Peru. The expedition caught the public imagination, especially in New Zealand. This was, after all, a period in which Māori were categorised in the national census as 'Caucasian'.

After the Announcer has set the scene, beautiful Tawhai rouses her husband, who is snoring. 'Wake volcano!'[41] Already Tawhai has both cooked and caught the breakfast, having risen at dawn. She asks him, talking about herself in the third person, 'I am a good wife? You are pleased with Tawhai?', before going on to tell him how in the early-morning mist she had seen a man of the faery people.[42] She explains how frightened she was, and Ruarangi chastises her for disturbing his breakfast. He is frightened by her story too: the eel he has eaten 'squirms and bites' inside his stomach.[43] They squabble, accusing one another of laziness, of eating too fast, being too fat, and of jealousy. Not only does Tawhai have an admirer from the world of 'ghosts, monsters and demons' but she has been seen keeping company with the warrior Tiki, who is younger and slimmer than Ruarangi.

In the second scene we meet Wera, Tawhai's mother, and her close friend Koura, who saw Tawhai with the patu paiahere. Wera goes looking for her daughter and finds her asleep in the fern. Koura and Tawhai talk about the faery, with red hair and gold skin, who is as tall as a tōtara tree. As the play progresses there is a little tension created by Ruarangi and Tawhai's father attacking Tiki as the reason for Tawhai's frequent absences from her whare. In truth she is spending time with Whana, the patu paiarehe, and in time-honoured fairy-tale style she is at first frightened of him and then wildly in love. In Stewart's version of the story, Whana is overlaid with the European idea of the incubus. Whana tells Tawhai:

> You have dreamed about me. All your life you have dreamed.
> I know you, Tawhai. You have had lovers, a husband,
> And lovers and a husband they were not to be despised;
> But always beyond them, Tawhai, there was a dream.
> You lay, I know you have lain, with your lover in the bracken,
> You have lain with your husband in the bed of fern in the whare,
> But who did you lie with in dreams? With your golden lover![44]

Tawhai's people try to make her rub herself with shark oil in order to put off her handsome suitor. Tawhai refuses, saying she is bewitched already, and runs away back to Whana. There are jokes about Ruarangi threatening to eat Tawhai's father's dog, and jokes at Ruarangi's expense because he is fat and hopeless with the axe, which is presumably a mere or taiaha. The play ends, as the legend does, with Tawhai giving up her lover and returning properly to her husband. There are variants in the means by which this comes about, but the Announcer has told us at the very beginning that the play is 'a free interpretation' of the original story as related by Cowan.

*

Douglas Stewart at his desk at home in St Ives, 1970s.
Michael Elton photographer, Meg Stewart collection

On that Boxing Day afternoon in 1972, Semmler mentions that *The Golden Lover* is having a bit of a run with Māori players in New Zealand. Stewart replies:

> Yes I've been terribly pleased about that. There are a couple of productions in the last two or three years, I think there's a Maori Theatre Trust over there and they operate sometimes with white groups, there might be one or two white actors perhaps – I think one was an all Maori cast and it had a reasonable press, was I think pretty good, it was essentially, you know, a small production, but it seemed to be the start of something I'd like to see carry on.

Semmler asks if there is a lack of indigenous material of the type that Māori could use to develop traditions in the theatre.

Stewart: I have been told by the last people that put it on that this was the only play they could find that expressed the spirit and feeling of the Maoris. It doesn't mean it's the only good thing that's been written about the Maoris, there's tons of very good short stories and novels but I don't think much has gone into plays as far as I know.

There is also, although Stewart doesn't mention it, emerging writing *by* Māori, as opposed to *about* them. He is aware, perhaps, of the publication of Witi Ihimaera's first collection of short stories, *Pounamu, Pounamu*, this very year. Ihimaera's *Tangi*, the first novel ever published by a Māori writer, will be published the following year, in 1973. He does not know that he was himself one of Ihimaera's main inspirations to become a writer, after reading the short story *The Whare* as a boy.

When Semmler asks Stewart about his other New Zealand-inspired play, the unpublished 'An Earthquake Shakes the Land', about the land wars of the 1860s, Stewart replies that he never cared very much for it. 'There's quite a good soliloquy MacDonald [the central character] makes to his shadow in it, I think. I think the Maoris are a bit statuesque in it; and it was a conscious attempt to analyse war which is too big a subject to analyse anyhow.'

Semmler: Is there a sort of thing for the Maoris in it, an indignation at the way the Maoris are treated?

Stewart: Yes there would have been but I don't think I set out to do that, it was an attempt to analyse war, it was written during the war, I think or just after it, but I think it's a bit too self-conscious and the Maoris don't come alive as people.

Written after *The Golden Lover*, 'An Earthquake Shakes the Land' was produced by the ABC in 1944. A copy of the manuscript is held in the State Library of New South Wales, re-titled 'Sunset in the Waikato'. As in *The Golden Lover*, there is an attempt to capture a 'Māori' sense of humour. It is one thing for a Māori writer to make jokes at the expense of Māori characters, quite another for a Pākehā to do it. The first joke is on the first page and plays on the fact that the visiting Māori have eaten not only minor chief Kimo's pigs but are starting on the matting of the whare. This is not just unlikely; it is also highly offensive to Māori. Kimo's first speech of any length is not humorous, but full of angst and despair. He is referring to land he sold to MacDonald, a Scots settler trying to wrest a farm from the bush on land he has procured from Kimo.

> KIMO: You gave me tobacco, and I have smoked the tobacco;
> You gave me rum, and I drank too much and was sick;
> You gave me flour, and I have eaten the flour,
> You gave me clothes, and now they are all holes;
> You gave me blankets and now they have worn so thin
> That even the fleas are cold. I gave you the land,
> And the land is still there; nobody eats the land,
> Nobody smokes it or drinks it, it doesn't wear out,
> It stands where it is for ever. I was a fool.
> You have the land, and all I have left of the price
> Is the tomahawk and the gun.[45]

MacDonald has a Māori wife, Ngaere, and a baby. We are shown MacDonald stopping Ngaere from drinking whiskey, not because it's bad for her, but because it's a man's drink. MacDonald is dour and hard-working, a kind of everyman settler, not based on any individual. He believes the wars have devastated the Waikato, and thinks of his unloved baby as a 'piccaninny'.

When Ngaere is questioned about her child, she answers:

He is my pakeha baby, MacDonald's baby.
The Maoris are finished. They talk and talk at their meetings,
But they all died years ago. New Zealand belongs
To the white man now. I belong to a white man.
And you, little sleepy, New Zealand belongs to you.
You will live in this house, you will have MacDonald's farm,
It is all for you, these hours and years that he works,
Sunrise to sunset, making a farm for his baby.

Pākehā writers of the 1940s tended to sympathise with the pioneering classes and gave characters such as Ngaere a sense of total defeat. After MacDonald tries to trade his wife and child in return for keeping his land, Ngaere takes up with Kimo, whom she has always loved.

A warrior called Rewi advises Kimo to get MacDonald off the land and take it back for his tribe. MacDonald has other ideas:

I'll never go.
I made this farm. Made it with my hands and my sweat.
I've sunk my life in it. I've grown a part of myself
In every pine and fruit-tree I've planted.
I've ploughed a part of myself into the ground
Whenever I've turned a furrow. My blood's in the grass.
The wheat grows out of my body. Would I leave all that
Because a few savages dance a dance in the night?

In the background, off stage as it were, the building of the Great South Road is going ahead, and Kimo is only too well aware that it will bring soldiers from Auckland. Among the chiefs, Rewi (Ngāti Maniapoto) wants to fight, Tamihana (Waikato) and Te Wherowhero (the future Māori king) do not. They are persuaded to go to war by MacDonald coming to tell them that Governor Browne is to be replaced by Governor Grey: 'The man of peace, the friend of your people.' Kimo is present when Grey meets Tamihana. In Rewi's absence, Kimo tells Grey, 'Next time you come to the Waikato, bring the soldiers.'

As the war begins, Rewi sends Kimo to collect Ngaere and the child and bring them back to the tribe. This is when MacDonald gives his soliloquy, which reads, in part:

Night. And a man alone. And the times bad.
A lamp and a bottle and a shadow. Shadow my lad,
Will you have a drink with me, Shadow? Drink with MacDonald,
For he drinks alone this night.

The next day he goes to the village with his gun to try to reason with the chiefs, but is shot by Māori warriors. It is Kimo who kills him, presumably because MacDonald is the one Pākehā who has damaged him more than any other.

To create crowd scenes, the play uses the convention of VOICE ONE, VOICE TWO, etc. In the final scene, we hear from soldiers with accents hailing from various parts of the United Kingdom. A Scottish accent has the last word, which may be read as an attempt to justify the war.

... Those brown gigantic men towering on the hill –
The sun stood here! The sun came out of the sky
And stood for three days on Orakau. Now it is dark,
No light, no laughter, no war-song, only the dead.
Yet something remains. The dark earth glowing, glowing!
Men will come here and fill their hands and their hearts
With light forever. They have made this hill a sunset.
(Haka, distant, fading)

No wonder Stewart had mixed feelings about this play, but there is something to admire in his attempt to dramatise the land wars at a time when few New Zealanders knew about the conflict, let alone based literary or artistic works on it. He was in some respects well ahead of his time in that he valued our stories over and above those he could have written centred further afield.

*

One of the final questions Semmler asks is about Stewart's love of Australian and New Zealand landscapes and animals. He says, 'There is to me a sort of simple and loveable way in which you write about these rivers and the countryside and so on, and I suppose it's – do you ever get a pulling apart, a dichotomy thing between your love for the Australian countryside and your memories of the New Zealand countryside, or do the things coalesce in your thinking and your love of the countryside generally?'

Stewart answers, 'I don't think I have any nostalgia at all for New Zealand now – it seems like, you know, a fairy tale to me it's so long since I lived there, and when I go back it all seems like something you dreamed … after a few years, you know I used to think it took about 10 years to get used to Australia and after that I think you just become Australian.'

Where is Margaret as the interview finishes? Perhaps she is in her studio painting, or perhaps she is outside. A poem that displays not only Stewart's impressive gift as a poet but also his great love for his wife describes her coming in from the garden. After Margaret's death, Meg has the poem etched on her mother's gravestone.

> My wife, my life, my almost obligatory love
> Heaven forbid that I should seem your slave,
> But perhaps I should say I saw you once in the garden
> Rounding your arms to hold a most delicate burden
> Of violets and lemons, fruits of the winter earth,
> Violets and lemons, and as you came up the path –
> Dark hair, blue eyes, some dress that has got me beaten –
> Noting no doubt as a painter their colour and shape
> And bowing your face to the fragrance, the sweet and the sharp,
> You were lit with delight that I have never forgotten.[46]

When the interview is finished, Semmler goes home with the tapes. He works away on his book, and after many trials and tribulations the biography is published by Twayne in 1974.

In September 1975 Douglas Stewart writes to Semmler: 'The book is certainly getting a wonderful run. In fact, if Twayne will send out review copies, it might be worth trying to continue the run in New Zealand. I get attacked a good deal over there, except for *The Seven Rivers*, but that doesn't trouble me.'[47]

I think it did trouble him, but not overly, not enough for him to lose sleep or fall into a depression. Douglas Stewart was far too level-headed for that. He did know, however, as many of us have learned since, that it is a rare artist or writer who produces work that straddles the Tasman.

In 1982, reviewing *Springtime in Taranaki*, historian Michael King wrote:

Douglas Stewart is one of New Zealand's forgotten literary pioneers. Though he has lived in Australia for more than 40 years, he was one of a small group of authors who set in motion a revolution in New Zealand writing in the 1930s. His New Zealand work included poetry, short stories and at least one play, one of the first New Zealand ones broadcast on radio.[48]

That could be the last word on Douglas Stewart. His close friendship with and/or support of writers like Eve Langley, Rosemary Dobson, Ruth Park, David Campbell, Gloria Rawlinson, Kenneth Slessor, R.D. FitzGerald, Judith Wright, Frances Webb, Mary Gilmore, A.D. Hope, Thomas Keneally and Christina Stead, to name only a few, was instrumental in creating twentieth-century literatures on both sides of the Tasman. However, I think the last word belongs to Stewart himself. In an interview with Geraldine O'Brien in 1984, a year before his death, he talked about the long three years it had taken for his autobiography to find a publisher.

'It was a comedy, really,' said Stewart, when asked about this. 'You see publishers believe Australians won't read about New Zealand and in New Zealand I'm not known or else wrongly thought an Australian!'[49]

A Comedy Really …

t was about 9.30 on the morning of 1 November 2014, a Saturday, on the road out of Whitecliff, that I killed an emu with a rented Kia. It was a fairly new Kia, a car designed in Korea for driving in cities and urban environments. It was not a sensible car to be driving on the road from Whitecliff, which is bitumen, but narrow, surrounded on all sides by low vegetation subscribing to desert. The flat, gently undulating land stretches for miles and miles and miles in every direction. On that road, with my husband Tim beside me, I totalled an emu. The bird smashed up against the windscreen, a pressing of brown and gold feathers and wildly scrambling talonous legs, then fell away. It gathered itself enough to run to the roadside, where it collapsed on its back, its three-toed feet and long powerful legs cycling in the air. The snake-like neck convulsed, the head banged up and down a few times. It was trying to stand, trying to get away, trying to survive – but we could see that it was, plainly, fucked. As fucked as the car which was steaming a long white plume. When we got out to have a look, we could see the bonnet was buckled. But who cared. Far worse was the spectacle of the giant bird trying to make its body obey its brain, convulsing as if it was having fits.

Get up. Run away.

'We can't leave it like that,' said Tim. He went to find a heavy stick.

I lit a cigarette and cried. I prayed for forgiveness. I couldn't believe I had killed an animal of such magnitude and beauty. I walked away so that I didn't have to watch Tim bash the emu on the head to put it out of its misery. I wondered if he'd gone mad, his slight figure lifting the stick above his head and bringing it down with all his strength. It was so out of character for him to do anything so brutal. And it was all my fault. I shouldn't have been doing 80k. I should have seen the emus before they ran across the road. I knew the animals were about. It was a cool spring morning. They hadn't yet sought the shade. We'd already seen wallabies around, and reduced our speed. It wasn't like the emus were hiding behind trees before they ran out. There weren't any to hide behind.

*

We were on holiday, which in our lives is a rarity. If we make a trip it's usually to Australia, most often solo, usually to spend time with friends or family, sometimes for work. This time we were having a proper holiday in Broken Hill, the nearest city to Whitecliff, which lies pretty much on the border of Victoria and New South Wales.

Broken Hill had always seemed to me a romantic name, a name that spoke of the heart of Australia, of heat and dust, industry and mining, the emergence of the labour movement that would inspire and govern so much of Australian politics in the twentieth century. It also spoke of camels, which you could ride! Riding a camel, a ship of the desert, swaying across the sandy bed of an ancient ocean, descendants of long-ago Afghan cameleers carrying cargo and working on the first railways. Broken Hill was the mural-mad hotel in which *Priscilla Queen of the Desert* was shot, surrounded by opal fiends with their molehills, desperate farmers, salt pans, and the world's longest dingo fence. My friend Rosie Scott and I had planned a trip there when I was six months' pregnant, but abandoned the idea in the final analysis: 13-hour train trips there and back while up the duff didn't seem like a good idea. That was in 1988.

Twenty-six years later I finally get here. It's a broken town. House after house is boarded up, abandoned. School rolls are dropping, some are threatened with closure. It's dusty and hot and poor, and knobs' hill barely qualifies as knobbish. People are leaving in their droves. Things have been tough since February 2009 when, without preamble, investor Zhonglin

Lingnan became the major shareholder in Perilya, the company that has owned the mine since 2002. Overnight, people lost their jobs. Depending on who you're listening to, the mine has only got 10 years left in it; or there are riches beyond compare to dig up, lead, zinc, and iron ore just waiting for discovery. In the year of our visit, the mine will lose $30 million. The Chinese company is having to pitch in to keep it afloat, as well it should, since it has the most chance of benefit from its success.

There are deep awnings over the main street; people are friendly and chatty. A giant glinting slagheap rises behind the Palace Hotel, a mountain 120 years in the making, monument to the dying mine. The last time it rained here was in 2012 and before that 2008. The drinking water stinks. In the chemist, buying sunblock, the pharmacist recognises my accent. He's a Pom. He says he and his wife would like to come to New Zealand because we have rain. He doesn't like the heat.

When I totalled the emu we were on our way back to Broken Hill from a couple of nights in Whitecliff, three hours away. We had slept in an underground hotel and met some of the locals. Most were diggers apart from the publican and the staff at the cave hotel and store. One sad old bloke was a farmer. The road into Whitecliff borders his farm and I hadn't seen a solitary beast. When I commented on that, he deduced that I was a New Zealander and therefore didn't know what I was talking about. There are cows, he explained, but a long way apart from one another, looking for food.

In much the same way the cattle hope for food, the diggers are looking for 'colour', giving opals the same name that pioneer goldminers used for gold. It's the same gripping fever. One man lives lonely in his cave while wife and kids live in an apartment on the Gold Coast. Another miner found a wife on an internet dating site and lives happily in his underground home with her and their four children.

In the scruffy pub with sagging veranda we met a digger who'd been married twice, each time to a gambler, and once saved $30,000. While he was underground the second wife was up top, supposedly in the pub selling opals to the tourists but instead playing the pokies until all his savings were gone. 'One gambler in the family,' he kept saying, 'upsets the whole apple cart.' He lived in one of the houses clustered on a southwest-facing hill with glowing late-afternoon windows meshed with fine dust.

Outside the pub there were dead and dying white locusts, great drifts of them on the dusty road and clogging the grilles of the four-wheel-drives. They were long legged and gauzy winged and in their millions: an excess of nature, a seemingly meaningless genocide or suicide. It was eerily beautiful, like bridal petals, but frightening in its magnitude. As far as the eye could see in one direction were fallen clouds of locusts. It seemed they'd come from the south.

It's the curse of our time that most of us, when observing any kind of die-off, will fret and worry that it is caused by climate change, or agricultural chemicals, or some new terrifying change in the balance of the world. The locals barely commented on the dying insects. It seemed almost as if it was poor form to even acknowledge them.

I sat outside and smoked with the old man whose ex-wives gambled away his savings. There was no one about. Away on the diggings a solitary big red kangaroo lolloped along through the rubble, where the cranes and lances poked up their bony elbows from the molehills and dust floated in the still, cooling air. My mate was kind, gruff, sad. He was going home to cook his dinner in a microwave, which he was adamant used as much electricity as a conventional oven. 'Don't be fooled, love,' he told me. 'But you don't have it on for as long,' I said. It seemed as if he thought he did, and he wouldn't be dissuaded. I had visions of his lonely dinners going round and round and round, nuked for hours.

Suddenly he started talking about the Māori people he had known. Australians will do this to let you know that they've worked out you're a New Zealander. It seemed there had long ago been a Māori woman working on the diggings with her Australian partner. One day in the general store, which is also the tearooms and the post office, she was trying to send a money order through to New Zealand and the postmistress couldn't understand the place names she was saying.

'Turned the air blue. Boy, did she lose it. C words and all. Never seen such fury in a woman.' He chuckled admiringly.

In another life he'd been a shearer and worked with Māori women in the shearing sheds. 'Best wool classers there are,' he said, 'best in the world. And work! They know how to work.' He'd never been to New Zealand, never been out of Australia. He got in his battered ute and drove the two blocks home.

*

When I hit the emu we were about 10 minutes out of Whitecliff in our rented tin-can city car on the road back towards Broken Hill, where we had been staying earlier in the week. We were talking about something – I have no recollection of what – when Tim suddenly yelled, 'Emus!' Three of them were crossing the road in front of us, pedalling the air and weaving their necks. I swerved wildly – missed the first, missed the second, hit the third. At the road edge the victim's fellow travellers paused for a moment and looked back as if they were wondering what had happened. They glanced, perplexed, at their mate rolling away from the car, and then gambolled away from the danger across the tundra.

The car was hissing and boiling, the bonnet caved in. After the emu was dead and we got back in, it wouldn't start. Eventually Tim got it limping along at around 30 kilometres per hour. Our phones had no coverage, and the nearest town, Wilcannia, was 80 kilometres away. Tim was mad with me for hitting the emu. I was mad with myself. I cried. He went silent, mad at himself for not killing the poor bastard with his first blow. Mad at the prospect of the thousands of dollars this was going to cost us. We hadn't got insurance. We'd rented a stupid car. We crawled on, not speaking. It got hot, the temperature tipping over 35.

At a T junction the Whitecliff Road joins Barrier Highway, the road that'll take you all the way from Adelaide to the middle of New South Wales. This is where the car stopped altogether, coaxed on to the edge by a signpost. Broken Hill lay to the right, nearly 200 kilometres south. Wilcannia was to the north. Tim got out and walked towards the town, his nippy stride and mop of silver hair disappearing out of sight, while I stayed with the car.

I was busting to go to the loo. Road trains with rigs as big as two-storey buildings roared by so close and so fast the car shuddered in the updraft. I waited. I looked out the window at the tussock and scrub, the red earth. I had killed an emu. If I had been going any faster I could also have killed Tim and me. On our way out from Broken Hill the road had been littered with carnage – emus, wallabies, kangaroos. Cars hit them all the time, four-wheel-drives fitted with roo-bars and high off the ground, and even they sometimes came to grief. I was so busting that I opened both the car doors on the passenger side and contemplated having a pee on the ground between them. There was nothing higher than my knee for a radius of hundreds of miles and I was in full view of the road.

An hour or so later a cop pulled up in a four-wheel-drive bristling with aerials and told me my husband was waiting for me in Wilcannia and that he'd rung a tow truck. Bladder burning, I climbed in.

Tim was sitting in Wilcannia's greasy-spoon, which marvellously had a Ladies. It was a three-hour wait for the towie to come from Broken Hill.

Wilcannia is the Australian equivalent of Stewart's Eltham, boarded up, declining and poor. Grand sandstone buildings stand disused; the bank, storehouses, warehouses, the courthouse all empty and window-less. On the banks of the Darling River, the town was once a stopping place for both boat and vehicle but now most just pass on through. The river is impassable, ravaged by pollution, and low and dank from years of drought. The town has a reputation for having an 'Aboriginal problem' with attendant street and domestic violence. It also has a history of Aboriginal protest.

Unaware of all of this, I went for an amble around the town while Tim read the paper. On the deserted main street group of kids and young teen-agers surrounded me, a couple of them asking for cigarettes. I declined, telling them I didn't want to get into trouble with their mothers. One them said he would hit me, I said he wouldn't, and we all ended up sitting on a low wall while they explained who was related to who, and how. It was very complex. They were full of laughter and jokes; some of them wanted to leave Wilcannia when they grew up and some of them didn't. Some of them came back into the shop with me, clutching pocket money to buy lollies and chips.

An Adelaide family had arrived in their Winnebago and were having hamburgers. They were a couple about our age with a family of foster chil-dren, all handicapped. Two boys and a girl, who was the youngest. She was Aboriginal and unable to talk or walk, and would later be fed in the van by a tube in her stomach. The boys were white Australian, and one of them had been kept in a dark room by his mother for the first four years of his life, never spoken to, neglected and starved. He was severely autistic as a result. The fostering couple were saintlike, kind and down to earth. Their own children were grown up and they were on their way to the Gold Coast for a daughter's wedding. The children liked travelling, and the boys especially liked the fast food available at every stop. The motion of the van and the close sleeping quarters were calming to them.

Not long after the family left, the towie arrived. He had already picked up the crumpled car. At the sight of it I wept again like a big booby. Poor emu!

'Oh don't worry about that, love,' said the towie, 'I kill millions of them. They go boof into the front of the truck and come out the back like a busted feather pillow.'

We sat three abreast across the front of the truck for the three-hour drive back to Broken Hill. The towie ate a sandwich while he drove with one hand. He told us how he had passed a cyclist on his way to collect us, and how he thought the guy was insane to be riding the distances on this road and in this heat. He drank a tin of Coke and chewed gum. He said he'd stop in an hour or so for a break.

'That emu you killed,' he said conversationally, 'that would have been an old lady emu. This time of year the boys are sitting on the eggs and the old ladies are out and about.'

Could it get any worse? Poor mother emu. Finally gets to go out with her girlfriends and I kill her. And I'm a feminist. I almost sooked again.

He reckoned Tim was a mug to hit it on the head. 'Got claws on them like razor blades. Rip your guts out.'

A disembowelled husband, a dying emu and me running round in tight circles screaming on the long empty road. It could have been that bad. We'd got off lightly.

By the time we got to the truckstop the day was roasting hot, so Tim and I went inside for the air conditioning and a cold drink. There was a cyclist there, the very same one the towie had talked about. He was in his bright lycra, eating a healthy option and examining a map. He showed us where he'd ridden from and where he was going. He was going to stay the night in some rooms they rented out the back of the place and set off in the morning. Outside, the towie chatted to a truck driver, ate another sandwich, drank a coffee and smoked about five cigarettes end on end.

Back in the truck the towie regaled us with a story of how it was when he went to visit his son in Melbourne. He didn't like the number of Asians coming in. He said he and his son were on a tram and they played 'Spot the Aussie'. He said he couldn't spot any Aussies at all that he recognised.

To cut him off, or at least change the subject, I told him how we had seen the cyclist in the truck stop.

'The very same one?'

We assured him it was.

'Sheez!' said the towie. 'He's got all the way here. That guy's so fit he's got muscles in his shit.'

What an image. What a poetical phrase for physical prowess. I laughed until my stomach hurt.

If there's a moral to the story it's that no matter how many tons of carbon you've burnt in your irresponsible lifetime, jetting back and forth across the Tasman and deluding yourself that you have some kind of trans-Tasman mentality, West Island will find a way to remind you how very different it is. That day was my reminder – an old lady emu dead by my own hand, a previously mild-mannered husband arming himself with a cudgel, a pair of saints travelling thousands of miles in a Winnebago, and a hyperfit cyclist with muscles in the strangest of places. I love you, Australia, you're like nowhere else.

Afterword

ntil *West Island* found its happy home with Otago University Press, it was rejected by one or two major trade publishers. An odd thing to note in an afterword – except that the reasons are pertinent to the subject of the book. It's a New Zealand book, said the Australian publisher. It's an Australian book, said the New Zealand equivalent. Australians don't want to read about New Zealanders, said the Australian. Vice versa, said the New Zealander.

The two countries were at one time so much closer than they are now. If any of our five subjects was alive today, how sad they would be about the major trans-Tasman stories featuring in our media in the past couple of years. On 25 July 2018 Radio New Zealand reported that there are more New Zealanders than people of any other nationality languishing in the infamous Australian immigration detention centres. Joanne Cox, spokeswoman for the organisation Oz Kiwi, explained that in accordance with changes to the Australian Migration Act in December 2014, many New Zealanders who have lived in Australia since childhood face detention and deportation for crimes committed many years earlier. This so-called 'bad character law' gives officials the power to cancel visas of suspected or convicted criminals. Special attention is given to those who have done more than a year-long stretch of imprisonment or who were convicted of sex offences.

In June 2018 News Hub reported on a 17-year-old boy who is being held in Melbourne Immigration Transit Accommodation (MITA), which is supposed to be for adults only. At 17, the detainee is still legally a child. His detention is in direct contradiction of the UN Convention on the Rights of the Child. He is denied access to his computer and cellphone, and MITA is around nine hours' drive away from his family. His one previous crime was of a non-violent nature. A few weeks after this story broke, the *Guardian* ran an article featuring New Zealand's Acting Prime Minister Winston Peters speaking of more than a thousand Kiwis forcibly deported from Australia since 2016.

In that year Greg Barns from the Australian Lawyers' Alliance predicted that New Zealanders would be sent home in their thousands: in other words, the figure given by Winston Peters was only the first trickle. The statistics are disturbing – roughly 23 detainees are deported each month. Forty per cent of those returning re-offend within months of arrival. The *New York Times* reported that more than 60 per cent of those deported are Māori or Pacific Islanders. The men repatriated – and they are predominantly men – frequently find themselves isolated and alone in New Zealand. Many have Australian accents, no family in Aotearoa to help them and no immediate means of earning a living. There has been at least one reported suicide. These people think of Australia as home, even though it is a home that no longer wants them. In the detention camps they call themselves the 501s, naming themselves after the clause in the change to the Immigration Act.

Just these few facts and figures speak volumes. Despite decades – centuries – of immigration from all over the world, Australia is racist. Representation in government by either the Indigenous people or those who grew up in households that spoke languages other than English is miniscule. The lucky country feels itself under siege. It is a global phenomenon, and New Zealand, it must be said, is not immune either. All over the world countries feel themselves plagued by unwanted arrivals, whether they are 'boat people', or desperate evacuees travelling overland in the face of climate change and geopolitical unrest.

Australia's situation, then, is not unique. But do they really have to turn against their nearest neighbour?

They have many reasons for doing so. Long-term resentment of migrants gaining New Zealand citizenship only to use it to get into Australia through the 'back door'; legions of young Kiwis getting into trouble on their first step away from home – and, equally, New Zealanders ousting Australians from top positions in commerce, media, the arts, industry, politics, sport, almost every field of human endeavour possible. It is well beyond the scope of this book to try to pick apart the reasons for our falling out of love, but they're behaving as if they hate us. When we are serious about becoming Australians we have to prove that all our links with New Zealand are broken – no property owned and no bank accounts held. Individually we have to earn a minimum of A\$53,000 for three years before we can apply for permanent residency. Teenage children, taken across the Tasman as babes-in-arms or toddlers, are unable to access tertiary education without paying enormous fees. The situation, in light of our shared history, is barbaric.

In 2016 HarperCollins Australia published a nice fat novel called *Jarulan by the River*. It is a big, sprawling saga about a trans-Tasman family written by a Gold Coast chick called Lily Woodhouse. She is Australian. And younger than me. After the book was published, I did all my radio interviews in an Australian accent. Sometimes the interviewer knew I was not really Lily Woodhouse. Sometimes, depending on whether they'd bothered to read the guff sent to them by the publisher, they thought she was the real deal. It was great fun and also, in retrospect, a strange thing to do. Maybe a little mad. I tried it out for a while, a return to the life I might have had if I'd stayed in Australia and not come back to New Zealand. Then Lily wrote another book, but the publisher knocked it back on account of her first book not selling in the numbers required. So my experiment is over before I've even earned my first 53 thousand.

I will live happily in New Zealand for the rest of my life. I know that now, as I zoom towards 60. But I miss Australia. I miss our son and youngest daughter who live there. I miss my dear West Island émigrée Rosie Scott who made her life there as a well-loved writer, mentor and social activist. She died on 4 May 2017.

15 August 2018

Notes

WHY?

1. Marjorie Quinn, *The Years that the Locust Hath Eaten: The memoirs of Marjorie Quinn*, introduced by Deborah McMahon and Kathryn Berryman, Melbourne: Arcadia, Australian Scholarly Publishing, 2011, 30.

POINTS OF ORIGIN

Wairarapa: Roland Wakelin and Dulcie Deamer

1. Thomas Henry Smith – Papers MS-283, Auckland Museum Library.
2. Quoted in Virginia Gerritt, 'Roland Wakelin – The Man', *Art and Australia*, 4, 4 March 1967.
3. Ibid.
4. Ref 1/1-013476-G, Alexander Turnbull Library, Wellington (ATL).
5. Wakelin Papers, E.H. McCormick Research Library, Auckland Art Gallery.
6. Joanne Drayton, *Frances Hodgkins: A private viewing*, Auckland: Godwit, 2005.
7. Peter Kirkpatrick (ed.), *The Queen of Bohemia: The autobiography of Dulcie Deamer, being 'The Golden Decade'*, Brisbane: University of Queensland Press, 1998, 4.
8. Ibid.
9. Hazel de Berg, Trove, ORALTRC 1/159, 10 May 1965.
10. Kirkpatrick (ed.), *The Queen of Bohemia*, 3, 5.
11. MS-Papers-0368, ATL.
12. de Berg, Trove, ORALTRC 1/159.
13. Kirkpatrick (ed.), *The Queen of Bohemia*, 3.
14. David Yerex, *Featherston, the First 150 Years: 1857–2007*, Featherston: Featherston Community Board, 2007), 124.
15. de Berg, Trove, ORALTRC 1/159.
16. Ibid.
17. *New Zealand Truth*, 135, 18 January 1908, Papers Past, National Library of New Zealand.

Taranaki: Douglas Stewart

1. Douglas Stewart, *Springtime in Taranaki*, Auckland: Hodder & Stoughton, 1983, 38.
2. Ibid., 13.
3. Ibid., 30.
4. Ibid., 44.
5. Ibid., 51.
6. Ibid., 54.
7. Ibid., 61.

8. Ibid., 155.
9. Ibid., 126.
10. Ibid., 136.
11. Ibid., 154.
12. Ibid., 156.
13. Ibid., 170.
14. Ibid.
15. Douglas A. Stewart, 5147, Box 16, State Library of New South Wales.
16. Stewart, *Springtime in Taranaki*, 184.
17. Ibid., 216.
18. Ibid, 218
19. Witi Ihimaera, *Māori Boy: A memoir of childhood*, Auckland: Vintage, 2016, 341.
20. Email correspondence with Meg Stewart, May 2017.
21. Stewart, *Springtime in Taranaki*, 218.
22. Ibid.
23. Douglas Stewart, *Selected Poems*, Sydney: Angus & Robertson, 1973, 10.
24. Douglas Stewart Papers, Box 16, 5147, State Library of New South Wales.
25. Douglas Stewart Papers, MS Folder 1.
26. Douglas Stewart Papers, Correspondence, Folder 1.
27. Ibid.
28. Email correspondence with Meg Stewart, May 2017.
29. Stewart, *Springtime in Taranaki*, 228.
30. Ibid., 230.
31. Ibid.
32. Stewart, *Selected Poems*, 16
33. Joy L. Thwaite, *The Importance of Being Eve Langley*, Sydney: Angus & Robertson, 1989, 280.
34. Correspondence, Folder 1, Mitchell Library.
35. Quoted in Meg Stewart, *The Shadows Are Different*, 5; in Thwaite, *The Importance of Being Eve Langley*, 280.
36. Thwaite, *The Importance of Being Eve Langley*, 280.
37. Douglas Stewart Papers, Correspondence, Folder 3.
38. Douglas Stewart Papers, Correspondence, Folder 1.
39. Ibid.
40. Stewart, *Selected Poems*, 4.
41. Douglas Stewart Papers, Correspondence, Folder 1.
42. Ibid.
43. Ibid.
44. Ibid.
45. Douglas Stewart Papers, Correspondence, Folder 3.
46. Ibid.
47. Ibid.
48. *New Zealand Observer*, 15 July 1937.
49. Stewart, *Springtime in Taranaki*, 254.

Collingwood, Dunedin and Wellington: Jean Devanny

1. Michael O'Leary, *Wednesday's Women: Women writers in New Zealand 1945–1970*, Wellington: Silver Owl Press, 2012, 23.
2. Patrick Evans, 'Maurice Duggan and the Provincial Dilemma', *Landfall*, 142, June 1982, 218.
3. Carole Ferrier (ed.), *Point of Departure: The autobiography of Jean Devanny*, Brisbane: University of Queensland Press, 1986, 7.
4. Ibid., 28.
5. Ibid., 35.
6. *Journal of the Nelson and Marlborough Historical Societies*, 2, 2 (1988), NZETC, Victoria University of Wellington.
7. Quoted in Carole Ferrier, *Jean Devanny: Romantic revolutionary*, Brisbane: University of Queensland Press, 1999, 55.
8. Ibid., 44.
9. Rollo Arnold, 'The Australasian Peoples and their World', in Keith Sinclair (ed.), *Tasman Relations: New Zealand and Australia, 1788–1988*, Auckland: Auckland University Press, 1987.
10. Ibid., 67.
11. Jean Devanny, *Dawn Beloved*, London: Duckworth, 1928, 76.
12. Ibid., 190
13. Ibid., 184.
14. Ibid., 15.
15. Ibid., 31, 45.
16. Ferrier, *Jean Devanny: Romantic revolutionary*, 13.
17. MS-Papers-7658 Levesque, Andree, fl 1950–2003, ATL.
18. Quoted in Ferrier, *Jean Devanny: Romantic revolutionary*, 29.
19. Ferrier (ed.), *Point of Departure*, 81.
20. Ibid., 81.
21. Jean Devanny, *Dawn Beloved*, London: Duckworth, 1928, 350.
22. In Vincent O'Sullivan (ed.), *The Oxford Book of New Zealand Short Stories*, Auckland: Oxford University Press, 1992, 67.
23. Jean Devanny (edited and introduced by Heather Roberts), *The Butcher Shop*, Auckland: Auckland University Press, 1981, 133.
24. Ibid., 161.
25. Ibid., 143.
26. Ibid., 169–70.
27. Quoted in Ferrier, *Jean Devanny: Romantic revolutionary*, 36.
28. MS-Papers-7658 Levesque, Andree, fl 1950–2003, ATL.
29. N. Scanlan, 'Banned by the Censors: *The Butcher Shop* too brutal: Novel by Wellington woman refused admission into New Zealand', *New Zealand Free Lance*, 26 May 1926, ATL.
30. Quoted in Ferrier, *Jean Devanny: Romantic revolutionary*, 49.
31. Ibid., 44.

32. Ibid., 48.
33. *New Zealand Observer*, 15 December 1935.
34. Chris Hilliard, 2006, quoted in Michael O'Leary's thesis, 'Social and literary constraints on women writers in New Zealand 1945–1970', later published as *Wednesday's Women.*

Auckland: Eric Baume

1. Arthur Manning, *Larger Than Life: The story of Eric Baume*, Wellington: A.H. & A.W. Reed, 1967, 25.
2. Eric Baume, *I Have Lived These Years, 1900–1941*, London and Sydney: George G. Harrap & Co, 1941, 21.
3. Ibid., 27.
4. Ibid., 34.
5. Ibid., 19.
6. Manning, *Larger Than Life*, 27.
7. *San Francisco Call*, 12 January 1916, California Digital Newspaper Collection, 18.11.16.
8. Baume, *I Have Lived These Years*, 35.
9. Manning, *Larger Than Life*, 31.
10. Baume, *I Have Lived These Years*, 81.
11. Manning, *Larger Than Life*, 36.
12. Baume, *I Have Lived These Years*, 97.

OUT INTO THE WORLD

1. Eric Baume, *I Have Lived These Years, 1900–1941*, London and Sydney: George G. Harrap & Co, 1941, 99.

LIFE IN WEST ISLAND

1913: The Painter: Roland Wakelin

1. Marjorie Quinn, *The Years that the Locust Hath Eaten: The memoirs of Marjorie Quinn*, introduced by Deborah McMahon and Kathryn Berryman, Melbourne: Arcadia, Australian Scholarly Publishing, 2011, 30.
2. Trove: *Kalgoorie Miner*, WA, 14 February 1913.
3. Leslie Walton, *The Art of Roland Wakelin*, Sydney: Craftsman House, 1987, 14.
4. Ibid., 15.
5. Quoted in John Hetherington, *Australian Painters: Forty profiles*, Melbourne: F.W. Cheshire, 1963, 13.
6. Hetherington, *Australian Painters*, 34.
7. Walton, *The Art of Roland Wakelin*, 15.
8. Ibid.
9. Elwyn Lynn, *The Australian Landscape and its Artists*, Sydney: Bay Books, 1977, 98.
10. Hetherington, *Australian Painters*, 32.
11. Ibid.

12. Ibid., 34.
13. Lynn, *The Australian Landscape and its Artists*, 98.
14. Quoted in Walton, *The Art of Roland Wakelin*, 21.
15. Jean Campbell, 'Roland Shakespeare Wakelin 1887–1971', in Henrik Kolenberg (ed.), *The Art Bulletin of Tasmania 1985*, Hobart: Tasmanian Museum and Art Gallery, 1985.
16. Drusilla Modjeska, *Stravinsky's Lunch*, New York: Farrar, Straus & Giroux, 1999, 272.
17. Hetherington, *Australian Painters*, 32.
18. Ibid., 33.
19. Ibid.
20. Christopher Johnstone, *Landscape Paintings of New Zealand: A journey from north to south*, Auckland: Godwit, 2013, 70.

1925: The Party Girl: Dulcie Deamer

1. Essay on Roland Wakelin, in Robert Lindsay (introduction and text), *Aspects of Australian Art*, Sydney: Art Gallery of New South Wales, 1976, 23.
2. Peter Kirkpatrick (ed.), *The Queen of Bohemia: The autobiography of Dulcie Deamer, being 'The Golden Decade'*, Brisbane: University of Queensland Press, 1998, 37.
3. Ibid., 24.
4. Ibid., 82, 83.
5. Ibid., afterword, 165.
6. Louis Nowra, *Kings Cross: A biography*, Sydney: New South Publishing, 2013, 116.
7. Kirkpatrick (ed.), *The Queen of Bohemia*, 37.
8. Ibid., 46.
9. Michael Sharkey, *Apollo in George Street: The life of David McKee Wright*, Sydney: Puncher & Wattman, 2012, 157.
10. Kirkpatrick (ed.), *The Queen of Bohemia*, 35.
11. Ibid., 29.
12. Ibid., 30.
13. Ibid., 47.
14. Nowra, *Kings Cross*, 120.
15. Kirkpatrick (ed.), *The Queen of Bohemia*, 16.
16. Nowra, *Kings Cross*, 117–18.
17. Kirkpatrick (ed.), *The Queen of Bohemia*, 122.
18. Ibid., 10.
19. *Australian Women's Mirror*, 9 June 1925.
20. Kirkpatrick (ed.), *The Queen of Bohemia*, 97.
21. Ferrier (ed.), *Point of Departure*, 107.
22. Introduction to Charles Ferrall (ed.), *Henry Lawson in New Zealand*, Wellington: Steele Roberts Aotearoa, 2011, 8.
23. Kirkpatrick (ed.), *The Queen of Bohemia*, 32.
24. Carole Ferrier, *Jean Devanny: Romantic revolutionary*, Brisbane: University of Queensland Press, 1999, 199.
25. Kirkpatrick (ed.), *The Queen of Bohemia*, 155.

26. Douglas Stewart, *Norman Lindsay: A personal memoir*, Sydney: Allen & Unwin, 1975, 56.

27. Quoted in Ferrier (ed.), *As Good as a Yarn with You*, 371.

28. Kirkpatrick (ed.), *The Queen of Bohemia*, 58.

29. Quinn, *The Years That the Locusts Hath Eaten*, 41.

30. Anna Hoffmann, *Tales of Anna Hoffmann*, vol. 1, Hawke's Bay: Batwing Press, 2009, 235.

31. Ibid., 241.

32. Ibid., 242.

33. Nowra, *Kings Cross*, 237; Kay Saunders, *Notorious Australian Women*, Sydney: ABC Books, 2011, 226–27.

34. *Sunday Sun*, 29 December 1955.

35. Hoffmann, *Tales of Anna Hoffmann*, 248.

36. Kirkpatrick (ed.), *The Queen of Bohemia*, 169.

37. Michael Costigan, National Office for the Participation of Women, Australian Catholic Bishops Conference, 2016: www.opw.catholic.org.au/latest-news/a-reflection-on-the-life-of-rosemary-goldie.html

38. Ruth Lee, *The Encyclopedia of Women and Leadership in Twentieth Century Australia*: www.womenaustralia.info/leaders/biogs/WLE0157b.htm

39. Kirkpatrick (ed.), *The Queen of Bohemia*, 45–46.

1939: The Beast: Eric Baume

1. Carole Ferrier (ed.), *Point of Departure: The autobiography of Jean Devanny*, Brisbane: University of Queensland Press, 1986, 176.

2. Eric Baume, *I Have Lived These Years 1900–1941*, London and Sydney: George G. Harrap & Co, 1942, 98.

3. Arther Manning, *Larger Than Life: The story of Eric Baume*, Wellington: A.H. & A.W. Reed, 1967, 42.

4. Bill Olson, *Baume: Man and beast*, Sydney: Horwitz Publications, 1967, 10.

5. Baume, *I Have Lived These Years*, 126.

6. Ibid., 127.

7. Ibid., 98.

8. Ibid., 13.

9. Ibid.

10. Marjorie Quinn, *The Years that the Locust Hath Eaten: The memoirs of Marjorie Quinn*, Melbourne: Arcadia, Australian Scholarly Publishing, 2001, 159.

11. Manning, *Larger Than Life*, 54.

12. Baume, *I Have Lived These Years*, 162.

13. Michael King, *The Penguin History of New Zealand*, Auckland: Penguin, 2003, 223.

14. Baume, *I Have Lived These Years*, 172.

15. Manning, *Larger Than Life*, 64.

16. Quinn, *The Years that the Locust Hath Eaten*, 132.

17. R.S. Walker, *Yesterday's News: A history of the newspaper press in New South Wales from 1920–1945*, Sydney: Sydney University Press, 1980.

18. Manning, *Larger Than Life*, 101.
19. Ibid., 106.
20. Ibid., 107.
21. Ibid., 136.
22. Ibid., 169.
23. Ibid., 18.
24. Martin Edmond in *New Zealand Books*, 99, 1 September 2012.
25. Eric Baume, *Half-Caste*, London: Falcon Press, 1950, 10.
26. Ibid., 29.
27. Ibid., 33.
28. Ibid., 34.
29. Ibid., 35–36.
30. Ibid., 36–37.
31. Ibid., 38.
32. Ibid., 40.
33. Ibid., 45.
34. Ibid., 47.
35. Ibid., 48.
36. Ibid., 50.
37. Ibid., 63.
38. Ibid., 91.
39. Ibid., 102.
40. Ibid., 128.
41. Ibid., 129.
42. Ibid., 139.
43. Ibid.
44. Ibid., 176.
45. Ibid., 187.
46. Ibid., 189.
47. Ibid., 190.
48. Ibid., 211.
49. In Tamara S. Wagner (ed.), *Domestic Fiction in Colonial Australia and New Zealand*, London: Pickering & Chatto, 2014, 174–75.

1951: The Communist: Jean Devanny

1. Clement Semmler Papers, State Library of New South Wales.
2. Jean Devanny, *Travels in North Queensland*, London: Jarrolds, 1951, 136–37
3. Carole Ferrier (ed.), *Point of Departure: The autobiography of Jean Devanny*, Brisbane: University of Queensland Press, 1986, 183.
4. Ibid., 105.
5. Ibid., 111.
6. Bill Pearson, 'The banning of *The Butcher Shop*', *Sydney Morning Herald*, 29 August 1929, 15.

7. Ferrier (ed.), *Point of Departure*, 126.
8. Ibid., 133.
9. Quoted in Jane Gleeson-White, *Australian Classics: 50 great writers and their celebrated works*, Sydney: Allen & Unwin, 2007, 108–09.
10. Ferrier (ed.), *Point of Departure*, 137.
11. Ibid., 320.
12. Carole Ferrier, *Jean Devanny: Romantic revolutionary*, Brisbane: University of Queensland Press, 1999, 128.
13. Ibid.
14. Ferrier (ed.), *Point of Departure*, 148.
15. Ferrier, *Jean Devanny: Romantic revolutionary*, 110.
16. Drusilla Modjeska, *Exiles at Home: Australian women writers, 1925–1945*, Sydney: Angus & Robertson, 1981, 148.
17. Lynley Cvitanovich, *Breaking the Silence: An analysis of the selected fiction of two New Zealand women writers*, Massey University Monograph No. 2, New Zealand Cultural Studies Working Group in association with the Department of Sociology, 1985, 28.
18. Ibid., 30–32.
19. Ferrier (ed.), *Point of Departure*, 176.
20. Carole Ferrier (ed.), *As Good as a Yarn With You*, Cambridge: Cambridge University Press, 1992, 75–76, 377.
21. Ferrier (ed.), *Point of Departure*, 322.
22. Jean Devanny, *Sugar Heaven*, Sydney: Modern Publishers, 1936, 36.
23. Ibid., 159.
24. Ibid., 199.
25. Ibid., 276.
26. Ibid., 305–06.
27. Dale Spender, *Writing a New World: Two centuries of Australian women writers*, London: Pandora, 1988, 260.
28. Ferrier (ed.), *Point of Departure*, 190.
29. Ibid., 105.
30. Ferrier (ed.), *As Good as a Yarn With You*, 318.
31. Ferrier (ed.), *Point of Departure*, 185.
32. Ferrier, *Jean Devanny: Romantic revolutionary*, 161.
33. Ferrier (ed.), *Point of Departure*, 227.
34. Jean Devanny, *By Tropic Sea and Jungle*, Sydney: Angus & Robertson, 1944, 58.
35. Ibid., 138.
36. Ibid., 16.
37. Ibid., 20.
38. Ibid., 178.
39. Ibid., 179.
40. Ibid., 219.
41. Ibid., 226.
42. Ferrier (ed.), *Point of Departure,* 320.

43. Ferrier (ed.), *As Good as a Yarn With You*, 334–35.
44. Ferrier (ed.), *Point of Departure*, 209.
45. Ibid., 302.
46. Ferrier (ed.), *As Good as a Yarn With You*, 346.
47. Ibid., 347.
48. Ibid., 246.
49. Ibid., 373.
50. Ibid., 50.
51. James Bennett, '*Rats and Revolutionaries': The Labour movement in Australia and New Zealand 1890–1940*, Dunedin: University of Otago Press, 2004, 85,
52. MS-Papers-7658 Levesque, Andree, fl 1950–2003.

1972: The Man of Letters: Douglas Stewart
1. *New Zealand Herald*, 10 April 2017.
2. Correspondence with Vincent O'Sullivan, 20 June 2016.
3. Ibid.
4. Douglas Stewart Papers, Box 22, Folder 2.
5. Peter Simpson, *Ronald Hugh Morrieson*, Auckland: Oxford University Press, 1982, 14.
6. Email correspondence from Peter Simpson, 19 June 2015.
7. *Dominion Post*, 3 August 2010.
8. Correspondence with Vincent O'Sullivan, 20 June 2016.
9. Box 23, Folder 1, Douglas Stewart Papers.
10. Peter Simpson (ed.), *Charles Brasch Journals 1945–1957*, Dunedin: Otago University Press, 2017, 493–94.
11. Douglas Stewart, *Norman Lindsay: A personal memoir*, Sydney: Allen & Unwin, 1975, 9.
12. Nancy Keesing, *Douglas Stewart: Australian writers & their work*, Melbourne: Oxford University Press, 1967, 9.
13. Simpson (ed.), *Charles Brasch Journals*, 494.
14. Correspondence with Vincent O'Sullivan, 20 June 2016.
15. K.S. Inglis, *This is the ABC: The Australian Broadcasting Commission, 1932–1983*, Melbourne: Melbourne University Press, 1983, 416.
16. Meg Stewart, *Autobiography of My Mother*, Sydney: Vintage Australia, 2006, 240.
17. Clement Semmler Papers. Where the context of Semmler's interview with Stewart is clear in the subsequent text, references have not been included in each instance.
18. Stewart, *Autobiography of My Mother*, 249.
19. Douglas Stewart, *Elegy for an Airman*, Sydney: Frank C. Johnson, 1940, 16.
20. *Lake Wakitipu Mail*, 3 September 1942, Papers Past, National Library of New Zealand.
21. Clement Semmler Papers.
22. Stewart, *Norman Lindsay*, 25.
23. Email correspondence with Meg Stewart, May 2017.
24. Stewart, *Norman Lindsay*, 116.

25. Douglas Stewart, *Selected Poems*, Sydney: Angus & Robertson, 1973, 193.
26. Clement Semmler Papers.
27. Stewart, *Selected Poems*, 156.
28. Keesing, *Douglas Stewart*, 4.
29. Stewart, *Selected Poems*, 188–90.
30. Correspondence with Meg Stewart, 2 June 2017.
31. Douglas Stewart, *The Seven Rivers*, illustrated by Margaret Coen, Auckland: Whitcombe & Tombs, 1966, 119.
32. Ibid., 121.
33. Keesing, *Douglas Stewart*, 59.
34. Both quotations are from Semmler, in Inglis *This is the ABC*, 88.
35. Stewart, *Autobiography of My Mother*, 245.
36. Clement Semmler, *Douglas Stewart*, Sydney: Angus & Robertson, 1977, 87.
37. Douglas Stewart Papers.
38. www.britannica.com/biography/Alfred-Domett
39. Maori Theatre Trust Papers, ATL 1/4-027626-F.
40. Douglas Stewart, *Four Plays*, Sydney: Angus & Robertson, 1958.
41. Ibid., 33.
42. Ibid., 35.
43. Ibid., 36.
44. Ibid., 61.
45. Douglas Stewart Papers.
46. 'Domestic Poem', in Meg Stewart, *Margaret Coen: A passion for painting*, Sydney: State Library of New South Wales Press, 1997, 30.
47. Clement Semmler Papers.
48. Michael King, 'Bookworld', *New Zealand Times*, 10 July 1982.
49. *Sydney Morning Herald*, 21 January 1984.

Bibliography

BOOKS

Baume, Eric, *Half-Caste*, London: Falcon Press, 1950

—— *I Have Lived Another Year*, London and Sydney: George G. Harrap & Co, 1942

—— *I Lived These Years 1900–1941*, London and Sydney: George G. Harrap & Co, 1941

Bennett, James, *'Rats and Revolutionaries': The labour movement in Australia and New Zealand 1890–1940*, Dunedin: Otago University Press, 2004

Barbara Brookes, Charlotte Macdonald and Margaret Tennant (eds), *Essays on Women in New Zealand: Women in history 2*, Wellington: Bridget Williams Books, 1992

The Bibliography of Australian Literature, Brisbane: University of Queensland Press, 2005

Cvitanovich, Lynley, *Breaking the Silence: An analysis of the selected fiction of two New Zealand women writers*, Massey University Monograph No. 2, New Zealand Cultural Studies Working Group in association with the Department of Sociology, 1985

Deamer, Dulcie, *Revelation*, London: Mr T. Fisher Unwin, 1921

Devanny, Jean, *The Butcher Shop*, edited and introduced by Heather Roberts, Auckland: Auckland University Press, 1981

—— *By Tropic Sea and Jungle*, Sydney: Angus & Robertson, 1944

—— *Cindie*, London: Robert Hale, 1949

—— *Dawn Beloved*, London: Duckworth, 1928

—— *Devil Made Saint*, London: Duckworth, 1930

—— *Sugar Heaven*, Sydney: Modern Publishers, 1936

—— *Travels in North Queensland*, London: Jarrolds Publishers, 1951

Doyle, Peter, with Caleb Williams, *City of Shadows: Sydney police photographs 1912–1948*, Sydney: Historic Houses Trust of New South Wales, 2005

Evans, Patrick, *The Penguin History of New Zealand Literature*, Auckland: Penguin, 1990

Ferrall, Charles, *Henry Lawson in New Zealand*, Wellington: Steele Roberts Aotearoa, 2011

Ferrier, Carole, *Jean Devanny: Romantic revolutionary*, Brisbane: University of Queensland Press, 1999

Ferrier, Carole (ed.) *As Good as a Yarn With You : Letters between Miles Franklin, Katharine Susannah Prichard, Jean Devanny, Marjorie Barnard, Flora Eldershaw and Eleanor Dark*, Cambridge: Cambridge University Press, 1992

—— *Point of Departure: The autobiography of Jean Devanny*, Brisbane: University of Queensland Press, 1986

Franklin, Miles, *Laughter, Not for a Cage*, Sydney: Angus & Robertson, 1956

Fyfe, Frank, *Wakelin, Father of Journalism*, Greytown: Wakelin House, 1990

Gleeson-White, Jane, *Australian Classics: 50 great writers and their celebrated works*, Crows Nest, NSW: Allen & Unwin, 2007

Goldman, L.M., *The History of the Jews in New Zealand*, Wellington: A.H. & A.W. Reed, 1958

Greer, Germaine, *Whitefella Jump Up: The shortest way to nationhood*, London: Profile Books, 2004

Hetherington, John, *Australian Painters: Forty profiles*, Melbourne: F.W. Cheshire, Melbourne, 1963

Hoffmann, Anna, *Tales of Anna Hoffmann* Volume 1, Hawkes Bay: Batwing Press, 2009

Ihimaera, Witi, *Māori Boy: A memoir of childhood*, Auckland: Vintage, 2014

Inglis, Kenneth Stanley, *This is the ABC: The Australian Broadcasting Commission 1932–1983*, Melbourne: Melbourne University Press, 1983

Johnson, Stephanie, *Playing for Both Sides: Love across the Tasman*, Wellington: Bridget Williams Books, 2016.

Johnstone, Christopher, *Landscape Paintings of New Zealand: A journey from north to south*, Auckland: Godwit, 2013

Keesing, Nancy, *Douglas Stewart: Australian writers & their work,* Melbourne: Oxford University Press, 1967

King, Michael, *The Penguin History of New Zealand*, Auckland: Penguin, 2003

Kirkpatrick, Peter (ed.), *The Queen of Bohemia: The autobiography of Dulcie Deamer, being 'The Golden Decade'*, Brisbane: University of Queensland Press, 1998

Lindsay, Robert (introduction and text), *Aspects of Australian Art*, Sydney: Art Gallery of New South Wales, 1976

Lynn, Elwyn, *The Australian Landscape and its Artists*, Sydney: Bay Books, 1977

Maconie, Janet, *Landmarks of New Zealand Writing to 1945*, Wellington: New Zealand Book Council, 1990.

Manning, Arthur, *Larger Than Life: The story of Eric Baume*, Wellington: A.H. & A.W. Reed, 1967

McCormick, E.H., *New Zealand Literature: A survey*, Auckland: Oxford University Press, 1959

Modjeska, Drusilla, *Exiles at Home: Australian women writers, 1925–1945*, Sydney: Angus & Robertson, 1981

——*Stravinsky's Lunch*, New York: Farrar, Straus & Giroux, 1999

Nowra, Louis, *Kings Cross: A biography*, Sydney: NewSouth Publishing, 2013

O'Leary, Michael, *Wednesday's Women: Women writers in New Zealand, 1945–1970*, Wellington: Silver Owl Press, 2012

Olson, Bill, *Baume: Man and beast*, Sydney: Horwitz Publications, 1967

O'Sullivan, Vincent (ed.), *The Oxford Book of New Zealand Short Stories*, Auckland: Oxford University Press, 1992

Park, Ruth, *The Witch's Thorn*, London, Melbourne and Sydney: Horwitz, 1966

Pearson, Bill, *Fretful Sleepers and Other Essays*, Auckland: Heinemann Educational Books, 1974

Quinn, Marjorie, *The Years that the Locust Hath Eaten: The memoirs of Marjorie Quinn*, Melbourne: Arcadia, Australian Scholarly Publishing, 2011

Roberts, Heather, *Where Did She Come From? New Zealand women novelists 1862–1987*, Wellington: Allen & Unwin, 1989

Saunders, Kay, *Notorious Australian Women*, Sydney: ABC Books, 2011

Semmler, Clement, *Douglas Stewart*, New York: Twayne Publishers, 1974

Sharkey, Michael, *Apollo in George Street: The life of David McKee Wright*, Sydney: Puncher & Wattman, 2012

Simpson, Peter, *Ronald Hugh Morrieson*, Auckland: Oxford University Press, 1982

Simpson, Peter (ed.), *Charles Brasch Journals 1945–1957*, Dunedin: Otago University Press, 2017

Sinclair, Keith, *Tasman Relations*, Auckland: Auckland University Press, 1987

Spender, Dale, *Writing a New World: Two centuries of Australian women writers*, London: Pandora, 1988

Stewart, Douglas, *The Broad Stream: Aspects of Australian literature*, Sydney: Angus & Robertson, 1975

—— *Elegy for an Airman*, illustrated by Norman Lindsay, Sydney: Frank C. Johnson, 1940

—— *Four Plays*, Sydney: Angus & Robertson, 1958

—— *A Girl With Red Hair*, Sydney: Angus & Robertson, 1944

—— *Norman Lindsay: A personal memoir*, Sydney: Allen & Unwin, 1975

—— *Selected Poems*, Sydney: Angus & Robertson, 1973

—— *The Seven Rivers*, illustrated by Margaret Coen, Auckland: Whitcombe & Tombs, 1966

—— *Springtime in Taranaki*, Auckland: Hodder & Stoughton, 1983

Stewart, Meg, *Autobiography of My Mother*, Sydney: Vintage Australia, 2006

Thwaite, Joy L., *The Importance of Being Eve Langley*, Sydney: Angus & Robertson, 1989

Tink, Andrew, *Australia 1901–2001: A narrative history*, Sydney: NewSouth Publishing, 2014

Wagner, Tamara S. (ed.), *Domestic Fiction in Colonial Australia and New Zealand*, London: Pickering & Chatto, 2014

Walker, R.S., *Yesterday's News: A history of the newspaper press in New South Wales from 1920–1945*, Sydney: Sydney University Press, 1980

Walton, Leslie, *The Art of Roland Wakelin*, Sydney: Craftsman House, 1987

Yerex, David, *Featherston, the First 150 Years: 1857–2007*, Featherston: Featherston Community Board, 2007

ARTICLES

Braunias, Steve, 'Steve Braunias on John Clarke', *New Zealand Herald*, 10 April 2017

Campion, Edmund, 'Catholic leader pushed for change: Rosemary Goldie 1916–2010', *Sydney Morning Herald*, 7 April 2010

Gerritt, Virginia, 'Roland Wakelin – The man', *Art and Australia 4*, 4 March 1967

Hyde, Robin, 'To England in the galley', *New Zealand Observer*, 15 July, 1937

Journal of the Nelson and Marlborough Historical Societies, 2, 2, 1988, NZETC Victoria

Pearson, Bill, 'The Banning of *The Butcher Shop*', *Sydney Morning Herald*, 29 August 1929

PAPERS AND UNPUBLISHING MANUSCRIPTS

Clement Semmler Papers, State Library of New South Wales

Douglas Stewart Papers (including some files labelled 'Correspondence'), State Library of New South Wales

An Open Letter to Douglas Stewart by Frank Sargeson, National Library of New Zealand
'Sunset in the Waikato' – first written as 'An Earthquake Shakes the Land', radio play by
     Douglas Stewart, State Library of New South Wales
MS-Papers-7658 Levesque, Andree, fl 1950–2003, National Library of New Zealand
Thomas Henry Smith: Papers MS-283, Auckland Museum Library
Wakelin Papers, E.H. McCormick Research Library, Auckland Art Gallery
Walsh, Fintan Patrick, 1894–1963: Papers, National Library of New Zealand

Acknowledgements

West Island would never have been written without the faith and generosity of the Randell Cottage Trust in Wellington, New Zealand. I was the grateful recipient of the Randell Cottage Residency in 2016 and it was there that I completed the research and first draft of the book.

Thank you to Douglas Stewart's daughter, Meg Stewart, for her support of the project, and who kindly corrected a few errors. Thanks, Meg, also for the photographs of Doug included in this work.

Bill Murray, Roland Wakelin's grandson and executor, was generous and encouraging. Thanks to Bill in particular for permission to reproduce the painting on page 125.

Thank you to Melbourne University Press, Australian Scholarly Publishing, Vintage New Zealand, University of Queensland Press, Silver Owl Press, NewSouth Publishing and Cambridge University Press for their generous permission to use quotes herein free of charge.

Thanks also to Dr Peter Simpson and Vincent O'Sullivan for sharing their impressions and personal knowledge of Douglas Stewart.

Thank you to Bridget Williams Books for permission to use an excerpt from *Playing for Both Sides: Love across the Tasman* by Stephanie Johnson (Wellington: Bridget Williams Books, 2016).

Thanks to my agent Sandy Wagner for her continued belief in this book.

Thank you to my parents-in-law Woody and Ursula for their generous hospitality on my research trips to Sydney.

Thank you to Helen Forlong for her generous hospitality in Featherston on a research trip to the Wairarapa.

Thanks to Lucy Treep and Aorewa McLeod for our conversations about Eve Langley and Jean Devanny respectively.

Special thanks to my dear friend Peter Wells for his reading of an earlier draft and for his encouragement.

And thanks as always to Tim Woodhouse, my favourite Australian in the world.

Index

154, 187; children 113–14, 131,
132–33, 135, 137, 147–49; early
life 25, 34–38, 141; I Felici, Letterati,
Conoscenti e Lunatici 138, 140–41,
166; interest in the paranormal and
occult 36–37, 135, 144–45, 147, 187;
and Jean Devanny 141–42; leopardskin
costume 12, 137–38, **139**, 142;
marriage 98, 113–14, 131, 132, 133–34,
135, 137; Queen of Bohemia 137–38,
140, 141, 143, 144, 147; and Rosaleen
(Roie) Norton 12, 37, 135, 143–47;
travels 40, 135–36; writing 35, 37,
38–40, 113, 132, 134, 135, 141, 142, 143,
145, 149–51, 154, 187, 224
Deamer, Dulcie, works: 'As it was in
the beginning' 38–40; *The Golden
Decade* 149; *Revelation* 149–51;
The Silver Branch 145; *The Suttee of
Safa* 113, 135–36; 'The Compleat Kisser:
A handbook yet to be written' 140;
Victory 154
Deamer, G.E. 35–36
Deamer, Isabel Mabel (née Reader) 35, 36,
37, 38, 40, 132–33, 135, 140, 141, 148,
151
Dempster, S.M. 8
Denison, Sir Hugh 157
Depression 59, 84, 123, 142, 156, 157, 159,
188, 191
Devanny, Erin 76, 77, 78, 113, 130
Devanny, Hal 11, 73–74, 75, 76, 77, 78,
130, 154, 191, 194, 197, 203, 205, 208,
209, 211, 212
Devanny, Jean (née Jane Crook) 113,
189, **203**, 215; in Australia 10, 11,
13, 21, 69, 84, 86, 96, 98, 141, 154,
187–88, 191–213, 218; and Dulcie
Deamer 141–42; early life 70–73,
141, 188; in Germany 192; politics 11,
73–74, 75, 77, 78, 84–85, 113, 130, 154,
191–92, 194, 196–97, 198, 203–04,
205, 207–09, 210, 211, 213; sexual
life 11, 77–78, 83–84, 130, 194, 196,
204, 207–08; in the Soviet Union 194;
talk, 'Literature and Morality' 191;
writing 69–70, 77–78, 83–84, 85, 86,
95, 130, 141, 154, 188, 190, 191, 193–94,
197, 198–202, 204, 205, 210–11; writing
about Māori 81–82, 83, 188, 190

Devanny, Jean (née Jane Crook),
non-fiction: *Point of Departure* 70, 75,
78–79, 202, 208–09, 210–11; *Travels
in North Queensland* 72, 187, 198, 209,
213; *By Tropic Sea and Jungle* 72, 187,
198, 205–07, 209
Devanny, Jean (née Jane Crook), novels
and short stories: *Bushman Burke* 188,
190; *The Butcher Shop* 11, 69, 77,
80–83, 86, 130, 188, 190, 191, 201;
Cindie 11, 70, 198, 201, 209, 211; *Dawn
Beloved* 75–76, 79, 86, 199, 200; *The
Ghost Wife* 197; *Lenore Divine* 77, 86;
Old Savage 86; *Out of Such Fires* 191;
Paradise Flow 154, 198, 204; *Poor
Swine* 193–94; *Riven* 86; *Roll Back
the Night* 198; *Sugar Heaven* 11, 154,
198–202, 204, 209–10; 'The Perfect
Mother' 79; *The Virtuous Courtesan* 197
Devanny, Karl 73, 84, 130, 154, 191, 197,
198, 202
Devanny, Patricia *see* Hurd, Patricia (Pat)
(née Devanny)
Deveson, Anne 171
Dobell, William 10, 124
Domett, Alfred, *Ranolf and Amohia* 238
Donne, John 230
Downstage Theatre Society 237, 238
Doyle, Mr 93
Drayton, Joanne 33
Drysdale, Russell 124
Duchamp, Marcel 117; 'Nude Descending
a Staircase' 116
Duckworth publishing house 79–80
Duff, Oliver 93
Duggan, Eileen 86
Dundas, Douglas 119, 120
Dunedin 38, 44, 61, 77, 78

Edger, Kate 88
Edmond, Martin 17, 173
Egan, John (Nora Kelly) 12–13
Ehrenfried, Catherine 93
Elder, Anne 13
Ellis, Havelock 227
Eltham 41, 42–46, 50, 51–52, 66, 219,
254; Bridge Street 42, 43, **43**
Eltham Argus 51–52
Eltham Public School 45
Endean & Holloway 91